KON-TIKI MAN

KON~TIKI MAN

An Illustrated Biography of Thor Heyerdahl

Thor Heyerdahl with Christopher Ralling

Chronicle Books • San Francisco

To Angela

First published in the United States in 1991 by Chronicle Books.

Copyright © 1990 by BBC Books. All rights reserved.
No part of this book may be reproduced in any form
without written permission from Chronicle Books.
© A/S Fred. Olson 1990
Maps © Line and Line 1990
Jacket design by Julie Noyes Long
Printed in Hong Kong

Library of Congress Cataloging-in-Publication Data
Heyerdahl, Thor.
    Kon-Tiki man: an illustrated biography of Thor Heyerdahl / Thor
Heyerdahl with Christopher Ralling.
        p.   cm.
    Previous ed.: The Kon-Tiki man / Christopher Ralling. 1990.
    Includes bibliographical references and index.
    ISBN 0-8118-0069-5 (pbk.).—ISBN 0-8118-0026-1 (hard)
    1. Heyerdahl, Thor.   2. Explorers—Norway—Biography.
I. Ralling, Christopher.   II. Ralling, Christopher. Kon-Tiki man.
III. Title.
G306.H47H49   1990
910'.92—dc20   91-22087
[B]   CIP

Extracts from previous books by Thor Heyerdahl reproduced
by kind permission of Allen and Unwin, United Kingdom.

10 9 8 7 6 5 4 3 2 1

Chronicle Books
275 Fifth Street
San Francisco, California 94103

FRONTISPIECE *Thor Heyerdahl confronts one of the 'sightless giants' of Easter Island.*
PAGE 7 *The young Thor enjoyed trekking through the Norwegian winter with his husky, Kazan.*

CONTENTS

FOREWORD

BY CHRISTOPHER RALLING

Thor Heyerdahl belongs to that small band of scientific adventurers who have undoubtedly left their mark on the twentieth century. In a life-time's work which has included ten books translated into all the major languages, hundreds of articles for magazines and scientific journals, and a dozen documentary films Heyerdahl has had his share of public attention; and in the course of it he has become widely known and admired. But for all that, the image remains diffuse. Many people feel that they know something about the man, and have read about his more spectacular exploits, but that they don't understand the pattern which holds it all together.

This book sets out to redress that balance: to put Heyerdahl's dreams, theories and journeys into context, to pull together what may at times seem a loose arrangement of scientific and anthropological threads and weave them into a single logical web. It is part biography, part autobiography – for who but Heyerdahl himself could describe adequately the experience of being swamped by heavy Atlantic rollers on a flimsy balsa wood raft, or the excitement of fitting together the pieces in the archaeological jigsaw of Easter Island? For the first time this book attempts to make his scientific achievements accessible to the general reader, and it is not therefore in any way a critical, academic assessment. That task is for the qualified anthropologists, archaeologists and oceanographers of the future, for although he is in his seventies Thor Heyerdahl continues to devote himself to his life's work; the web is not yet complete.

My gratitude goes out to many more people than I

have space to record. But I would particularly like to express my sincere thanks to the Sebrafilm team, who made the TV series which this book accompanies; to the publishers of Heyerdahl's own books, who have co-operated with us so generously; to Clodagh Wallace, who frequently took the tiller when the going got rough; to John Gau, who pitchforked me into the project in the first place; to Annette Ewington, without whom nothing would ever have got finished; to Snorre Evensberget, whose unflappable professionalism was an example to us all; to Sheila Ableman, Frank Phillips and Esther Jagger, who handled the English edition with such style and enthusiasm; to Fred Olsen, the architect of all our endeavours; to my wife Angela, whose name should really be on the cover of this book; and above all to Thor Heyerdahl, for allowing me to poke around inside his life with complete trust, which has led, I hope, to an enduring friendship.

We shall go

Always a little further; it may be

Beyond that last blue mountain barred with snow,

Across that angry or that glimmering sea;

White on a throne, or guarded in a cave,

There lives a prophet who can understand

Why men were born.

James Elroy Flecker, 'Hassan'

Larvik

27762
Wilse. Enere

1

NATURE'S CHILD

'It's not only in geography that we can
make discoveries.'

It is of course an over-simplification, but a useful one
none the less, to think of Thor Heyerdahl as the man
who, some forty years ago, dropped a pebble into a
rather large pond. The pond was the Pacific, and ever
since the ripples caused by that pebble have been
spreading outwards across all the other oceans of the
world. They are spreading still.

But the pond can also be seen as the academic world
at that time, or those parts of it which were concerned
with archaeology, anthropology, ethnology, ocean-
ography, botany, zoology and other related subjects.
Before the arrival of the young Thor Heyerdahl on the
scene, there were very few ripples to disturb the surface
of that great ocean of knowledge which might loosely be
called Pacific Studies. Then Heyerdahl dropped his
pebble, and the waves began to lap around a thousand
islands of specialist endeavour. Almost immediately the
smooth pattern of the ripples was criss-crossed by the
wash of angry, dissenting voices, woken from their
slumbers. For most of his working life, Thor Heyerdahl
has had a bumpy ride. He has no complaints about that.
Even now, in his seventies, he thrives on controversy in
the pursuit of knowledge. There is only one thing that
he cannot abide; and that is to be misquoted.

It is very easy, looking back over the life of an individual, to perceive a pattern that was never really there. So
much of what we experience along the way, so much of
what we eventually become, is the result of events
entirely beyond our control. Accidents, wars, chance

FAR LEFT *Thor's parents, Thor
and Alison Heyerdahl, were
already in their forties when
their son was born in 1914 in
the little coastal town of Larvik*
(ABOVE). LEFT *The two-year-
old Thor.*

encounters – all play their random part. And yet, looking back at the broad shape of Thor Heyerdahl's life, it is
hard to escape from the sensation that there does seem
to be a pattern there, like some giant moving shadow
beneath the surface of everyday events. In the words of
one celebrated Scandinavian prince, 'There's a divinity
that shapes our ends, rough-hew them how we will.'

Not that divinity, in the theological sense of the word,
played much of a part in his early upbringing. Thor's
mother was a militant atheist; his father a nominal
Christian. Between them, they banged the question of
his immortal soul back and forth like a sort of evangeli-
cal tennis ball. His mother Alison, being much the
stronger character, was the easy winner. But throughout
his life Thor has always retained a sense of spiritual
wonderment at our universe, and everything in it; perhaps that was due to his father's influence. In almost
every other way, however, it was his mother who was
the dominant influence throughout his early life.

A tall, striking woman with fixed opinions, Alison was
what we would today call a liberated woman. Her
marriage to Thor Heyerdahl senior, owner of the local
brewery in the little whaling port of Larvik in southern
Norway, was her third and his second. Thor was an only
child, born in 1914 to parents already in their forties.
This marriage, unfortunately, was to fare no better than
the earlier ones: marriage is one of those institutions
that the Heyerdahls have never got the hang of. The
young boy was only dimly aware of it, but throughout
his childhood his parents were drifting further and further apart.

As a result he was rather a lonely little boy. Important
though he was to both of them – in fact he was probably
the one thing that kept them together – neither showed
him much physical affection in the presence of the
other. Except for mealtimes, the two parents would seldom stay in the same room together for very long. And
when they did there was an atmosphere of strain that
the small boy could sense, but could not understand. It
wasn't a carefree household, but Thor has no recollec-
tion of being consciously unhappy.

Thor's father's work caused him to spend a good deal
of time out of the house. If his son saw him at all, it was

usually in the evenings when he used to come up to the boy's bedroom for little chats – rather vague attempts to modify the outspoken opinions of his forceful wife. He would sometimes read the Lord's Prayer, or a passage from the Bible, but if she caught him at it she would scold him for filling young Thor's head with silly, super-stitious notions. His father never stood his ground; he would simply walk off. And the time was to come when he would walk off once and for all.

Over-dominant mothers often have the opposite effect on the development of their sons from the one they intend. Apron strings can strangle. Being a highly educated woman, well versed in Freud, Thor's mother knew this very well and did her best to shape his child-

Thor photographed in the winter of 1918, proudly wearing his first pair of skis. The 'toughening-up' process which his father tried to impose on him failed, but some years later Thor discovered the outdoor life for himself.

hood without smothering his personality. Oddly enough, although she had rebelled against her own puritanical upbringing at the hands of two maiden aunts, she still insisted on the simple puritan virtues of cleanliness and punctuality when it came to her son. Compared to most of his friends he was kept on a very short leash. On the other hand, of all the adults he had so far encountered she was the least prudish; Alison was the one person at that time with whom he felt he could discuss virtually anything.

As for her atheism, she refused to believe in a god who could take away her own mother when she herself was only six. Indeed, that tragedy alone was enough to convince her that no such being could possibly exist. At Thor's primary school she was the scourge of the teaching staff, berating them fiercely if she thought they were deviating from the principles of logical thought and scientific deduction. Mysticism and make-believe had no place in her world. Alison's hero, the one person who had come close to explaining the mysteries of our planet, was Charles Darwin, with his theory of natural selection through the survival of the fittest. (Her son was definitely going to be one of those.) It would have been not unexpected if Thor had rebelled against all of this; but he didn't. It was his mother who taught him to have a deep respect and love for the natural world, which has never left him. Indeed it is probably true to say that much of his own work has been based on the solid rock of Darwinism.

Thor's father, on the other hand, must have been rather disappointed in his young son. Fearful perhaps that he was in danger of becoming something of a 'mother's darling', Heyerdahl senior did his best to interest the boy in more manly pursuits like hunting; he went so far as to bribe him with offers of extra pocket money, but to no avail. Even as a boy, Thor could no more bring himself to shoot an animal for sport than to shoot a human being.

Thor had one over-riding passion as a boy – collecting biological specimens for his own personal museum. It could equally well have been an anthropological museum, but as he remarked many years later, in a small Norwegian whaling town you can't very well go out in search of Red Indians and Eskimos with a view to sticking pins in them. So he had to be content with sea shells, butterflies, bats, lemmings and hedgehogs. Despite his aversion to hunting, he didn't have any qualms about murdering these smaller specimens for his collection. Apparently they died in a good cause.

On one famous occasion he managed to catch an adder alive; the only problem was how to get it home. A couple of hours later, his mother got the scare of her life. She opened the front door to find her son standing there holding up a venomous reptile by its tail. For four miles

Thor with his mother in 1920, at their typical southern Norwegian house. This was his childhood home until he moved with her to Oslo in 1933.

he had carried the creature at arm's length, while it thrashed about doing its best to bite him. Each time one of his arms got tired, he gingerly transferred it to the other. Up to that point, his mother had been an enthusiastic supporter of Thor's natural history collection, which was housed in a disused outhouse at the brewery, proudly labelled 'Zoological Museum'. But this was too much.

Then, quite suddenly, a new trait began to reveal itself in his character: a strength of will which, up to that time, no one had suspected he possessed. Others were probably quite right to call it stubbornness. But it certainly helped a shy, introverted boy to emerge from his chrysalis and become, of all things, the leader of the local gang. To be sure, it wasn't just the force of his personality which singled him out – he also had the advantage of being a Heyerdahl, which gave him the chance to maintain his hold over the gang with offers of lemonade and soda pop from his father's brewery. But the willpower was there as well. The only question was whether he would put it to good use or bad.

Summer holidays were always spent at a log cabin in the mountains above Lillehammer, now a flourishing ski resort about eighty miles from Oslo. It was perched on the edge of the Hoy Fjell, a wild plateau among the central mountains, far from the encroachments of civilization. In those days it was a full three days' journey from Larvik. On the long, hot summer days Thor and his mother would take a packed lunch and a flask of water, and set off across the windswept moors.

The hermit Ola Bjorneby and Thor photographed each other outside the tent they shared on Hoy Fjell. The adolescent Thor was deeply influenced by Bjorneby's philosophy and way of life.

There was a purpose in this. His mother wanted him to take a look from the outside at all the trappings that the modern world calls progress, and see them for what they were. One day, in the remotest part of the Hoy Fjell, they came across a man living the life of a hermit. His name was Ola Bjorneby. He had practically no possessions beyond a few knives and a cooking pot; even his clothes and the rough furniture inside his log cabin he had made for himself. Although the life he was leading was the very opposite of that enjoyed by the sophisticated town-dweller, he seemed to Thor just as cultured as most of the people he had encountered during his first fourteen years, and much more amusing. Ola was far from being an illiterate tramp. He told the Heyerdahls that he came from a wealthy land-owning family away to the east, and had taken to this lonely life as a matter of choice when his father lost all his money. He appeared to fit naturally into the environment he had chosen for himself, and to be quite content with it.

Thor began to spend more and more time with his new hermit friend, and, rather to his surprise, his mother raised no objections. In fact she positively encouraged him: he was acquiring the lore of the wilderness at Ola's side. In fact, some of the things he had declined to be taught by his father, like hunting and fishing, he was happy enough to pick up from Ola. He learned how to keep rowing for hours on end, and to sleep with nothing but a stone for his pillow. In short, he learned hardship.

The influence of this most lovable of hermits was profound, and Thor became much stronger in mind as well as body. After that summer on the Hoy Fjell he felt more prepared to join the local boys on skiing trips and cross-country runs. They pulled sledges behind them, loaded with tents and provisions, and slept out in the mountains on the coldest of nights. All over Norway young boys were doing the same; it was a normal part of growing up. Yet deep down, Thor felt he was preparing himself for something more; and already, in the secret world of his own thoughts, he sensed what it might be.

Back in Larvik he had started middle school; here he met a large, intellectually minded boy called Arnold Jacoby, who years later was to write a book about Thor's

OVERLEAF *The Hoy Fjell, the wild, high plateau of central Norway.*

BELOW *At this time Thor went off on frequent long mountaineering expeditions with companions such as his friend Edvard Barth. Sometimes they slept rough in snow dugouts.*

life called *Señor Kon-Tiki*. In many ways they were an odd pair, but they became very close. Young Jacoby was quite unlike the sort of youths with whom Thor had previously been friends; he was interested in music and poetry, and the two boys had deep philosophical discussions far into the night. Eventually Thor decided that this was the one person in the entire world to whom he could confide his secret. He told Arnold that when he grew up he intended to become an explorer, and that nothing in the world would deflect him from it. In his book, Jacoby recalls the exchange of views which followed.

❛Thor thought the reading of fiction was a poor substitute for reality; he wanted to experience life for himself, in close contact with nature, to set out on journeys of discovery to strange and distant lands. My argument was that there was nothing more to discover.'

'Africa,' I said, 'is no longer the dark continent. Australia was drawn on the map years and years ago. Only the Amazon has still a certain number of twilit spots, but it's not an undiscovered country.'

'It's not only in geography that we can make discoveries,' said Thor. 'There are still many great challenges in the world, among other things the mystery of Easter Island.' Those were his very words. **)**

If this account is correct, then it was certainly the most remarkable premonition of Thor Heyerdahl's entire childhood.

With all the impetuosity of youth, the two boys began to question the entire basis of modern civilization. Arnold Jacoby recalls those intense night-time conversations.

(Thor was convinced that modern man had his brains stuffed full, not so much with his own experience, but with opinions and impressions derived from books, magazines, radio and motion pictures. The result was an over-loaded brain and reduced powers of observation. Primitive man, on the other hand, was an extrovert and alert, with keen instincts and all his senses alive. . . . Civilization might be compared with a house full of people who had never been outside the building. None of them knew what their house looked like, although

OPPOSITE ABOVE *On some of his mountain expeditions Thor's only companion was his husky, Kazan. The powerful dog could pull a 100lb sledge in winter.*

OPPOSITE BELOW *In the twenties and thirties Thor and Edvard Barth (seen here) used their skis as a practical means of travel, but soon these mountain slopes would become a playground for winter sports enthusiasts.*

BELOW *Another regular companion on these mountain treks was Erik Hesselberg, who many years later was to join the* Kon-Tiki *expedition.*

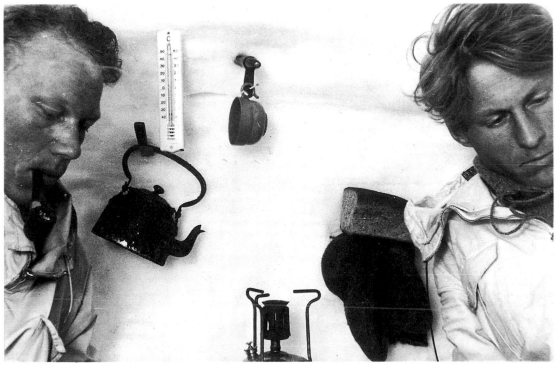

Das große Abenteuer

HEFT

9

September
1971

they lived in it. It was necessary to go outside to see the house as it really was. . . . If, said Thor, he could be sure that his views were the right ones, he would return to nature, and accept the consequences. *'*

Of course there was nothing particularly new in all of this. The French philosopher Jean-Jacques Rousseau had put forward the doctrine of the 'Noble Savage' nearly two hundred years earlier. The difference was that the young Thor Heyerdahl was determined to put it into practice.

There is a drawing that he made at the age of eight, which shows a little house built on top of a pole, just off the shore of some lush tropical island in the South Seas. The sun shines down on palm trees and cactus plants, and the tendrils of an exotic creeper have somehow managed to entwine themselves round everything. He was never attracted to the frozen Arctic wastes that had held such fascination for his famous countrymen

OPPOSITE *The cover of a German magazine, published just after the Ra expeditions, showing Thor as a young man on one of his early adventures in the mountains of Norway.*

ABOVE *Arnold Jacoby was the only friend in whom Thor felt he could really confide his dream of turning back to nature. Thirty years later Jacoby was to write a biography of him, entitled* Señor Kon-Tiki.

Nansen and Amundsen. It may have been nothing more than a dislike of the cold, but even at that early age it was the warmer climate of the Pacific, and the mysterious islands of Polynesia, that formed his vision of Paradise. Now, at seventeen, his heart and mind were set on going there one day soon.

But meanwhile, with Thor on the verge of manhood, other events were taking place on the domestic front. There was no further reason for his parents to maintain the façade of a relationship which had ceased to exist. As the years passed, his father had grown more successful and wanted to enjoy the fruits of that success, while his mother had become increasingly ascetic. By now Thor senior was a powerful figure in the local community, owning not only the brewery but also several properties and large tracts of forest, as well as being chairman of a local bank. On one occasion he and Alison had taken young Thor out to lunch at a tourist hotel in the hills nearby. Increasingly frustrated at the poor service, his father pronounced that the only solution was to buy the hotel, which he promptly did. The boy was thrilled at such grandiose behaviour, but his mother was disgusted.

It is probably true that in Scandinavia, then as much as now, marital breakdown was not always regarded as an occasion for tears. The decision of Thor's parents to live apart, she in Larvik and he in Oslo, caused no bitterness, and to him personally the minimum of distress. It was a lesson which stood him in good stead when his own turn came to face the ever-shifting intricacies of his personal life; and in any case he had his own plans for the near future.

His mother, as mothers will, had been in the habit of saying, 'Thor doesn't care for girls. The only thing that interests him is zoology.' How wrong she was. He had become desperately interested in girls, although too awkward and inexperienced to know how to approach them. But now the hunt was on to find one of these fairy-like creatures, infinitely fascinating but not really human, who would drop everything (quite literally, he hoped) and come with him on a one-way ticket to the South Seas.

From a very early age Thor dreamed of travel, of a life far away from the ice and snow of Scandinavia. This is his idea of Paradise, somewhere in the South Seas, drawn when he was eight years old.

2

ALL THE WAY

'What would you think about going
back to nature?'

Impressionable boys are apt to go around telling
people that they intend to run away to sea, join the
Foreign Legion, or live on a desert island; while for
their part, adults give knowing smiles and tell each
other that it won't be long before 'little Johnny grows
out of it'. Such notions are regarded as the naive
fantasies of youth – not something to be taken seriously.
But in the early 1930s the young Thor Heyerdahl was
deadly serious.

He was in a torment of frustration. In a small town like
Larvik it was possible to know all the girls, by sight if not
by name. In his imagination he had interviewed all of
them for the job; and not one had measured up. Worse
still, the problem was compounded by the fact that he
was far too shy to approach the prettier ones at all. Then
along came Liv. It is almost impossible to describe
Thor's first meeting with her without making it sound
like an absurdly sentimental piece of romantic fiction. It
was absurd and romantic, but it happened none the less.

Schooldays were over at last, and it was the night of
the matriculation ball. Since he was still as gauche with
girls as he had ever been, and a truly terrible dancer, it
wasn't an evening Thor had been looking forward to.
Everyone else seemed to be enjoying themselves, but
he sat alone at an open window, watching the reflection
of the moon tremble in the wake of small boats as they
passed to and fro on the black waters of the fjord.

Suddenly, his melancholy reverie was interrupted by
the appearance of a girl he had never seen before. She

OPPOSITE *Liv Torp, who was to become Thor's first wife, was tall and slender, with striking good looks and a strong will.*

had come from another town not far away and hardly knew anyone; now she found herself parked on Thor by a friend. To both of them it looked like being an encounter of awkward introductions and agonizing pauses. But there was something in her manner, a sort of forthright directness, that told him his search might be at an end.

Her looks were typically Scandinavian: she was slender as a birch, with bushy blonde hair and laughing blue eyes. Marvelling at his own boldness, Thor suggested a walk down to the beach. She readily agreed. There beside the jetty, with the lights of the whaling ships winking at the night sky, he turned to this perfect stranger and asked her: 'What would you think about going back to nature?'

She might have slapped his face, or run away; those were unliberated days. Instead, she just looked at him with steady eyes and said, 'It would have to be all the way.' A few years were to pass before that fragile, youthful dream turned into reality, but from that moment neither Liv nor Thor wavered in their resolve. It was a solemn pact, made in a moment, and not even sealed with a kiss.

To outsiders Thor must have seemed like many another callow youth with a lively imagination, dreaming of faraway places. His mother knew better. She had amassed a considerable library reflecting her own scientific interests, and she had watched her son steadily work his way through it. Then, in the autumn of 1933, when they both moved to Oslo, he had a stroke of luck. A wealthy wine merchant called Bjarne Kroepelien, who was also a family friend, decided to help him. As a young man, he himself had visited Tahiti and fallen in love with the daughter of the great Polynesian chief Teriieroo. Tragically, the girl had died, but Kroepelien then started collecting everything he could lay his hands on to do with Polynesia. In his Oslo house he had the finest private library on the subject to be found anywhere in the world. Delighted to find a young man who shared his passion for the South Seas, he let Thor come and go just as he liked; and as time went by, he began to treat him almost as if he were his own son.

It had already been decided that Thor would study zoology at Oslo University, but this did not prevent him from taking an intense interest in all the related subjects to do with the Pacific. The fact that as yet he had had no formal academic training proved to be a virtue. He was already coming to the conclusion that narrow specialization tended to obscure the wider view. Now, in the wonderland of Mr Kroepelien's library, he became convinced of it. Thor's one immense advantage, as he described it later, was that he came to the study of the Pacific by the window instead of the door. At that time, the earliest settlement of that glittering rope of islands in the South Seas known as Polynesia was one of the world's great anthropological mysteries. In cheerful ignorance of where one discipline ended and the next one began, he read huge volumes about botany, ocean currents and the formation of atolls which most zoologists would have regarded as lying outside their field.

It was a year before Liv followed him to Oslo University; and even then, since she was reading social economics they didn't see much of each other. She was also spending a good deal of time in the company of a rather sophisticated young man. It began to look as if the prospect of going 'all the way' with Thor to some distant tropical island was something she had already put out of her mind. But this was not so. She told Thor she had never been able to forget their discussion, and was as willing as ever to put it into practice. Her only fear was that he might have changed his mind about her. Even when Thor told her flatly that if the experiment succeeded he had no plans to return home, that 'all the way' might mean forever, she didn't hesitate. In spite of her popularity and the evident fact that she was having a good time at the university, she shared his dislike of the modern industrialized world, a world of overtime and overdrafts, divorced from the natural rhythm of the earth. He could hardly believe his luck.

In their exuberance, it never really occurred to either of them that choosing a partner, albeit a sexual partner, for an expedition might not be the same thing as choosing a partner for life. They were both so preoccupied with their plans that they hardly spoke of love. Thor was infatuated by this attractive, open, uncomplicated girl – not least because she fitted so perfectly into his grand idea.

Thor and Liv met for the first time at a graduation party in 1933. Until that moment he had been excruciatingly shy with girls, regarding them as 'creatures from another planet'.

Thor on the roof of a typical Norwegian log cabin. Years later he was to build himself a similar turf-covered log cabin on the shores of the Mediterranean.

Now came the difficult part: to persuade their respective parents that they were in earnest. The stark truth was that they needed money as well as good wishes. With all the guile of experienced campaigners, they chose the softest target first – Thor's mother. She was as forthright as ever, but once she understood what he was planning to do there she began to put her doubts aside. One of Thor's zoology professors, Kristine Bonnevie, whom Alison liked and admired, had suggested a project. Thor was to find an isolated Pacific island that had risen sterile from the bottom of the ocean through volcanic activity, and try to discover how the local animals had found their way there; the research would form the basis for a thesis. Later, he would substitute human beings for animals; in the meantime this was to prove the ideal prelude to his life's work.

The next step was to convince Thor's father, whose view of the matter was quite different. He had no objections to the project itself ('It'll make a man of you'), but the idea of taking a white girl to those primitive parts he saw as completely insane. Thor knew that the old man was missing Alison dreadfully, and that gave him his chance: he arranged a meeting so that the three of them could discuss the whole idea. And so Thor senior came home, for an hour or two at least, after years of lonely separation; he sat sipping tea on the settee like any bashful suitor. By the time he left, he had withdrawn his objections and agreed to provide an indefinite loan to cover the cost of their fares.

A coloured sketch by Thor depicting an expedition with Liv to the forests of Hornsjo in 1936. He called it: 'One of our nights with a fire in the open.'

Thor and Liv were married on Christmas Eve, 1936, and the following day they set out on their long journey to the South Seas.

Liv's parents were another matter. They were a conventional, bourgeois couple who had given their daughter a much stricter upbringing than Thor had received. Unwisely perhaps, Liv decided to break the news in a letter. There was a lot to break: her intention to marry a young man they had never heard of; the abrupt end of her university career without a degree; a life without clothes, comfort or prospects on some faraway islands in the South Seas. An ancient encyclopaedia confirmed her father's worst suspicions. The islands were cesspits of depravity, where cannibalism and lasciviousness flourished side by side.

It was Thor's father who saved the day. When the young couple went to call on Liv's parents, he came too. Calmly but firmly, he convinced them that his son too came from a respectable and prosperous background. Furthermore, behind this apparently hare-brained scheme there was a serious scientific purpose that he personally was prepared to support. Above all, he told them that he thought their daughter was a sensible and lovely girl who knew her own mind. It was enough. Liv and Thor were married on Christmas Eve, 1936. She was twenty, and he was twenty-two. Next day they were bound for the island of Fatu Hiva – their personal Garden of Eden.

3

A TICKET
TO PARADISE

'A single virgin speck among the thousands
of islands and atolls.'

Going back to nature' is one of the recurring
myths of Western society. As an idea, it has no
particular potency in Hindu, Buddhist or
Islamic cultures. Indeed, among Asian countries it is
only in overcrowded and industrialized Japan that the
notion holds any attraction at all. But in Europe and the
United States the picture is quite different. Almost
everyone dreams of escaping from the claustrophobia
of the office, or the clamour of the production line, even
if few of us ever turn our fantasies into reality.

As a panacea for the world's ills, it is of course an illu-
sion. On this overcrowded planet, there is no longer
enough 'nature' to go round; and what remains
diminishes year by year. Thor and Liv were well aware
of this half a century ago. The experiment was to be
more an escape from civilization than an attempt to find
a practical paradise. Both of them felt that modern man,
in his ceaseless pursuit of material progress, had somehow lost his way. This was to be an inner journey as
much as an outward one.

Later, in *Fatu Hiva: Back to Nature*, Thor recalled the
difficulties they had experienced in finding a suitable
island:

❜ For the thousandth time we pored over the colourful
map of the South Seas. For the thousandth time we
sailed around on the vast ocean, our eyes scanning the
blue paper, hoping to find a little speck suitable for us. A
single virgin speck among the thousands of islands and
atolls. A speck which the world had overlooked. A tiny

...lv og Thor
...eser om
...arquesas.

EN HELLIG RØD ÅL SOM LEVER ALENE I EN KULP

MASSEVIS AV FUGL
SKILPADDER
KOKUSPALMER

ATU OVA
HIVA OVA
NUKUHIVA
TAIPI VALLEY
DET ER 13 ØER I ALT

TEMPERATUREN ER CA 25°
ET IDEELT KLIMA UTEN REGNT...
STAUTE OG VAKRE MENNESK...
GJESTEVENLIGE FOLK

EN HVIT KOLONI MED FRANS...
GUVERNØR
EN KATOLSK KIRKE MED EN FRANSK...
ET HOSPITAL
FARVERIKE FISK I LAGUNEN
EN HERLIG KRYDDERAKTIG LU...
TARORØTTER
SØTPOTETER SOM VEIER OPTIL 2...

...BBER SOM GÅR I TRÆRNE
...VILLETE HESTER OG KVEG
...SER, HØNER, KATTER OG HUND
...SSEVIS AV VANNFALL
...RØDFRUKTTRÆR
...VRIMLER AV FUGL
...NESIERNE GÅR KLÆDT I =
PAREU
...FORSKJELLIGE SORTER BANAN
...KSPRUT ER POLYNESIERNES =
LIVRETT.
...ER AV VULKANSK OPPRINDELSE.
...JELL SOM GÅR 1400m STEILT OP FRA HAVET.
...DE INNFØDTES RUSDRIKK ER KAWA.
...POLA GAUGUIN'S GRAV LIGGER DER

BARE ET TUSENBEN SOM STIKKER
SOM EN HVEPS
INGEN GIFTIGE ELLER FARLIGE DYR

free port of refuge from the iron grip of civilization.

But every tempting little speck was already swept off the map with a little pencilled cross. It didn't suit us. That could be learned from heavy volumes of geographical literature. . . .

To live with bare hands like early man demands a lot from an environment. It would have to be fertile and luxuriant, and unclaimed by others. But wherever there was fertile land it was densely inhabited. Wherever it was uninhabited the environment was too poor to sustain man unaided by some degree of culture. . . .

Just below the equator, where the mild trade-winds flowed westwards across the map as red arrows, lay the thirteen islands of the Marquesas group. They had already become thirteen crosses. But we returned to these alluring islands with an eraser when the entire map was filled with crosses and every single island rejected.

. . . Once upon a time a hundred thousand Polynesians were supposed to have lived in the Marquesas group. Today a mere two thousand were left, with only a

OPPOSITE *A page from Thor's journal, in which he and Liv are seen poring over maps. Choosing an island for their experiment was not easy, for those that were uninhabited usually lacked food and water.*

ABOVE *Thor and Liv's first sight of tropical abundance was on the Caribbean island of Martinique. Would life be like this, they wondered, when they reached their final destination?*

handful of white men. The Polynesian islanders were dying out at a tremendous rate. And Fatu Hiva was the most luxuriant island in the South Seas. . . . **,**

The decision was made. Spectacularly beautiful, with mountains rising high above the green coastline, Fatu Hiva offered everything necessary to sustain them for at least a year, if not forever.

So Thor and Liv boarded a French ocean liner at Marseilles, and after six weeks at sea arrived at Tahiti – as far as any shipping line then travelled. Its legendary beauty did not disappoint them. As they stood at the ship's rail watching the island get closer and closer, 'verdant as a huge flower basket sailing on the sea', there seemed little point in looking further for their Garden of Eden.

But the mirage faded as soon as the ship docked. Immediately they were confronted by French police and customs officers, a sharp reminder that this was a colony like any other. Thor and Liv spent just two nights in the capital, Papeete, before taking a bus eastwards to the beautiful valley of Papenoo on the north coast. This was the dwelling place of Chief Teriieroo, the most

One fellow passenger's contribution to the journal was his prediction of how the great experiment in 'going back to nature' might well end up!

Thor and Liv had been given an introduction to the Tahitian chief Teriieroo. He and his wife taught them much about living off the land and adopted the couple as their children, renaming them 'Mr and Mrs Blue Sky'.

VELKOMSTDRIKK I KOKUSMELK.

senior of Tahiti's seventeen chiefs and about to become an important influence in Thor's life. Teriieroo was overjoyed to hear that they were friends of Bjarne Kroepelien. Ever since his daughter Tuimata had died during the Spanish flu epidemic that devastated the island after the First World War, Teriieroo and Bjarne had managed to keep in touch; Thor and Liv were carrying letters and gifts from Norway.

Teriieroo was a man large in both girth and spirit, imbued with strong principles of justice, holder of the Légion d'Honneur, and an exceptional orator in both French and Polynesian. Unlike many islanders, he took pride in his inheritance and was critical of many of the 'advances' which the white man had brought. For instance, he considered it barbaric to put metal in one's mouth: it destroyed the taste of the food. He insisted that Liv and Thor stay in his own bungalow until they could catch a schooner to Fatu Hiva, almost a thousand miles away. In the weeks ahead he was to instruct them in the Polynesian art of living, in which man lives in tune with nature; the land and the sea are tapped for life's necessities, but never exploited for wealth alone.

While Liv learned from Faufau, the chief's wife, how to cook roots and fruits over an open oven, Thor went off with Teriieroo to catch prawns and fish, or in search of wild pigs. It was vital to know what made good eating and what was poisonous. Everyone ate with their fingers, and in silence except for appreciative grunts and belches.

The high point of their stay on Tahiti was the farewell party given by Teriieroo. The setting, decorated with banana leaves and sweetly scented flowers, could not have looked more romantic; and the food was delectable. In his speech the chief told his guests that,

although he already had twenty-nine children, he proposed to adopt two more. However, as the Tahitians found 'Liv' and 'Thor' impossible to pronounce, they received the names of Terie Mateata Tane and Terie Mateata Vahine – Mr and Mrs Blue Sky.

A week later they departed on a little copra schooner, the *Tereora*; Thor and Liv slept with other Polynesian passengers on the cabin roof to escape the stifling heat below. The ship was commanded by another exile from civilization, an old seafarer who, as Thor noted at the time, was well aware that he was steadily destroying what he loved best in all the world.

'The trading schooner was the culture-bringer and a profitable business enterprise. It carried a well-stocked store below deck, and by selling at high prices doubled its business by getting back with a profit the same money paid to the islanders in return for working copra. . . .

'It's all crazy,' said Captain Brander . . . 'but they want it, like everybody else. I detest our own civilization; that's why I am here. Yet I spread it from island to island. They want it, once they have a little taste of it. . . . Why do they want sewing-machines and tricycles, or underclothing and canned salmon? They don't need any of it. But they want to tell their neighbours: look here, I've got a chair while you are squatting on the floor. And then the neighbour also has to buy a chair, and something else not possessed by the first one. The needs increase. The expenditure. Then they have to work although they hate it. To earn money they don't need.'

It took three weeks to reach the savagely beautiful Marquesas islands, spaced out across the Pacific as if scattered by some giant hand. They circled Fatu Hiva, looking for a suitable landing place; but the first possibility, Hanavare, a valley so extraordinary that it looked like a theatre setting, was ruled out by the captain who knew that the people there were plagued by elephantiasis, the most dreaded disease in the Pacific. Finally they agreed to be put ashore at a place called Omoa, and after some emotional farewells Captain Brander set a course for the south. Liv and Thor stood on the beach and watched until there was nothing to be seen except a vast expanse of sparkling blue sea. So this was it. They

had no provisions, no weapons and very few possessions. They must live on what they could gather by their own ingenuity and endeavours. This was the challenge of 'all the way', as Thor wrote in *Fatu Hiva*:

❝ There we were on the beach, with our luggage beside us on the boulders. Two big suitcases containing Liv's wedding gown, my dinner jacket suit, and all the usual apparel we had needed on the long journey as first-class honeymoon passengers from Norway. Nothing was useful now. . . .

The sun and the singing tropical birds warmed us up. The sandy turf above the beach abounded in aromatic flowers, and the feeling of high adventure and happiness overtook us anew. Then we suddenly noticed people standing among the trees. There were many of them. Watching us. Nobody moved and nobody greeted us. Some were in loincloths and some in tattered rags of European make. Copper-coloured to brown, all were varieties of the Polynesian stock. Most faces looked more cruel than those of their friendly relatives in Tahiti and the Tuamotu atolls. But a couple of the younger women and most of the children were beautiful.

Seeing that we hesitated, an old crone was the first to get into action. . . . She ventured forward, followed by the rest, and to my surprise and fear she headed for Liv rather than for me. She licked her thin finger and

The island of Fatu Hiva, Liv and Thor's chosen Garden of Eden, as they would have seen it for the first time from the deck of the Tereora.

41

Having anchored the Tereora *in deep water, the captain sent eight of his men to row the young couple ashore. Then the schooner sailed away, and Liv and Thor were left alone on their tropical island.*

rubbed it against the cheek of Liv, who in her surprise was incapable of speech. The old woman scrutinized her own finger and nodded with an approving smile. Only later were we to learn that the spectators had trusted me for what I seemed to be, but they were sure that Liv was a Tahitian girl dressed up and white-washed. The old crone did not believe there were women in Europe. The vessels anchoring on twenty-four hour visits to the island had brought ashore many white men, but not one white vahine. White men always came ashore for the brown girls, but no white women ever came for a brown man. **❯**

They spent their first night in a wooden shack with a corrugated roof, as hot and uncomfortable as a furnace room. Their gentle host was Willy Grenet, keeper of the

local store, whose father, a European, had been a friend of the artist Paul Gauguin when he had lived in the Marquesas. Liv and Thor talked to Grenet in French until well into the early morning, compiling a dictionary of useful Polynesian words – not an easy task as the local dialect seemed to consist entirely of vowels, making words sound very alike to untrained European ears. The word for 'no' appeared to be *aoe*, the word for 'I' was *oao*, and the word for 'he' was *oia*.

Later Thor recalled their first day in their chosen tropical paradise, a place of paradoxes:

❝ Adam and Eve, when God drove them out of the Garden of Eden, must have felt the very opposite of us as we started our walk into the lush valley of Omoa at sunrise next morning. They left; we were returning. The song of

TOP OF PAGE *This illustration from the journal was signed by Pola Gauguin, son of the great French Post-Impressionist painter who lived and worked in the Marquesas.*

ABOVE *A wooden rifle butt carved by Paul Gauguin himself, which Thor brought back to Europe from the island of Hivaoa.*

GLOSSAR.
MARQESANSK - NORSK
OVERSATT VIA FRANSK   VED WILLY GRELET.

Norsk	Marqesansk		Norsk	Marqesansk
Höre	ono, Hakaono		Kokůstre	Tŭmŭeehi
Hår	oŭoho		Komme	Hemai
Höne	Moa		Kostbar	Hoonŭi
Hövding	Hakaiki		Krabbe	Pŭava
Idag	Teneia		Kreps	Koŭa
Ild	Ahi		Kropp	Timo
Ildsted	Ŭmŭ		Kŭ	Koivi eifa
Imorgen	oioi		Kŭnde	Knanw
Ingen, intet	Aoe		Kvinne	Vahine

KAOHA   GODDAG

Norsk	Marqesansk		Norsk	Marqesansk
Is (sne)	Vaianŭ		Kylling	Moa
Ja	E		Land	Fenŭa
Jeg	oaŭ		Langt	Memao
Jeg forstår ikke	Aoe vivini		Le	Ata
Kald	Amŭ, Makaii		Leve	Pohoe
Kano	'vaa		Like	Maimai
Katt	Potŭ		Liten	Memiono
Klær	Kahŭ		Lysning	Adama
Klatre	Pii		Mange takk	Kaoha (nu)
Kniv	Kohe		Mann	Ahana
Koke	Tŭmŭ		Mange, meget	Menŭi
Kokůsmött	Eehi		Mat	Kai
- " - (modern)	Pŭoho		Mave	Opŭ

To help them learn the language Liv and Thor began to compile a glossary of useful, everyday words. They quickly discovered that the Marquesan dialect depends far more on pronunciation than on spelling.

the colourful tropical birds resounded from all parts of the valley as they joined the Marquesas cuckoo in the early morning concert. The temperate air seemed green with jungle aroma. Whatever unknown we were heading for, we felt we were returning to a luxurious lost garden that was ours for the mere asking. . . .

It was the old overgrown royal path we followed inland. Away from the village. The red dented ridge which soared skywards at the bottom of the valley disappeared from sight as the jungle began to close above our heads. First, young coconut palms, resembling giant ferns; next, mighty jungle trees with moss-studded branches bearded by parasitic growths and pendent ropes of lianas. At intervals we could hardly see the rays of the sun playing on the upper foliage, which was filled with hooting, fluting, fiddling and piping creatures. There was life everywhere, although all we saw were little fluttering birds and butterflies, and lizards and bugs pattering away from the exposed trail. . . . We were keen on getting away as fast and as far as possible from the little cluster of village houses where a complete lack of sanitation seemed to have brought all kinds of diseases upon the natives. We had waved to the last ones in the outskirts of the village. They waved back, shouted *kaoha*, and chattered unintelligibly. 'Good day,' we answered in their own language, 'nice, nice; good day.' . . . They seemed very happy despite their diseases, though some of them could hardly walk, their legs being as thick as their bodies. The elephantiasis from which they suffered had come to the island when the white man unintentionally brought the mosquito ashore. The last we saw was a little group of women sitting waist deep in a pool of the river washing themselves in milk-coloured water . . . while others were filling their gourd-containers with drinking water a few yards further downstream. They knew nothing about hygiene or contagion.

Just above the village the river water, filthy lower down, became clean and fresh. The trail followed the stream, occasionally winding across the transparent water on smooth stones, and sometimes cutting into the rusty red soil of the river bank. At the beginning the trail was kept wide and clear of intruding bush, but as we advanced ever deeper inland it became narrower and we often had to use our long machete knife. Willy had picked our guide, Ioane, his own Marquesan brother-in-law. He had a very definite idea of the place he would show us for our future homestead. The site of the last island king. . . .

Far up the valley . . . the trail was gradually lost. Here we left the water and the valley bottom and began climbing in a complete wilderness of boulders, bush, and giant trees. . . .

Finally Ioane stopped. A spring of cold clear water gushed forth at our feet. Next to it was an artificial plateau so overgrown it was impossible to get a view of the

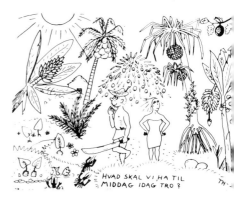

Food was so abundant on Fatu Hiva that all they had to do was cut down their lunch from the nearest tree.

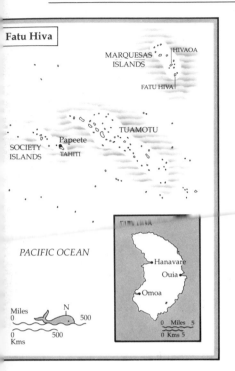

valley or an impression of the place itself. This was the royal terrace. Here the last queen had lived. It did not look too inviting, but trunks of coconut-palms and of breadfruit trees could be distinguished in the impenetrable chaos of foliage, and we spotted the huge leaves of bananas and of taro, besides the largest lemon tree we had ever seen, loaded like a Christmas-tree with golden fruits. **"**

Their second night on the island was as idyllic as the first had been unbearable. Thor quickly cleared the ground and they fell asleep under a magical starry sky. 'Sleeping in a tent is the next best thing to sleeping in the open,' wrote Thor, but the place was new to them and the night sounds bizarre and unidentifiable.

" With nothing but a cloth wall to separate you from your surroundings you participate in the faintest sound around, particularly so in an unfamiliar kind of forest. . . . What made that ghastly cry as it seemed to leap across the canvas? It could croak like a toad and creak like a rusty door. There, something was rummaging in a pile of stones nearby. Was it a wild pig? Higher up in the valley something hooted like an owl. And we clearly heard the mewing of a cat somewhere just below our terrace.

As the breeze increased at night and shook the lofty palm leaves, ripe nuts loosened, and, heavy with milk, they made the silent night jungle resound with a sharp report each time one plummetted to the ground. One of the tallest palms was waving against the stars right above our heads; one tent stay had been lashed to its trunk. In a hurry we untied the stay and pulled the little tent away into safety. A nut from that palm would rip the tent and be as fatal as a bomb if it hit us. . . .

As the sun rose above the Tauaouoho mountains, hardly a ray fell upon our plateau. We were well walled in by the dense jungle, and not even the faintest breeze could enter and brush away the mosquitoes. We decided to clear the entire terrace and build some kind of dwelling, strong enough to keep out the jungle beasts. **"**

Breakfast consisted of bananas and other fruit, washed down by crystal-clear water from the spring. The machete, which Chief Teriieroo had insisted they bring, was constantly in use during the next three days,

cutting through banana stems, breadfruit trees, creepers and ferns, to clear the thick undergrowth and let in the sunlight. From the lower terrace there was a splendid view of the valley and the mountains beyond.

They were just beginning the construction of their home when Ioane appeared, struggling uphill with their suitcases, which they had deliberately left behind with Willy. There would be no getting rid of him until he had seen the contents of these mysterious packages from across the ocean. Obligingly, Liv and Thor opened them up; and immediately regretted it. They might have no use for the suits and evening dresses which tumbled out, but to Ioane it was like treasure trove.

Recovering from his astonishment at such marvels, Ioane turned his attention to the hut. He roared with laughter and told them it would be quite useless: as soon as the rains came, it would disintegrate. Much better to hire him and his friends to build a proper bamboo cabin. And so it was arranged, for a fee of 17.50 francs per day, or in Marquesan dialect, *etoutemonieuatevaso-diso.* Or something like it, anyway.

Next morning Ioane, his wife and four other islanders arrived with a gift of pineapples. Out came the suitcases once more, and after the newcomers had shrieked with

Their first home in the forest was built of plaited bamboo, with a roof of woven coconut palm leaves.

47

Joane Naheekua

BANANER · NESTE PLATÅ · FEI · PAPAYA · KA · FEI
KOKUSPALME
KOKUS
TIL FJELLS
TATOVERINGS-PLANTER.
KJEMPEPOTETER.
FEI
BRØDFRUKT
BAMBUSHYTTA
3 ETAGES HYLLE
SENG · VINDU
BRØDFRUKT · VINDU
THOR · PINNE-STOL
BORD · KASSE
VINDU
DØR
BRØDFRUKT
FEI
GU
FEI
KAFFE VANILJE
BRØDFRUKT · TARO
PALMETAKS-KJOKKENET
STENOVN · KASSE
VED · KASSE
SATERN TARO
STENPORT
TIL KILDEN 20 m.
TIL ELVEN OG VIDERE TIL LANDSBYEN STI
APPELSIN
BRØDFRUKT
PAPAYA
KOKUS-PALME
TIL LANDSBYEN
STENPORT
KOKUS · PIA LUFTPOTETER · APPELSIN · BANANER · KOKUS · PA · BANA
KONGSSTOLEN
RØD BLOMST
STENSENGEN
K P
BRØDFRUKT · FEI

Det er så yndig å følges ad for dem som gjerne vil så...

joy at such items as Thor's binoculars, microscope and shaving mirror, they set to work. First, the frame was constructed of narrow poles tied together with rope and made from hibiscus bark. Then the roof was tiled with overlapping coconut leaves. Plaited bamboo sheets covered the walls and floor. Ingenious bark hinges were fitted to the door and the three shuttered windows. Thor and Liv realized that they were benefiting from centuries of trial and error: their new home was a green and shady delight.

The work took many days, and was frequently interrupted by banquets of fish and chicken brought up from the village, followed by long afternoon siestas. In the end it was paid for from the contents of their suitcases. The villagers much preferred the status conferred by exotic European goods to uninteresting money. Thor managed to hang on to his cameras and a few bits of scientific equipment; the rest vanished.

Left alone at last, they busied themselves with the construction of an outside kitchen, with a stone-lined oven. Thor made a table, two stools and a little shelf from split branches spliced together. They found shallow pearl shells to use as plates, and their cups were coconut shells. No pampered prince or princess could have been happier than these two honeymooners on their royal terrace. In *Fatu Hiva* Thor described their idyllic life:

❛The day begun when a spectacular, parrot-coloured Marquesan cuckoo awoke the slumbering jungle with its resounding trumpet calls. Not losing a moment, all the other birds of the forest began their chorus of joy.... The growing light stole in through the bamboo-framed window-opening with the last gusts of the chilly night breeze. The temperature would turn from chilly to pleasant the very instant that daylight was fully turned on. The dark dragon crest across the valley was itself a spectacle as it reddened in the dawn twilight to flame out like a cock's comb in the morning sun....

As the early morning concert trailed off we were already out of bed and down by the cool spring. We often surprised a beautiful wild cat with distant domestic ancestry that had the habit of sharing the spring with us.... Our sense of perception seemed to be tuned into a

DEN FØRSTE NATT I BAMBUSHYTTEN
PÅ DE UTDØDDE KANIBALERS RUINER

ABOVE *Thor's drawing of their first night's sleep in the bamboo hut, constantly interrupted by strange nocturnal noises from the surrounding forest.*

OPPOSITE ABOVE *Thor's sketch of the layout of the Royal Terrace. In the centre is their bamboo cabin, containing a bed, table, two chairs and a shelf. The little kitchen on the left had a stone oven and two packing cases to sit on. Outside grew various fruit trees and vegetables. The path, marked top left, led to the village.*

OPPOSITE BELOW *An imaginary drawing by a fellow passenger on the* Tereora *of the life that awaited Thor and Liv on Fatu Hiva.*

different and clearer reception, and we smelt, saw and listened to everything around us as if we were tiny children witnessing nothing but miracles. All these little things were everyday matters, such as a little drop of water shaping up to fall from the tip of a green leaf. We let drops spill from our hands to see them sparkle like jewels against the morning sun. No precious stone polished by human hands could shine with more loveliness than this liquid jewel in the flame of the sun. We were rich, we could bail them up by handfuls and let them trickle by the thousands through our fingers and run away, because an infinity of these jewels kept pouring out of the rock. The melodious dance of the little stream below us, formed of this treasure, tempted us to shake pink hibiscus flowers from the branches and let them sail away, rotating and leaping down the tiny rapids between the smooth boulders. . . .

To rise from the spring and put our feet on the silky clay, in the soft mud or on a hard warm slab, felt marvellous. From the day the natives left us, our contact with nature was complete. . . . The fine climate made it a relief to strip off the clothes which the white man from cool countries was now imposing on the tropical islanders and which cling to a sun-baked body like wet paper. . . . Our ever-wrapped skin was at first tender like that of a reptile casting off its slough and hiding until the new covering toughened. But gradually the jungle withdrew its long claws and instead it felt as if its leaves and soft branches stroked us in friendship as we passed. . . . Rather than feeling poor and naked, we felt rich as if wrapped in the whole universe. We and everything were part of one entirety. **❱**

Any couple accustomed to a varied social environment, sophisticated entertainment and the companionship of friends, and who suddenly find themselves spending their days in the company of just each other, may begin to suffer deep feelings of deprivation. Even the shortest of honeymoons can have its bleak moments. But in all Thor Heyerdahl's writings, either at the time or shortly afterwards, there is no hint of the strain of isolation. Could his relationship with Liv really have been so idyllic, day after day for an entire year? Or was this an aspect of their lives that he preferred not to

ABOVE *Their bathing pool lay in the shadow of palms and tropical vegetation: 'If we so much as touched a branch, pink hibiscus blossoms would fall into our bathtub.'*

OPPOSITE *Half a century later, Thor returned to the same rock pool where he and Liv had felt the cool water flowing over their bodies in the golden light of summer afternoons. It was as close as they came to finding an earthly Paradise.*

describe, out of respect for the feelings of his partner?

Half a century later he still felt sure that his memory had not played him false. There had been long discussions between them, even occasional disagreements, but no rows or emotional upheavals of any consequence. He put it down, not just to their equable temperaments, but to the fact that they were so busy. During every waking hour, around the camp and in the forest there was something to be attended to. Although they never consciously worked for it, the result was harmony.

Inevitably, their days revolved around the quest for food. Bananas and the red mountain plantain called *fei* grew close to their cabin; no doubt they had been cultivated by the area's former inhabitants. *Fei* became their bread; they never tired of it, roasting it over the fire and spicing it with a variety of sauces. Coconuts provided oil for cooking and balm for their sun-dried skins. Breadfruit, and a wild tuber called *taro* that was rather like a potato when roasted, varied their staple diet. Fruit was abundant: papayas, mangoes, oranges, lemons and tiny tomatoes.

Thor was always searching the forest for animals and insects for his zoological collection. These varied according to the vegetation in different parts of the island. The key to it all was the Tauaouoho mountain ridge, running right down the middle and rising to over two thousand feet. Where there were lofty peaks to bring down the rain, the surrounding land was covered with lush, impenetrable rain forest; elsewhere the clouds sailed serenely by, resulting in parched, barren areas. The difference was clearly marked because the wind always seemed to blow from the same direction – from the east. And the currents which raced past the island flowed the same way.

Each day produced fresh discoveries: stone terraces and platforms, old bones and skulls hidden away in caves and crevices, even an occasional primitive stone giant. Confronted by these ghosts from the past, Thor's imagination was beginning to stir.

❛I began to acquire a less strictly academic approach to anthropology than I used to have at my own desk at home, when trying to digest the many conflicting

OPPOSITE *The cover of Thor and Liv's 'Visitors' Book'. In the course of a year on Fatu Hiva, they achieved a grand total of six signatures.*

*Monarch of all he surveys,
Thor tries on an ancient
Marquesan crown.*

theories of scholars, few of whom had seen a trade-wind cloud and still fewer had set foot ashore a Polynesian island. The problem of how Polynesian tribes had found their way to these islands long before the days of Captain Cook, Columbus, or Marco Polo, began to interest me more than the itinerary of irrational celeopters and gastropods. **❯**

Other matters began to concern him, too. Even now, half a century before ecological awareness became a burning issue, Thor was becoming uncomfortably aware of how man abused the natural world:

❮ Weeks passed. What gradually burned itself into our memories more than any artifact or animal was the feeling of being an integral part of the environment, rather than something combating it. Civilized man had declared war against his own environment and the battle was raging on all continents, gradually spreading to these distant islands. In fighting nature man can win every battle except the last. If he should win that too he will perish, like an embryo cutting its own umbilical cord.

... Living with nature was far more convincing than any biological textbook in illustrating the fact that the life cycles of all living creatures are interdependent. As city people we had been second-hand customers of the environment; now we were directly part of it and had the strong impression of nature being an enormous cooperative where every associate unwittingly has the function of serving the entity. Every associate except man, the secluded rebel. Everything creeping or sprouting, everything man would spray with poison or bury in asphalt to make his city clean, is in one way or another his humble servant and benefactor. Everything is there to make the human heart tick, to help man breathe and eat.

The way in which our clean valley river was polluted by the ignorant village people before it reached the sea is followed on a larger scale by modern industry and all the cities of the world. Nothing has been found too venomous or poisonous to be piped into the sea. **9**

After a few weeks, their vegetarian diet began to pall; they found themselves dreaming of tender steaks and other carnivorous pleasures. This prompted Thor to make a bamboo trap to catch river prawns. One day, while he was fishing, a native suddenly appeared; to their surprise he spoke in French. He turned out to be the Protestant pastor on the island, and had once lived on Tahiti, where he had become a good friend of Chief Teriieroo. His name was the Reverend Pakeekee. A few days later he invited Thor and Liv to his home, where they feasted for three days on all the things they had been dreaming about.

Tioti the sexton, the only other Protestant on the island, was also there; he became a very good friend, and took Thor and Liv on expeditions. One day, Tioti said he wanted to show them a fish of stone, or, as he called it, *i'a te kea*. After an exhausting journey inland, cutting their way through the thick vegetation with machetes, he pointed excitedly to a rocky promontory above them, as Thor later recalled in *Fatu Hiva*:

6 There it was, over six feet long, head, tail, fins and all, clearly outlined on the rock. Not a fossil but the first petroglyph ever discovered on Fatu Hiva. The only one of this kind known in any part of Polynesia. Petro-

glyphs, or line incisions, of small human figures had been reported from a couple of other islands in the Marquesas group, but there was a fish larger than a man and covered with cup-shaped depressions and symbolic signs. The dominant signs were sun-symbols carved as a dot surrounded by concentric rings, some representing eyes in masks. I drew the machete from its sheath and started cutting down the surrounding bush . . . a large number of other figures emerged from beneath the black soil.

'*Tiki*,' Tioti whispered solemnly. '*Menui tiki*.' Gods. Many gods.

Old magic masks with huge eyes stared once more into the daylight. One that was depicted behind the dorsal fin of the fish was a deity with a right eye only, and this was carved as large concentric circles. Some masks had eyes and mouths only, and huge eyes were sometimes carved in isolation, always as concentric circles, scattered over the stone. Elsewhere on the rock were complete human figures with hooked legs and arms, a turtle, nondescript symbols, and something that puzzled me for years: a crescent-shaped ship with a curved bottom, a very high bow and stern, a double mast and rows of oars. The vessels used in the Marquesas group since the arrival of Europeans were dug-out canoes and flat rafts, both shaped from trunks or poles so that their bottoms were as straight as logs. This crescent-shaped ship looked more like the reed boats of ancient Egypt and Peru, not like a rectilinear Polynesian canoe. . . . **9**

That night Thor turned over this intriguing riddle in his mind. Who had done these carvings? Had it been a spontaneous flowering of cultural endeavour? Or did these people have their roots somewhere else? He knew from his studies in Oslo that most scientists accepted the view that the original Polynesian migrants must have come from Asia. But that would have involved a succession of journeys against the prevailing winds and currents; journeys which defied common sense. From this point in his life, Thor Heyerdahl's interests began to shift away from animals towards man; from zoology to anthropology.

OPPOSITE *The forest was full of burial sites and old stone foundations, long since abandoned. Thor noted that the masonry techniques had more in common with the pre-Inca culture of Peru than with anything in Malaysia or Indonesia.*

4

THE BIRTH OF AN IDEA

'I sat and marvelled at this sea which never stopped
proclaiming that it came . . . from the east, from
the east, from the east . . .'

One day, Thor and Liv were bathing in the river when a horseman arrived, looking sick and drawn. He brought news which chilled their hearts: 'the plague' had arrived with the copra schooner *Moana*. Almost everyone in the valley was affected, and within a few days they too began to feel unwell, and braced themselves for the worst. For them it proved to be no more than slight influenza; but the local population, already debilitated by other illnesses including tuberculosis, elephantiasis and venereal disease, were hit very hard. Tioti arrived in a pathetic condition and asked them to take a photograph of his last remaining son; 'the plague' had carried away all the others.

They found conditions in the village grim. Gone were the garlands of flowers and happy faces. People were lying on the floor of their huts, the dead and the dying side by side. There was no medical assistance, no hygiene and no understanding of the concept of quarantine. The people simply coughed into each other's faces. Liv and Thor did what they could, then hurried home to the airy freshness of their royal terrace. Now they were starting to appreciate that their idea of 'getting away from it all', of turning their backs on so-called civilization, encompassed more hidden complexities than they had originally realized. In *Fatu Hiva* Thor wrote of their thoughts at this moment:

❛Here in the wilderness we were safe, far away from anybody. But something bothered us both: something was not quite what we had expected. We had come to this island to rid ourselves of all links with a civilization whose true virtues we had begun to doubt. Yet we had just seen fellow beings down in the village who were in desperate need of some sort of cultural progress. Medicine. Knowledge of germs.

'Medicine is civilization,' Liv commented laconically.

I could not contradict her. Medicine was one of the blessings of civilization. . . .

It was nature that had given us disease, and man had developed medicine for his own defence. . . . Liv pointed out. . . .

I had to agree, but insisted that Liv should bear in mind the reason why nature imposed more diseases on man than on any other living species.

'Because we live an unhealthy, unnatural life,' Liv admitted.

'That too,' I said, 'but even more because we have defied perhaps the most fundamental law of the biological environment: the vital equilibrium between the species.'

Then the rainy season arrived, turning the ground into a sea of mud. Everything became damp and mouldy, and squadrons of mosquitoes kept up an unrelenting attack day and night. Liv was soon covered in unsightly boils, a tropical affliction called *fe-fe*. Thor was spared the boils, but whenever his legs brushed through the undergrowth he developed sores which showed no disposition to heal. It became imperative for them to leave the island in search of medical help.

But the nearest island, Hivaoa, was over sixty miles away, and it might be weeks before the next copra schooner called. Eventually they found an old, abandoned wooden lifeboat amongst some reeds, and set out with a few intrepid natives to act as crew. It was a fearful journey, which affected Thor's attitude to conventional wooden boats for the rest of his life. Day and night they were in danger of being swamped by the heavy seas; it was only by constant bailing that they kept afloat at all.

Hivaoa was only marginally more sophisticated than Fatu Hiva, but Liv and Thor knew of a native there called Terai, who had learned some basic medicine in Tahiti. He agreed to treat their legs with mysterious ointments; it took many weeks, but gradually the sores began to

OVERLEAF *Liv and Thor's new home was on the east coast of Fatu Hiva, at the foot of the Ouia valley, far from the mosquitoes and elephantiasis that plagued the western part of the island.*

59

Half a century after his first visit Thor re-encounters the wind and currents of eastern Fatu Hiva, which combine to create a very different weather pattern from that on the opposite side.

heal. However, the time was not wasted.

One day they accompanied Terai on his monthly trip round the island to care for the sick. At the end of a day's riding through spectacular mountain scenery they came down through the isolated Puamau valley to a little house on the beach. The man who came out to greet them was astonished to hear himself addressed in his own language, Norwegian. His name was Henry Lie. Thirty years previously he had come to the islands working as a cabin boy, and was so enchanted by what he saw that he had decided to jump ship. He had been living in the Marquesas ever since, making a living by growing copra. He introduced them to his Polynesian wife and their son Aletti, and Thor told him of his growing interest in the origin of the Polynesian peoples. 'In that case,' said his new-found friend, 'there are one or two things on this island that might interest you.'

Next morning they set off, with Aletti as their guide. 'Suddenly we saw them,' wrote Thor in *Fatu Hiva* of this, one of the seminal experiences in his life. 'The giants.'

❛ Aletti had been silent as we approached and merely pointed as he held the foliage aside. They stared at us from the thickets with round eyes as big as life-belts and grotesque mouths drawn out in diabolical grins wide enough to swallow a human body. . . . The giants of the cliff-girt Puamau valley displayed such a contrast to the lazy Polynesians down on the beach that the question inevitably came to mind: who put these red stone colossi there, and how? They must have weighed many tons. . . .

We approached the tallest, which stood on an elevated stone platform. It took two of us to measure its fat belly, and with a deep pedestal sunk into the platform masonry the image was some ten feet tall, carved entirely from one block of red stone, a kind of stone that did not exist anywhere locally. . . .

The red statues had obviously been raised on some outdoor temple ground. We found that there were walls and terraces everywhere as we began looking around in the underbrush, and a few statues lay half buried in the ground, their heads or arms broken by force. There were also huge round heads gazing at us from between creepers and ferns, heads that had been carved as independent stone images without busts or bodies.

There are incidents in everyone's life that may be casual and yet prove to have vital consequences in future development, even to the extent of side-tracking an entire life. My introduction to the Puamau stone giants during an attempt to return to nature later resulted in switching me on to a new track that was to guide my destiny for many eventful years to come. It set me asail on rafts, led me into continental jungles, and made me excavate Easter Island monuments as high as buildings of several storeys. All in an effort to solve a mystery which puzzled me from the day I began to suspect that an enterprising people with the habit of creating stone colossi had reached the eastern headland of Hivaoa before the Polynesian fishermen arrived. **'**

Henry Lie was an erudite man with an impressive library. From him Thor learned of the legend, known throughout Polynesia, that another people with reddish hair and fair skin, who claimed descent from the sun-god, were already living on the islands before the present Polynesian population arrived. The belief was so widespread that when Captain Cook's ship *Endeavour* first appeared over the horizon in 1768, he and his men were welcomed as returning members of this earlier people.

While they were discussing these matters they were joined by an elderly Frenchman, whom Lie introduced

simply as 'my friend'. After listening to their conversation for a while, the Frenchman produced a thick book containing pictures of statues very similar to the giants they had seen that morning. But amazingly, these were in South America, due east of the Marquesas. Pre-Inca, they had been discovered by the Spanish conquistadores half hidden by the jungle. They stretched over a wide band from the northern Andes to Lake Titicaca, but were most numerous at Tiahuanaco, at the southern end of the lake. Here the local people, the Aymara Indians, informed the Spaniards that they had been made, not by their own ancestors, but by a fair-skinned race who had subsequently set sail on balsa wood rafts, across the Pacific in the direction of the setting sun.

Thor spent some time minutely examining all the sculptures and ruins he could find on the island. Cutting back the turf and undergrowth, he measured and took notes, all the time surprising even the local people with his discoveries. Then, with the job finished and their legs now healed, he and Liv decided to return to Fatu Hiva.

It was too soon to admit defeat, but it was never going to be quite the same again. The jungle had reclaimed their little clearing with amazing rapidity. Even the posts that supported their cabin had taken root, and were cheerfully sprouting leaves. Most depressing of all, the dreaded mosquitoes which carried elephantiasis seemed to have multiplied a thousandfold. It was impossible for them to stay. They would do better to move to the coast, where the sea breezes drove the mosquitoes away.

But the unhygienic squalor of the villages on the west coast had little appeal. They resolved to try and cross the high mountain wall that divides the island, and see what the east coast had to offer. Hiring a couple of pack horses, and with Tioti as their ever-faithful guide, they began the long and difficult ascent. At one point they were shocked and saddened to notice that, beneath his European-style trousers, one of Tioti's ankles was grotesquely swollen with elephantiasis. Fatu Hiva was looking less and less like Paradise.

On the summit of the ridge they were confronted by a sheer escarpment on the eastern side. After a nightmare

OVERLEAF *The bay on the west coast of Fatu Hiva where Thor had first landed with his young bride in 1937.*

OPPOSITE *The ever-encroaching jungle: during Thor and Liv's few weeks' absence from Fatu Hiva the framework of their cabin had caved in and the poles that supported the kitchen roof had begun to sprout leaf-covered branches.*

ABOVE *The old chief Tei-Tetua, said to be the last man still living on Fatu Hiva who had tasted human flesh. It was he who told Thor about the legend of Kon-Tiki.*

OPPOSITE ABOVE *A quiet evening on the terrace: Liv and Momo, the former cannibal chief's adopted daughter, listen while Tei-Tetua plays his nose flute. 'We never saw Momo without a smile on her face,' wrote Thor.* OPPOSITE BELOW *Half a century later, he shows Momo a book containing photographs of their first encounter.*

descent, at the foot of the precipice they followed a river down the Ouia valley until they came to a golden beach, with the Pacific glittering beyond in the morning light. It was the Polynesian dream they had long awaited.

The only inhabitants seemed to be an old man, naked except for a loincloth, and a young girl. The old man's name was Tei-Tetua; the girl, whom he introduced as his adopted daughter, was called Tahia-Momo. Both of them were delighted to have some extra human company, and they all celebrated with a feast of roast hog. Soon they were such good friends that the old man entreated them to stay. Wild pigs and fruit were plentiful, and the water was excellent. They needed little persuading. Next morning they began building a cabin on the beach, separated from Tei-Tetua's house by the stream.

The sole survivor of a thriving community, including his twelve wives, who had once lived on the eastern side of the island, Tei-Tetua was a true relic from the past. He remembered the days when cannibalism was practised throughout the Marquesas, and proved to be the last islander who had tasted human flesh. (Another reason perhaps, Thor thought, why the rest of Fatu Hiva's population preferred to live on the other side of the mountains.) But whatever his past, he was now a fine, generous old man, eager to share everything he had with his unexpected guests. Little Momo attached herself to Liv and taught her the old Marquesan arts: how to make paper from breadfruit bark, and how to weave *leis* from the flowers that grew all around. At night, this unlikely foursome would sit around the fire under the breathtaking canopy of the Polynesian sky, its darkness pierced by stars of extraordinary brilliance.

One evening, Thor managed to steer the conversation round to the subject of cannibalism:

❛Tei began to tell us about his father, Uta, who was the greatest and most savage warrior of the Ouia valley. He rarely ate any meat but human flesh. But he did not want it fresh, the way most of his friends ate it. No, he waited until it was old and tender before he headed for the burial platform to fill his *poe* or calabash-bowl. . . .

Human flesh was sweetish, like *kumaa*, or sweet potato. The victim was usually baked, like the pork he prepared for us; that is, rolled up in banana leaves between hot stones in an earth-oven. Some people ate human flesh from hunger, as there were too many people then for all of them to have enough food. But usually human flesh was eaten as a religious ceremony, and as a sort of revenge.

The choicest piece was supposed to be the forearm of a woman. 'A white woman,' Tei added, looking at Liv with a grin. . . . **'**

Tei-Tetua would often play his nose flute, or sing songs about Tiki, the god-king. Thor listened closely and questioned the old man about the legends of his people.

'It was Tiki in flesh and blood who had led Tei-Tetua's ancestors across the ocean to these islands.

'From where?' I asked, and was curious to hear the old man's reply.

'From Te-Fiti, from The East,' answered the old man and nodded towards that part of the horizon where the sun rose, the direction in which there was no other land except South America.

I was puzzled. Every scientist had taken it for granted that these islanders had come from the very opposite direction. From Asia. But the Marquesans themselves had always alluded to their ancestral fatherland as Te-Fiti, literally 'The East'. . . .

I looked across the moonlit sea. America was indeed far away. Still, Asia was more than twice as remote, and winds and currents came continuously down upon us from South America. It dawned upon me that we were in fact sitting on the one island of all the isles and atolls in Polynesia that had been first hit upon by Europeans. . . . And the first Europeans had come here from South America. . . . For, when the Spanish Mendana expedition discovered Polynesia in 1595, they came sailing this way straight from Peru down upon Fatu Hiva. It was the Incas of Peru who had told the Spaniards that there were inhabited islands far out here in the ocean. At that time the Europeans had known the coasts of Asia for almost three centuries without learning of inhabited islands in the Pacific. . . .

Could it not be, then, that Tei-Tetua and the other islanders remembered the truth, when they said that

Tei-Tetua had a realistic view of death and had already dug his own grave, decorated with a cross that a missionary had given him. His home-made coffin hung in the kitchen: when the time came, he told Thor and Liv, he would simply climb in and close the lid.

their ancestors really had come from the east?

After all, the scientists who had studied the physical types in Polynesia had stressed that the Polynesians contrasted with the Malays and Indonesians in nearly every respect: head form, nose form, hair colour, hair texture, stature, complexion, beard and body hair; everything was different. The only scholar who had made a special study of Marquesan somatology, the noted American anthropologist, L. R. Sullivan, had found that these islanders were far closer to certain American Indians in physical composition than to any Mongols, and there was nothing at all to support an Indonesian parentage.

For the first time I really started to wonder whether these islands could have been reached first by one of the many different kinds of culture people who had succeeded each other before the Inca dynasty in ancient Peru. **,**

Thor would have been keener still to unlock the old man's store of memories if he had known then what he was to discover in the years ahead. For the full Inca name for the god-king who had left Peru to travel westward was Con-Tici Viracocha. While he still ruled in Tiahuanaco, he was known simply as Tici, or Tiki.

From his new vantage point on the east coast of the

island, Thor began to look for supporting evidence that might link Fatu Hiva, and by inference the whole of this part of Polynesia, with the South American mainland. He felt sure that the pieces of the jigsaw were there to be found, waiting to be pieced together by someone who was not afraid to bridge academic disciplines. Much of the vegetation – the papaya, the small native pineapples, the sweet potatoes – originated in South America. Yet here they were, well established in this part of Polynesia long before the first Europeans arrived. Fruits and tubers could hardly have floated across such a breadth of ocean, since they rot rapidly in salt water.

There were other remarkable similarities. In the medical field trepanation, the surgical repair of skull fractures, was practised in ancient Peru. Yet the old man said he had seen it performed with his own eyes in Ouia by a medicine man named Teke. But the huge stone

Revisiting Fatu Hiva in the 1980s, Thor reminisces round a camp fire with Tei-Tetua's son.

giants they had uncovered in the jungle remained the most striking evidence of all. No one could say *they* had accidentally arrived on a piece of driftwood.

❛We sat there, staring at the drifting clouds and the heaving moonlit sea. Tei took a stick and stirred the dying embers of his little fire. He picked up his bamboo nose-flute, pressed it against one nostril and began to play. . . . Our own nostrils were filled with the scent of luxuriant foliage and salty air, and we listened to the delicate tones from the island's past; the nose-flute, the wind rustling in the coconut palms, and the cannonade which drowned out all other sounds each time a mighty roller broke against the boulder barricade we sat on. I sat and marvelled at this sea which never stopped proclaiming that it came this way, rolling in from the east, from the east, from the east. . . . ❜

One day life was suddenly interrupted by the arrival of people from the other side of the island, no doubt attracted by Tioti's stories of plentiful food. They soon revealed themselves to be noisy troublemakers, who began to brew beer from local oranges. Even old Tei started drinking, and was no longer his normal, generous self. It was time to go. Once again Thor and Liv made their way up the precipitous mountain passes.

Their original cabin was now uninhabitable, and the villagers of Omoa unfriendly and unwashed. It was Tioti who once again came to their rescue. He led them to a cave by the sea where they would at least be safe from disease and the worst of the rainy season. It wasn't Paradise; they even found deadly moray eels under the wet boulders inside the cave itself. But at least it was clean and free of mosquitoes. Above all, perhaps, it gave them time to consider their situation.

❛For several days neither of us spoke out. Perhaps we felt uncertain of each other, perhaps we felt uncertain of ourselves. . . .

'What to do if we see a schooner?' Liv asked one day, after we had been sitting all morning doing nothing but watching the waves on the horizon.

'We hurry to Omoa,' I replied. 'And if it arrives at night Tioti will come and fetch us.'

'Why?' asked Liv. Her voice was gently challenging. . . .

'I know,' she said. 'We are just running away from

ABOVE *Thor examines a papaya tree, a special variety which could only have been brought to Fatu Hiva by aboriginal voyagers from the South American mainland.*

OPPOSITE *A cave on the mountainside provided some welcome shelter from the midday sun on the journey back to the west coast of the island.*

everything here. This is not what we came to do.'

She had taken the words out of my mouth.

'We are just killing time now,' I admitted. 'Like the village people, sitting waiting for their coconuts to fall.'

We had confessed openly what both of us felt at the bottom of our hearts. . . .

Yet Liv stressed that she would not have missed our experience on this island for all the treasures in the world. That went for me too. . . .

'But do you realize something?' I said to Liv. 'If things had worked out differently, we should still have left Fatu Hiva. If we had found that man could rid himself of all modern problems by going straight back to nature, we should have been pestered by guilty consciences until we went home and told others.'

Something of the insect is within us. An ant has invisible ties to the ant-hill. A bee finds no satisfaction in hiding from the hive and licking its harvest in solitude.

'But do you know something?' interrupted Liv. 'If things had worked out the way we had expected, we still couldn't go home and recommend a mass migration back to nature. Think of our map.'

She was referring to the way we had been forced to cross out continents and islands . . . before we encircled Fatu Hiva as the only place that seemed possible for our back-to-nature experiment.

'There is nothing for modern man to return to,' I admitted. I said it most reluctantly, for our wonderful time in the wilderness had given us a taste of what mankind had abandoned and what mankind was still trying to get ever farther away from.

'We are in the middle of a long road. There is no way back, but don't let that ever make us believe that just any road ahead is progress,' I added. **)**

When the first available ship appeared on the horizon, they knew that they would indeed bring the experiment to an end. They were mellower in their judgments now; some might say they had grown up. But Thor still retained the deeply felt belief that man had taken the wrong turning, and was busy destroying the very planet on which he depended for his survival.

(We like to think of progress as modern man's struggle to secure better food for more people, warmer clothing

and finer dwellings for the poor, more medicine and hospitals for the sick, increased security against war, less corruption and crime, a happier life for young and old. But as it has turned out, progress involves much more.

It is progress when weapons are improved to kill more people at a longer range. It is progress when a little man becomes a giant because he can push a button and blow up the world. . . . It is also progress when reality gets so damned dull that we all survive by sitting staring at entertainment radiating from a box, or when one pill is invented to cure the harm done by another, or when hospitals grow up like mushrooms because our heads are overworked and our bodies underdeveloped, because our hearts are empty and our intestines filled with anything cleverly advertised. It is progress when a farmer leaves his hoe and a fisherman leaves his net to

Liv and Thor's last home on Fatu Hiva was a cave by the sea, where they lived like Stone Age people. The great experiment was over, and now they were waiting for the first schooner to appear over the horizon and take them back to civilization.

step on to an assembly line, the day the cornfield is leased to industry, which needs the salmon river as its sewer. It is progress when cities grow bigger and fields and forests smaller until ever more men spend ever more time in subways and bumper-to-bumper car queues . . . and blow exhaust all over their babies. When children get a sidewalk in exchange for a meadow, when the fragrance of flowers and the view of the hills and forests are replaced by air-conditioning and a view across the street. '

Then, one morning, the long wait was over.

' Suddenly I was torn out of my reveries as I focused my eyes on one point on the horizon.

'Liv,' I shouted. 'A sail!' . . .

We both climbed on to a lava outcrop and gazed at the majestic white sail of a schooner fixed in one spot among the changing white-caps on the horizon. It grew bigger. It came from Tahiti and was heading for Fatu Hiva. . . .

We hated leaving. We hated going back to civilization. But it was something we could not resist. We had to do it.

We were sure then, and I still am, that the only place where it is possible to find nature as it always was is within man himself. There it is, unchanged, now as always. Man has succeeded in changing his environment and his own attire. Some peoples have resorted to tattooing and body-paint, head-flattening, ear-extension, filing their teeth, and stunting the growth of their feet. Men shave and cut their hair, and women dye and curl their hair, paint their faces and put on false eyelashes, but below the skin nothing is ever altered. We cannot get away from ourselves. . . .

When we sat on the thwarts of the life-boat and our Polynesian friends rowed us out to the anchored schooner, I fumbled in a mouldy suitcase for our return vouchers.

'Liv,' I said, 'one can't buy a ticket to Paradise. '

5

THE HIGHWAYS OF THE ANCIENT WORLD

There are three great ocean currents, mightier than the mightiest river, that lead to the New World.

Liv and Thor got back to Norway in March 1938. Immediately both of them were pestered by friends and relatives. Had they truly found Paradise? Would they do it all over again? Had it been worth it? The answers were as complex as the questions. For the truth was that they were not the same two people who had set out in a mood of boundless optimism and naivety, baldly announcing to the world that there was more than a chance they might never return. Now here they were: thinner, wiser, and much chastened by their experience, but not in ways that were easy to put into words.

Thor remained convinced that mankind was somehow off the rails, intent on material progress at the expense of harmony with the natural world. But he was no longer so sure that he had any answers. The one thing above all that Fatu Hiva had taught him was that Paradise has no geographical location. If it lies anywhere, it lies within.

With Liv now pregnant, they settled for a piece of Norwegian wilderness instead of a Pacific one: a log cabin overlooking the town of Lillehammer where Thor had come for holidays as a boy. To keep some money coming in he wrote a Norwegian version of their experiences under the title *In Search of Paradise*, and undertook a series of lectures. Sadly, Liv never resumed her own academic studies, and for that reason may have felt the beginnings of resentment against Thor.

Much to the disappointment of his parents, Thor now

After returning to Norway in 1938 Thor and Liv moved into a cabin in the mountainous region around Lillehammer, where he wrote his first book, In Search of Paradise. *Later a revised, extended version was published as* Fatu Hiva: Back to Nature.

abandoned academic zoology and within weeks of returning handed over all his specimens from Fatu Hiva – fish, butterflies and beetles – to the Oslo University Museum. His prime interest – obsession, even – had become the Polynesian people themselves.

When the first maritime explorers from Europe found their way into the vast expanses of the eastern Pacific in the mid-eighteenth century, on every island they visited they were welcomed by people of very similar type. All spoke the same basic language, with only minor differences of dialect. For the most part they were fairly tall, with bronze skins and flat noses. They kept pigs and chickens. They had pineapples, sweet potatoes and bananas. But on none of the islands was there any trace of pottery, weaving or the use of the wheel. When, how and from where had these people reached their vast, watery homeland? The answer to those questions was still a mystery to anthropologists and ethnologists.

In Bjarne Kroepelien's library in Oslo Thor had discovered that over thirty theories had been put forward to account for the peopling of Polynesia – all different, and some mutually contradictory. Experts in linguistics, cranial measurement, adze heads and the distribution of blood groups – all trapped, in Thor's view, within the blinkers of their own specialist subjects – had put forward starting points as far afield as Korea, Japan, Sarawak, Malaya, Borneo and even Egypt.

These theorists did have one thing in common, however: they all agreed that the Polynesian migration must have been from west to east. Any movement the other way would have been impossible for lack of adequate ships to cover the vast distances. With the exception of the uninhabited Galapagos, at least two thousand miles of ocean lay between the American mainland and the nearest of the islands.

There was plenty of evidence to support the general theory of a migration from Asia: there were strong linguistic roots, strengthened by the presence of breadfruit, sugar cane, yams, taro and outrigger canoes, all of which echoed Asian cultural patterns. Who was Thor Heyerdahl, a lone student working outside his own academic field, to cast doubt on all of this?

And yet, in his mind's eye he could still see the breakers on the eastern shore of Fatu Hiva as they rushed in foaming from the sea; still hear Liv's words as they sat watching for hour upon hour: 'It's queer how there were never breakers like this on the other side of the island.' Another, still more potent image haunted his mind – the image of Tiki, the god-chief, worshipped by old Tei-Tetua, last of his cannibal race. The more Thor read in the libraries of Oslo, the more certain he became that this same Tiki was the one represented by gigantic monoliths on the shores of Lake Titicaca in the Andes.

There was one area of crucial importance to which no one seemed to be paying any attention: the true nature and contribution of the oceans. Up to very recent times, all scholars concerned with human migration routes had shared the same gigantic misconception – that before 1492, when Columbus sailed to America, the oceans were impassable barriers between one culture and another. It had to follow that all major migratory routes had been across land, or at the very most had involved island-hopping through some archipelago.

If this was the case, then the most isolated landmass in the world, the continents of North and South America, must have developed culturally without any influence from elsewhere – the widely accepted isolationist theory. But the more Thor read about the oceans, the less easy it became to accept that theory's validity. In the first place, it is easy to forget that the Equator is in fact a circle: a journey from east to west may be just as long, or short, as one from north to south. From the navigator's point of view, a second factor is even more important. The voyaging distance between two geographical points is quite different from the 'dead' distance, for every vessel has to contend with ocean currents. When considering the question of migration routes by sea, their importance can hardly be exaggerated. Yet Thor was already discovering that, in all the attempts to unravel the mystery of Polynesia, the true nature of the sea had been largely ignored.

There are three great ocean currents, mightier than the mightiest river, that lead to the New World: two on the Atlantic side and one on the Pacific. There are also three currents that lead away from it: two on the Pacific side, and just one on the Atlantic. They play a vital part

One of the great stone monoliths at Tiahuanaco on the shores of Lake Titicaca in the Bolivian Andes. When Thor visited the place, what he saw convinced him still further that the first people to reach eastern Polynesia must have come from America.

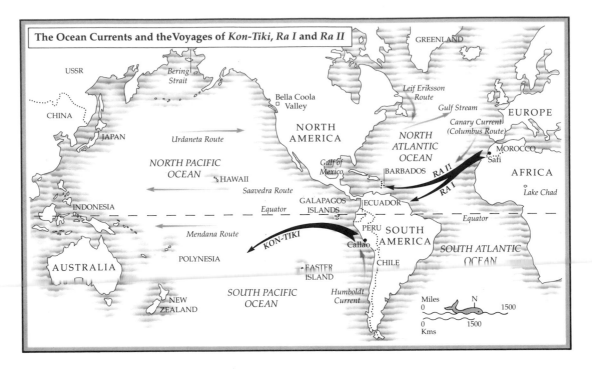

The Ocean Currents and the Voyages of *Kon-Tiki*, *Ra I* and *Ra II*

in this story; indeed, without them there would be no story to tell.

The shortest approach on the Atlantic side is the Leif Eriksson Route, a fast current that runs along the coast of Greenland before sweeping south-west towards Labrador and Newfoundland. It is now known that the Vikings in their longboats used this route for at least five voyages to the New World more than two hundred years before Columbus set out. The Columbus Route itself offers much more gentle climatic conditions (outside the hurricane season), and extremely favourable prevailing winds. It originates along the north-west African coast and runs, with the Canary Current, straight to the West Indies and the Gulf of Mexico. This was the route the slaving captains took, their ships loaded to the gunwales with human cargo. On the return leg these slavers, loaded now with bananas and sugar cane, used the one west–east route across the Atlantic which flows towards the British Isles – the Gulf Stream.

On the Pacific side the behaviour of the currents is quite different. Although European explorers reached the Asian side of the ocean long before they found a way through from the Atlantic, no crossing of the Pacific was attempted from west to east. The reason is simple: in the

Southern Ocean, the prevailing winds and currents are all in the other direction. The principal high road of the South Pacific is the Mendana Route, named after the first European to set eyes on the lush tropical islands of Melanesia and Polynesia. Magellan, Drake, Cook and many more made good use of the Mendana Route; and it certainly saved the lives of Captain Bligh and his companions when they set off in an open boat after the famous mutiny on the *Bounty*. Somewhat to the north of this current lies the one known as the Saavedra Route, from Mexico to Indonesia. It is very long, but favoured all the way by strong following trade winds, and almost invariable good weather. The Spanish galleons used this route to reach their colonies in the Philippines.

Only one major current crosses the Pacific in the opposite direction, towards the New World – the Urdarneta Route. But before it reaches its destination it takes a wide sweep up past the coasts of China and Japan, before curving round below the Arctic waters kept at bay by the Aleutian Islands to the south of Siberia and Alaska. This was the current which now caught Thor Heyerdahl's imagination. At first sight it is difficult to see what bearing it could have on the populating of the South Seas. But the more he considered the question, the more convinced he became that this route might bring together all the conflicting evidence.

While Thor was excitedly putting together his new theory, changes were taking place on the domestic front. On 28 September 1938, their first son, another Thor, was born. Naturally there was great rejoicing; and it must have seemed to both their families that the days of chasing after fantasies were at last behind them. But within a few days something happened, something quite small and apparently insignificant, which sent the wanderlust racing through the new father's veins once more.

In the course of a radio talk Thor had mentioned some of the rock carvings and other artefacts on Fatu Hiva. The radio at that time was a prime source of information and entertainment, especially among isolated communities; and it was no particular surprise when next day a local farmer congratulated him on the broadcast. The surprise came when he insisted that Thor should come to his house to examine some photographs. They had been taken in British Columbia by his brother, who happened to be staying with him. He was called Iver Fougner, and had served as a judge among the Indian community on the rugged west coast of Canada.

The photographs, mainly of the Indians and their way of life, were not very good – but Thor was transfixed. Here, in a homely Norwegian kitchen, were images of Fatu Hiva. But they were not Fatu Hiva. Here were rock carvings, stone adzes and the faces of people that he recognized immediately from his travels in Polynesia. But these were not Polynesians.

Closely questioning Iver Fougner, he learned that all the photographs depicted a seafaring people who had occupied the Bella Coola valley, directly inland from the coast about midway between Alaska and the United States. Fougner told Thor that they were quite unlike other North American Indians; it seemed that they had more in common with the peoples of Indonesia, or perhaps the Philippines.

Just a few days earlier Thor had been studying the movement of the Urdaneta Current, which runs up from Indonesia, past the Philippines and Japan, then heads straight for this mysterious Bella Coola valley before joining the trade winds down past Hawaii towards the Marquesas and Tahiti. Thor's new-found informant knew nothing of this mighty current, and yet he was talking as if its existence was a foregone conclusion.

Thor went back to the library to check the facts. Yes, there was a tribe of Indians in the north-west whose clothes were not woven but made from the inner bark of trees, and who seemed to be entirely ignorant of both iron and pottery – just like the people found by the first European explorers of the eastern Pacific. But were they the ones who inhabited the Bella Coola valley? This could prove to be much more than just another piece in the jigsaw – it could be the headstone, holding the great arch of the Pacific together. If he was right, and the migration route to Polynesia from Asia ran north, then east and finally south, all sorts of anomalies would suddenly fall into place. Thor knew that his next expedition must be to the Pacific coast of Canada: to the Bella Coola valley in British Columbia.

6

DISTANT THUNDER

*'In due course you will be exercising your skills
in special operations behind enemy lines.'*

By the time Liv and Thor set out for Canada in the autumn of 1939, Germany was already at war with Great Britain and France. That in itself is an illustration of how detached they felt from the events which were about to plunge the world into turmoil. Once before, they had put what they saw as the corrupt values of Europe behind them. They were about to do it again.

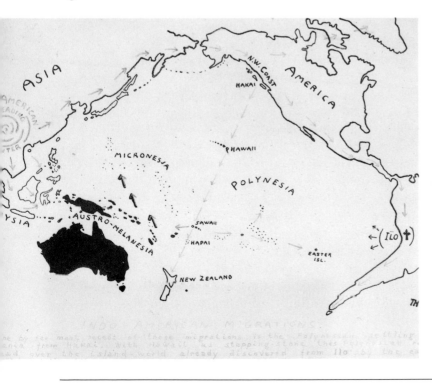

The sketch map drawn by Thor before his expedition to British Columbia. It illustrated his then revolutionary theory that migration from South-East Asia followed a circular route using the ocean currents, sweeping first north to North America, then south to Hawaii.

When Thor's Indian guide in the Bella Coola valley had to shoot a black bear, the killing reinforced Thor's aversion to all forms of hunting: 'The forest rang with howls that I shall never forget.'

As soon as Liv had Thor's assurance that he had no plans for further experiments in primitive living, she was eager enough to escape from being a housewife and mother in Lillehammer. But in some ways the northwest coast of Canada promised to be just as tough a proposition as the tropical island of Fatu Hiva. They would be cold; and they would be poor.

It was now that Thor Heyerdahl began an association that has proved to be one of the mainstays of his working life. The most important Norwegian shipping line, then as now, was run by that pioneer in the field, Fred Olsen. In every major port in the world his name was widely respected. Thor was a firm believer in the maxim that 'He who doesn't ask, doesn't get.' With all the brashness of youth, he presented himself at the office door of Fred Olsen's son Thomas, who had a senior position in the company; and by the time he came out he had secured, for a purely nominal sum, a passage to Vancouver for his family.

Thor hoped to find detailed evidence to support the North American end of the twin theory beginning to develop in his mind. At the heart of it lay the growing conviction that there had been two quite different waves of migration to eastern Polynesia. He first published this theory in a New York magazine called *Inter-*

national Science in May 1940. Taking as his title 'Did Polynesian Culture Originate in America?', in his summary Heyerdahl wrote:

❛After a year of research along the British Columbian coast, I believe that I possess sufficient material to trace two separate migrations from the American mainland to the Polynesian island world. (a) A pre-Incan civilization, with its centre near Lake Titicaca, and along the Peruvian coast below, seems to have swept the islands at a comparatively early period; while (b) a later migration, the descendants of which dominate the present Polynesian race, reached the islands via Hawaii, from the Bella Coola area of British Columbia, about AD 1000.❜

American and Canadian academics like to think of Indian studies as their own private preserve, and they were in no mood to think of their Indians as coming from, or going to, anywhere. In fact it was the redoubtable Margaret Mead, author of *Growing Up in Samoa*, who forestalled any serious debate on Thor's new theories. In answer to a journalist's question, she said that if any artefacts similar to Polynesian ones had been found on the North American mainland, the likelihood was that they had been left there by Captain Cook after visiting Hawaii. It was a hasty and stupid comment by

The Heyerdahl boys were only allowed to take their canoe out after their father had fitted it with South Sea-type outriggers. Whatever antics their pet got up to, the boat would not capsize.

RIGHT *Before returning from Canada to occupied Europe Thor was trained as a wireless operator. The orphaned bear cub Peik, who lived with the Heyerdahl family, became a mascot for him and his companions.*

BELOW *Thor with his young sons before departing for Europe. Despite having to leave his family behind he felt he was doing something important for his homeland: 'Never since has any arrival in Norway filled me with such profuse joy.'*

that eminent lady, but there was no time for Thor to refute it. Norway had been invaded.

There is a well-worn story that, when he heard the news, Thor said 'By whom?' It is hard to believe that his unconcern for world affairs stretched quite as far as that: Thor knew that, with or without his family, he had to try and get home. Each week new reports came in of the suffering and privations being inflicted on Norway. Having tried to turn his back on the war, he was determined now to be in the thick of it. Until Hitler had been dealt with, everything else must wait.

He began by joining a special training unit in Canada known as I Group or 'Little Norway'. They were to receive special training as radio operators and parachutists. 'In due course,' they were told, 'you will be exercising your skills in special operations behind enemy lines, among Norway's rugged mountains and fjords.' That was the plan, but as the months stretched into years it became more and more apparent that at best they were a nuisance, and at worst a forgotten body of men for whom no one appeared to have any use at all.

When at last Thor received notice to transfer to active service in Europe, Liv and the child suddenly became a major problem. It was Thomas Olsen once more who came to the rescue, by offering Liv an indefinite wel-

come at his mansion outside New York. It seemed an ideal solution, but it was to prove a fatal one.

Eventually, after many weeks of muddle and uncertainty, Thor arrived by Arctic convoy at Murmansk on the north coast of Russia. For a few brief months he was active behind the German lines, and his portable radio spluttered and crackled to some purpose. Then it was over; and immediately the situation was reversed. Having spent the best part of the war trying to get on to the field of play his problem now was how to get off it; apparently Heyerdahl the unwanted had suddenly become Heyerdahl the indispensable. But by then he had learned a thing or two about the military mind. Members of the armed services the world over are

Thor (centre) on active service behind enemy lines in Norway, where his task was to establish contact between the Resistance and the government in exile in London. On the left is Bjørn Rørholt, who was later to help provide urgently needed funds at a crucial stage in the planning of the Kon-Tiki *expedition.*

After the war Knut Haugland, one of the great heroes of the Norwegian Resistance, was to join Thor on the Kon-Tiki *expedition. Today he is Director of the Kon-Tiki Museum in Oslo.*

trained to respond to rank and official-looking bits of paper; perhaps a combination of the two might do the trick.

First he obtained a leave pass to go down to Oslo; Liv was arriving home from America. There he marched boldly into headquarters, found a piece of headed notepaper and typed out an order for his own discharge. The next step was to find some cog in the machine who was even more junior than he was. Spotting a harassed-looking second lieutenant, he brusquely ordered him to pass the document through the proper channels with the utmost despatch. In a matter of days his official release came through.

Thor made many friends during the war years, but two especially were to play a key part in the adventures that lay ahead. The first was Torstein Raaby. He had been dropped by parachute near the fjord where the *Tirpitz*, the pride of the German Navy, had her base, and for nearly a year he observed her movements, sending almost daily reports to London. Acting on information supplied by Raaby, two midget submarines severely damaged the *Tirpitz* in September 1943, and eventually the RAF bombed and sank the great ship at her moorings. Thor's second wartime comrade was Knut Haugland. In February 1943 he was one of a party of Norwegian saboteurs who attacked the heavy water plant in the Rjukan valley; it was this raid which prevented the Germans from developing an atomic bomb ahead of the Americans. Nothing that happened to Thor Heyerdahl in the war was to prove of more lasting significance than his chance meetings with these two Norwegian patriots.

7

T HE UNWELCOMING CITY

'You know, here in America, people turn up
with so many queer ideas'

After years of enforced separation Liv was looking forward to a husband with a normal job. It
was certainly no surprise to her to find that
Thor's obsession with the Pacific was as strong as ever,
but by now there were two children – their second son,
Björn, had been born in September 1940 – and it
seemed reasonable to her that the responsibilities of
fatherhood should come first. Thor, however, saw
things differently. All through the wasted years of war,
he had been nursing a dream. In that dream he was
bound for America once more, with just one purpose in
mind: to convince the scientific world that he had the
answer to the great mystery of Polynesia. Liv let him go
without complaint, but she knew before he did that the
bonds holding them together were already weakening.

There were other, less specific factors, too. Couples
separated by war often find they have become different
people by the end of it. They cannot start again as if
nothing had intervened. To a large extent Liv had been
insulated from the grim realities of the struggle against
Hitler: the arrest in the night, the hostage-taking, the
executions. With her infectious gaiety, she had become
a popular member of the New York social scene. On
Fatu Hiva, in the early days of their marriage, they had
seemed in almost perfect harmony when it came to fundamental questions. Now Liv was less liberal in her
political views, and where religion was concerned she
seemed to have adopted a sort of strident atheism, quite
out of tune with Thor's own searchings for a kind of

OVERLEAF *A drawing by the
famous German explorer Baron
von Humboldt of the kind of
balsa log raft that was in
common use along the Pacific
coast of Peru in the eighteenth
century.*

89

intelligence that might give meaning to the universe.

Through his connections with the Olsen family, Thor availed himself of a spare bunk on a ship bound for New York. But America was not about to open its doors, nor its ears, to this brash young intruder. In *The Kon-Tiki Expedition* Thor wrote of his first meeting with Dr Herbert Spinden, President of the Explorers' Club and Director of the Brooklyn Museum, to whom he had sent a copy of his manuscript 'Polynesia and America'.

❛'Arguments!' he said. 'You can't treat ethnographic problems as a sort of detective mystery!'

'Why not?' I said. 'I've based all the conclusions on my own observations and the facts that science has recorded.'

'The task of science is investigation pure and simple,' he said quietly. 'Not to try to prove this or that.'

He pushed the unopened manuscript carefully to one side and leaned over the table.

'It's quite true that South America was the home of some of the most curious civilizations of antiquity, and that we know neither who they were nor where they vanished to when the Incas came into power. But one thing we do know for certain – that none of the peoples of South America got over to the islands in the Pacific.'

He looked at me searchingly, and continued:

'Do you know why? The answer's simple enough. They couldn't get there. They had no boats!'

'They had rafts,' I objected hesitatingly. 'You know, balsa-wood rafts.'

The old man smiled and asked quietly:

'Would you like to try a trip from Peru to the Pacific islands on a balsa-wood raft?'

I could find nothing to say. It was getting late. We both rose. The old scientist patted me kindly on the shoulder as he saw me out and said that if I wanted help I had only to come to him. But I must in future specialize on Polynesia or America, and not mix up two separate anthropological areas. He reached back over the table.

'You've forgotten this,' he said, and handed back my manuscript. ❜

Wherever Thor went, in Washington, Boston and New York, the reception was much the same. Academic opinion could not be shifted. 'You know, here in

America,' he was told patronizingly, 'people turn up with so many queer ideas.'

Soon Thor's funds had grown so low that he had to move into the Norwegian Sailors' Home in Brooklyn. From these rough mariners there were lessons to be learned about the behaviour of the oceans, which lay outside his own experience. He had not realized, for instance, that the open sea has fewer terrors for the sailor than waters closer to the shore, where winds and currents are frequently at their worst. And when it comes to the danger of a vessel breaking up in a storm, a small craft that can ride the waves like a gull stands a much better chance of surviving than a bigger one that may get caught between one wave and the next. However, when it came to the sea-going properties of rafts, his new-found friends were rather less encouraging. In fact they were positively scornful.

In October 1946, Thor set out on paper for the first time the plan that was forming in his mind. He wrote to a friend, Erling Schjerven, back in Oslo:

❝One of the main arguments of my opponents is that the coastal inhabitants of Peru used a kind of log raft before the time of Columbus, and that these could not manage the voyage from Peru to Easter Island, which is two thousand miles. . . . If I cannot gain a hearing in any other way, my plan is to build a faithful copy of the log rafts of which we have detailed descriptions. . . . It is my intention . . . to prove that the voyage is feasible, since I shall have the ocean current and the trade wind behind all the way. In other words I intend to re-enact a voyage from South America to the South Sea islands on a primitive Inca raft. . . .❞

The vast canyons of New York can be as lonely as a wilderness. Thor was desperate for a kindred spirit, and just at that time chance provided one. The cheap but excellent food at the Sailors' Home had attracted another Norwegian landlubber – Herman Watzinger, an engineer from Trondheim. Watzinger was the first human being Thor had spoken to for many weeks who didn't actually think he was mad. On the strength of nothing much more than an open face and boundless enthusiasm he became Thor's first recruit, and in effect his second-in-command.

That chance meeting seemed to change Thor's luck. A few days later he took Watzinger to the Explorers' Club in Manhattan, where they ran straight into the Danish Polar explorer Peter Freuchen. In a letter home, Thor described the encounter:

❛Freuchen has the blessed quality of never disappearing in a crowd. As big as a barn door and bristling with beard, he looks like a messenger from the open tundra. A special atmosphere surrounds him – it is as though he were going about with a grizzly bear on a lead. We took him over to a big map on the wall and told him about our plans for crossing the Pacific on an Indian raft. His boyish blue eyes grew large as saucers, and he tugged at his beard as he listened. Then he stamped his wooden leg on the floor and tightened his belt several holes. 'Damn it boys, I should like to be going with you!' The old Greenland traveller filled our beer mugs and began to tell us of his belief in primitive peoples' vessels. . . . He himself had travelled by raft down the great rivers of Siberia, and towed natives on rafts astern of his ship along the coast of the Arctic. ❜

Peter Freuchen's contribution to the *Kon-Tiki* expedition was to take it seriously. Thanks to his support and enthusiasm, suddenly the hare-brained scheme was being talked about. They were taken up by the Scandinavian press. Backers emerged from the woodwork with offers of cash. For a few heady weeks it looked as if Thor's financial problems might be over; but where funds are concerned, life is never so simple. In the weeks ahead, almost all the offers were either withdrawn, or so hedged around with conditions as to be virtually useless.

On Boxing Day 1946, in a mood close to despair, Thor wrote out a page of diary notes and put them in a sealed envelope. It was Arnold Jacoby who opened it sixteen years later.

❛. . . Success and humiliation have followed one another step by step for many years, and in turn. Today they have both risen side by side to dangerous heights, so dangerous that one of them must collapse in the next few days. For long months I have been moving alone in a metropolis with a manuscript which no one would read. Day by day my money grew less. Before it was too

late I decided on the raft trip and staked my whole life on the plan, leaving no way of retreat open, in order to be able to concentrate on the way forward. I've gone straight ahead as never before in my life, I have believed and willed, and the obstacles have collapsed, one after another, until today. Many are still willing to contribute their name, some are willing to contribute from the government's abundance. But no one is willing to give anything of his own. We have arrived at a point where we have attracted abundant interest, have obtained most of the important equipment, but have not a penny with which to start the expedition. . . . There is one way forward, and none back. I believe it will work out; and I am determined that it shall work out. But I should like to remember this day, this struggle and this experience for

An historic meeting at the Explorers' Club in New York. Among the few who took Thor's planned Kon-Tiki *project seriously at this time were the bearded Greenland explorer Peter Freuchen and (second from left) Herman Watzinger, who was to join the crew.*

95

the rest of my life, till the day I shall be forced to give up my very breath. ❩

That was the lowest point. The following day Thor had a call from the Norwegian military attaché. Sensing that he and Watzinger were at the end of their tether, he pulled out his chequebook and handed over an indefinite loan of $500. In fact the attaché was not a complete stranger. His name was Bjørn Rørholt, and Thor had worked briefly with him during the war. In gratitude he now offered Rørholt a place aboard *Kon-Tiki*; but it was declined.

As for the rest of the crew, Thor had already decided that he did not want professional sailors, whose very skills would invalidate the experiment. Talking it over with Herman, it seemed sensible to think in terms of six watches of four hours each. With two men on duty for every watch, that meant they were looking for a crew of six. Of these, at least one would need to know how to use a sextant, understand the basics of navigation by the stars, and plot their course on a chart. The man Thor had in mind was an old boyhood friend, Erik Hesselberg. When he told Herman that he was also full of fun and could play the guitar, no further persuasion was needed. Herman in turn was convinced that they would have to have a radio, whether such things were known to the Incas or not. He was delighted at the suggestion of Knut Haugland and Torstein Raaby, who between them probably had more experience of operating radios under adverse conditions than anyone else alive.

Never for a moment did Thor expect that any of these men would be in a position simply to drop everything and come, and his letter must have caused a good deal of mirth at three Norwegian breakfast tables: 'Am going to cross the Pacific on a wooden raft to support a theory that the South Sea islands were peopled from Peru. Will you come? I guarantee nothing but a free trip to Peru, and the South Sea islands and back, and you will find good use for your technical abilities on the voyage. Reply at once.' At that time Thor hadn't seen Erik for many years, and he certainly wasn't a close friend of either Knut or Torstein. There was a strong chance that they would treat the invitation as a fanciful schoolboy prank or even a practical joke. But they didn't. That same day Torstein Raaby despatched a telegram with just one word on it: 'Coming.' Erik and Knut also accepted without demur. It hardly seems likely that all three of them were suddenly seized with a desire to solve the mysteries of the Pacific: a more probable explanation is that, after the excitements of the war, the peace was proving rather dull.

They still needed one more volunteer. But there was no hurry; in due course Thor felt sure that the right man would present himself. He gave a lot of thought to the possibility of awarding the last place to a woman, but in the end he decided against the idea. It wasn't so much the fear of emotional entanglements but the sort of publicity it would undoubtedly attract. In many ways, it was a pity. He knew very well from old Spanish accounts that the early navigators had sailed their rafts up and down the coast with whole families aboard.

Francisco Pizarro encountered balsa wood rafts off the coast of South America long before he discovered the Inca Empire itself. In 1526, his pilot Bartolomeo Ruiz pushed south from the Panamanian isthmus in order to explore the coast south of the Equator. To his astonishment, he suddenly saw another vessel sailing north towards him. It was a large raft, roughly equal in size to his own caravel, but much less manoeuvrable. On board were twenty Indians, both men and women, whom he had little difficulty in overpowering. With that casual cruelty for which the Spaniards of that period were notorious, eleven were thrown overboard to provide food for the sharks. Five were taken prisoner, and the remaining four were left on board their own craft, but not before Ruiz had given it a thorough examination.

The raft was composed of nine balsa logs, the lightest wood in the forests of South America. The longest log was placed in the middle, and progressively shorter ones on either side, which gave the craft a prow at one end. At right-angles to the logs, and raised several inches above them, was a deck made from slender canes, which remained dry while the logs beneath were permanently awash. Indeed, there was no attempt to prevent the water from running between them. Both logs and canes were held in place by lengths of henequen rope, not unlike hemp. The raft was a very good load carrier: the Spaniards estimated that it had a capacity of thirty-six tons. They were equally impressed with the rigging, which 'carried masts and yards of very fine wood, and cotton sails in the same shape and manner as on our own ships'.

But however impressed the Spaniards were in the sixteenth century, academic experts writing in the twentieth were not. They all agreed with the pronouncement of Dr Samuel Lothrop of Harvard University, who in 1932 had published a treatise called *Aboriginal Navigation of the West Coast of South America.* In it, he reached the conclusion that any craft made of balsa had one unavoidable weakness: the wood absorbs water so quickly that a raft would be bound to sink in a comparatively short time. He concluded that after using them the Incas probably dismembered their rafts and dried out the logs in the sun before reassembling them for another short journey. Using such craft for long ocean-going voyages would be quite out of the question. This was the expert view that Thor Heyerdahl was about to challenge as he flew south over the endless rain forests of the Amazon basin.

8

THE BUILDING OF
KON-TIKI

'A flippant naval attaché bet all the whisky the
expedition could drink if they reached a
South Sea island alive.'

On one point Thor Heyerdahl was quite clear.
Although he intended to copy the ancient raft
designs as closely as possible, using no modern
materials such as nails or wire, the balsa logs themselves
must come from newly felled trees. Old logs would
absorb water at much too fast a rate; but new logs, still
full of sap, should be much more water-resistant. The
problem was to find them.

Their plane had brought them to Guayaquil in southern Ecuador. Situated at the mouth of several rivers, it
seemed the obvious place to find balsa wood. But there
was none to be had: all the trees on the coast had been
cut down to meet wartime demands for aircraft manu-
facture. In six months' time the rains would be over,
their genial hosts comforted them, and then the roads
into the interior would be open again. In the meantime,
why not settle down and enjoy local hospitality?

Six months in Guayaquil: it sounded like a life sen-
tence. Knut, Torstein and Erik had already left Norway,
and once they arrived the expedition's slender funds
would evaporate. For the umpteenth time Herman and
Thor pored over the map to see if a route could be found
through the swollen network of waterways that would
lead them up into the interior.

Then, in a flash, Thor had the answer. He simply
turned the map the other way round. Instead of trying to
go up from the coast, they must come down from the
Andes and penetrate the rain forest from the north. A
couple of days later the two of them were strapped into a

As each balsa tree was selected, it was named after one of the legendary figures supposed to have accompanied the man-god Tiki across the sea towards the setting sun. The first to be cut down was called Ku.

hired cargo plane circling over Quito, the capital of Ecuador, nestling nine thousand feet up in the mountains. There were still two hundred miles to go before they reached the logging camps of Quivedo, south-west of the capital. But fortunately the American military attaché had heard about the proposed expedition. By this time, Thor's powers of persuasion were so finely tuned that the poor man never stood a chance. The next day an army jeep drove up to their hotel, loaded with petrol, spares and rations of all kinds. They were on their way to the balsa forests at last – and in style.

In those days Quivedo consisted of a couple of rows of tarred wooden houses, watched over by several hungry vultures. Thor had an introduction to a plantation owner called Don Federico; and in *The Kon-Tiki Expedition* Thor recalled their first foray into the jungle:

❛Soon after sunrise Don Federico sent his men out on horseback in all directions to look for accessible balsa trees along the paths . . . we soon found our way to an open place where there was a gigantic old tree of which Don Federico knew. It towered high above the trees round about, and the trunk was three feet thick. In Polynesian style we christened the tree before we touched it: we gave it the name Ku, after a Polynesian deity of American origin. . . .

From time to time we heard creaking and crashing and a heavy thud somewhere in the virgin forest. Don Federico nodded with a satisfied air. It meant that his half-breed Indians had felled a new giant balsa for the raft. In a week Ku had been followed by Kane, Kama, Ilo, Mauri, Ra, Rangi, Papa, Taranga, Kura, Kukara and Hiti, twelve mighty balsas, all christened in honour of Polynesian legendary figures whose names had once been borne with Tiki over the sea from Peru. **,**

The logs, each weighing about a ton, were dragged to the River Palenque, first by horses, then by tractor. After that they were lashed together to form two temporary rafts, which were loaded with bananas and lianas. The moorings were cut and they were off, caught up by a fast surge of water which propelled them to Guayaquil. Herman was to transport the logs from there by steamer to Peru, while Thor went to Lima by plane, in search of a suitable place to build the raft.

During a visit to the United Nations some weeks earlier, a Chilean archaeologist had given Thor a letter of introduction to the President of Peru. He was rumoured to be a rather unapproachable man whom very few Peruvians had actually seen in the flesh. But two days later Thor found himself ushered into the presence of a small man in a neat white suit. What Thor

The twelve balsa logs were lashed together with lianas to form rough rafts, and were then floated down the Palenque river to the Pacific.

Erik Hesselberg, Thor's boyhood friend and now a crew member, made many drawings of the expedition. In the naval dockyard at Callao one admiral was very pessimistic about their chances of survival, and made Thor sign a document absolving the Peruvian Navy from all responsibility.

wanted above all was a secure place, preferably within the naval dockyard at Callao, where they would be free to build the raft away from public gaze and the risk of vandalism. But since he had the ear of the President himself he decided to throw in a few extras as well, like the use of the naval workshops and dry dock should they require them. In due course they would also need a vessel that could tow them out into the Humboldt Current to begin their voyage.

After a few sharp questions, the President smiled and issued the necessary orders. 'If it is possible that the Pacific islands were first discovered from Peru,' he said, 'then Peru has an interest in this expedition. Let us be partners.' With that he shook Thor firmly by the hand.

But others were not so pleased. When the Minister of Marine, who was in charge of the naval dockyard, came down to inspect the frail craft he took Thor aside and made him sign a paper exonerating the Peruvian Navy from any responsibility in a venture so obviously destined to end in disaster.

It was now that the last member of the *Kon-Tiki*'s crew presented himself. This is how Thor described that first meeting:

❛I . . . was sitting in my hotel writing to Herman about the site for building the raft, when I was interrupted by a knock on the door. In came a tall sun-burnt fellow in tropical kit, and when he took off his white helmet it looked as if his flaming red beard had burned his face and scorched his hair thin. That fellow came from the wilds, but his place was clearly a lecture-room.

'Bengt Danielsson,' I thought.

'Bengt Danielsson,' said the man, introducing himself.

'He's heard about the raft,' I thought, and asked him to sit down.

'I've just heard about the raft plans,' said the Swede.

'And now he's come to knock down the theory, because he's an ethnologist,' I thought.

'And now I've come to ask if I may come with you on the raft,' the Swede said peaceably. 'I'm interested in the migration theory.' ❜

One by one the rest of the chosen team arrived in Lima. For the next few weeks, one inanimate object dominated all their working hours – the raft itself. In *The*

Kon-Tiki Expedition Thor described the scene:

❝ Down in the naval dockyard lay the big balsa logs from the Quivedo forest. . . . Fresh-cut round logs, yellow bamboos, reeds and green banana leaves lay in a heap; our building materials, in between rows of threatening grey submarines and destroyers. Six fair-skinned Northerners and two brown naval ratings with Inca blood in their veins swung axes and long machete knives, and tugged at ropes and knots. Trim naval officers in blue and gold walked over and stared in bewilderment at these pale strangers and these vegetable materials which has suddenly appeared in their midst, in the dockyard of all places. . . .

The ultra-modern dockyard gave us wonderful support . . . we had the run of the carpenter's and sailmaker's shops, as well as half the storage space as a dump for our equipment, and a small floating pier where the timber was put into the water when the building began. ❞

The construction, Thor wrote, was a faithful copy of the old vessels in Peru and Ecuador, with the exception of some low splashboards in the bows – which subsequently proved entirely unnecessary.

❝ Nine of the thickest logs were chosen as sufficient to form the actual craft. Deep grooves were cut in the wood to prevent the ropes which were to fasten them and the whole raft together from slipping. Not a single spike, nail or wire rope was used in the whole construction. The nine logs were first laid loose side by side in the

For the first time in hundreds of years, a balsa raft was being built in Callao Bay. 'Six fair-skinned northerners and two brown naval ratings with Inca blood in their veins swung axes and long machete knives, and tugged at ropes and knots.'

water so that they might all fall freely into their natural floating position before they were lashed securely together. The longest log, forty-five feet long, was laid in the middle and projected a long way at both ends. Shorter and shorter logs were laid symmetrically on both sides of this, so that the sides of the raft were thirty feet long, and the bow stuck out like a blunt plough. Astern the raft was cut off straight across, except that the three middle logs projected and supported a short thick block of balsa wood which lay athwart ship and held thole-pins [in place of rowlocks] for the long steering oar. When the nine balsa logs were lashed securely together with separate lengths of inch and a quarter-inch hemp rope, the thin balsa logs were made fast crossways over them at intervals of about three feet. The raft itself was now complete, laboriously fastened together with about three hundred different lengths of rope, each firmly knotted. A deck of split bamboos was laid upon it, fastened to it in the form of separate strips, and covered with loose mats of plaited bamboo reeds. In the middle of the raft, but nearer the stern, we erected a small open cabin of bamboo canes, with walls of plaited bamboo reeds and a roof of bamboo slats with leathery banana leaves overlapping one another like tiles. Forward of the cabin we set up two masts side by side. They were cut from mangrove wood as hard as iron, and leaned towards one another, so that they were lashed together crosswise at the top. The big rectangular square-sail was hauled up on a yard made of two bamboo stems bound together to secure double strength.

The nine big logs of timber which were to carry us over the sea were pointed at their forward ends in native fashion, that they might glide more easily through the water, and quite low splash-boards were fastened to the bow above the surface of the water.

At various places where there were large chinks between the logs we pushed down in all five solid fir planks which stood on their edges right down in the water under the raft. They were scattered about without system and went down five feet into the water, an inch thick and two feet wide. They were kept in place with wedges and ropes, and served as tiny parallel keels or centreboards. Centreboards of this kind were used on all the balsa rafts of Inca times long before the time of the discoveries, and were meant to prevent the flat wooden rafts from drifting sideways with wind and sea. We did not make any rail or protection round the raft, but we had a long slim balsa log which afforded foothold along each side. 〞

A stream of distinguished visitors came down to the docks to inspect work in progress. Not one of them thought the Scandinavians had a glimmer of a chance. One admiral who inspected the craft told them they were as good as dead already. In his book Thor recalled all the objections of these Job's comforters:

〝In the first place, the raft's dimensions were wrong. It was so small that it would founder in big seas, and at the same time it was just long enough to be lifted up by two lines of waves at the same time, and with the raft filled with men and cargo the fragile balsa logs would break under the strain. And, what was worse, the biggest balsa exporter in the country had told [the admiral] that the porous balsa logs would float only a quarter of the distance across the sea before they became so completely water-logged that they would sink under us.

. . . Gales and perhaps hurricanes would wash us overboard and destroy the low and open craft, which would simply lie helpless and drift in circles about the ocean before wind and sea. Even in an ordinary choppy sea we should be continually drenched with salt water which would take the skin off our legs and ruin everything on board. . . . High wagers were made as to how many days the raft would last, and a flippant naval attaché bet all the whisky the members of the expedition could drink in the rest of their lives if they reached a South Sea island alive.

Worst of all was when a Norwegian ship came into port and we took the skipper and one or two of his most experienced seadogs into the dockyard. We were eager to hear their practical reactions. And our disappointment was great when they all agreed that the blunt-bowed, clumsy craft would never get any help from the sail, while the skipper maintained that, if we kept afloat, the raft would take a year or two to drift across with the Humboldt Current. The boatswain looked at our lash-

Erik Hesselberg's drawing of the naming ceremony. Such was the press of officialdom, diplomats and friends that Thor confided in his diary: 'We decided that if the raft went to pieces outside in the bay, we would paddle to Polynesia, each of us on a log, rather than dare come back in here again.'

ings and shook his head. We need not worry. The raft would not hold together for a fortnight before every single rope was worn through, for when at sea the big logs would be continually moving up and down and rubbing against one another. **"**

The next step was to provision the raft. Under the bamboo deck they stowed enough military rations to last six men for four months. This didn't leave much of a margin if they were becalmed or the raft was seriously damaged. Thor estimated that the voyage would take around a hundred days; they had sufficient food for a hundred and twenty. But he hoped this would be supplemented by fish caught during the voyage.

Next, they drove high into the mountains to load up fifty-six small cans with crystal-clear spring water; if one small can sprang a leak, or became contaminated with salt water, the rest would be safe. There would be less than half a gallon per man per day; there was simply no space for more. Fruit, vegetables and coconuts were stowed on deck at the last minute, in large wicker baskets. The only other cargo consisted of eight wooden boxes: two for storing films and delicate equipment, and one per man for personal belongings.

It was now that they acquired a seventh member of the crew – a bright green parrot with a sharp temper and an even sharper beak. He was none too popular in the early days, and might easily have ended up in the pot. But as the voyage progressed, he more than earned his place.

The last few days in Callao were filled with scenes of chaotic bustle and near disaster. The captain of the tug *Guardian Rios*, which was to tow them out to sea, decided to begin the job when only Thor and the parrot were actually on board. The rest of the crew, who were ashore buying newspapers and having a few farewell beers, were quite unaware that the *Kon-Tiki* had already started on her fateful voyage. A few hours later they were off once more, this time in earnest and with a full ship's company. Press photographers, naval officers, dock workers and pretty señoritas packed the quayside, most of them quite convinced that the mad Scandinavians would never be seen again.

In the middle of the bay, where the sea was already sufficiently lively to make the *Kon-Tiki* buck like an angry bronco, their first mishap occurred: the tow rope snapped. It proved alarmingly difficult to manoeuvre the raft alongside the tug without crashing into her iron sides – or, worse, being sucked underneath. Finally, after a hard struggle, they managed to grab the rope again. The towing then went on all night while they took turns to keep watch on the tow rope and snatch a little sleep.

‘When it grew light next morning, a thick mist lay over the coast of Peru, while we had a brilliant blue sky ahead of us to westward. . . . It was chilly, and the green water round us was astonishingly cold for 12° south. This was

The crew of Kon-Tiki. *Left to right: Knut Haugland, Bengt Danielsson, Thor, Erik Hesselberg, Torstein Raaby and Herman Watzinger.*

the Humboldt Current, which carried its cold masses of water up from the Antarctic and swept them north all along the coast of Peru till they swung west and out across the sea just below the equator. It was out here that Pizarro, Zarate and the other early Spaniards came for the first time upon the Inca Indians' big sailing rafts, which used to go out for fifty to sixty sea miles to catch tunnies and dolphins in this very Humboldt Current. . . .

We took a ceremonious farewell of all on board [the tug], and many strange looks followed us as we climbed down into the dinghy and went tumbling back over the waves to the *Kon-Tiki*. Then the tow-rope was cast off and the raft was alone again. Not till the black column of smoke had dissolved and vanished over the horizon did we shake our heads and look at one another.

'Good-bye, good-bye,' said Torstein. 'Now we'll have to start the engine, boys!'

We laughed, and felt the wind. It blew up from the south-east quietly and steadily. Soon the sail filled and bent forward like a swelling breast, with *Kon-Tiki*'s head bursting with pugnacity. And the *Kon-Tiki* began to move. **9**

9

IN THE WAKE OF
THE SUN-GOD

'To us on the raft the great problems of civilized
man appeared false and illusory, mere perverted
products of the human mind.'

Even now, after a lifetime of journeys by sea and
land which have taken him to the uttermost parts
of the earth, the voyage of the *Kon-Tiki* remains
the single most important event in Thor Heyerdahl's
life. Throughout the voyage he kept a diary, which in
due course became the basis for *The Kon-Tiki Expedition*.
It was the first great post-war adventure story to catch
the imagination of the world: over twenty million copies
were sold, and it was translated into every major language. The extracts which follow are not an attempt to
relate the whole story; but through their vividness and
immediacy, readers may catch something of the flavour
of that extraordinary journey.

   Their first day alone in the Pacific, out of sight of land
or any other vessel, was 29 April 1947.

❛. . . the steering arrangements were our greatest
problem. The raft was built exactly as the Spaniards
described it, but there was no one living in our time who
could give us a practical advance course in sailing an
Indian raft. . . . As the south-easterly wind increased in
strength it was necessary to keep the raft on such a
course that the sail was filled from astern. If the raft
turned her side too much to the wind, the sail suddenly
swung round and banged against cargo and men and
bamboo cabin, while the whole raft turned round and
continued on the same course, stern first. It was a hard
struggle, three men fighting with the sail and three
others rowing with the long steering oar to get the nose
. . . round and away from the wind. . . .

The steering oar, nineteen feet long, rested loose between two thole-pins on a huge block astern. It was the same steering oar our native friends had used when we brought the timber down the Palenque in Ecuador. The long mangrove-wood pole was as tough as steel, but so heavy that it would sink if it fell overboard. At the end of the pole was a large oar-blade of fir-wood lashed on with ropes. It took all our strength to hold this long steering oar steady when the seas drove against it, and our fingers were tired out by the convulsive grip which was necessary to turn the pole so that the oar-blade stood straight up in the water. This last problem was solved by our lashing a cross-piece to the handle of the steering oar, so that we had a sort of lever to turn. **9**

Meanwhile, the wind was increasing.

6 By the late afternoon the trade wind was already blowing at full strength. It quickly stirred up the ocean into roaring seas which swept against us from astern. . . . Whether things went well now would depend entirely on the balsa raft's good qualities in the open sea. We knew that from now onwards we should never get

Life in the tiny bamboo cabin on board the raft was crowded, but with goodwill and organization everyone seemed to manage. Bengt Danielsson had brought along seventy-three scientific books, of which he read seventy-two during the voyage.

another on-shore wind or chance of turning back. . . . There was only one possible course, to sail before the wind with our bows towards the sunset. And, after all, that was just the object of our voyage, to follow the sun in its path, as we thought Kon-Tiki and the old sun-worshippers must have done when they were chased out to sea from Peru. **❜**

Soon they became aware of the force of the great current that was bearing them towards their destination.

❛As the troughs of the sea gradually grew deeper it became clear that we had got into the swiftest part of the Humboldt Current. . . . The water was green and cold and everywhere about us; the jagged mountains of Peru vanished into the dense cloud-banks astern. When darkness crept over the sea our first duel with the elements began. . . . When, swallowed up by the darkness, we heard the general noise from the sea around us suddenly deafened by the hiss of a roller close by, and saw a white crest come groping towards us on a level with the cabin roof, we held on tight and waited uneasily to feel the masses of water smash down over us and the raft. But every time there was the same surprise and relief. The *Kon-Tiki* calmly swung up her stern and rose skyward unperturbed, while the masses of water rolled along her sides.

The round logs astern let the water pass as if through the prongs of a fork. The advantage of a raft was obviously this: the more leaks the better – through the gaps in our floor the water ran out, but never in.

About midnight a ship's light passed in a northerly direction. At three another passed, on the same course. We waved our little paraffin lamp and called them up with flashes from an electric torch, but they did not see us . . . this was our last ship and the last trace of men we should see till we had reached the other side of the ocean. **9**

The warnings given to the crew on shore were never far from their thoughts. It was apparent that the balsa logs had already absorbed much water. Unobserved, Thor broke off a piece of sodden wood, threw it overboard and watched it sink. Later, he noticed two or three of the other men quietly performing the same ceremony. Similarly, they were anxious about the enormous friction inflicted on the ropes.

Apart from his artistic accomplishments, Erik Hesselberg was also a musician and folk singer.

6 In the daytime we were so busy that we thought little about it, but when darkness had fallen and we had crept into bed on the cabin floor, we had more time to think, feel and listen. As we lay there, each man on his straw mattress, we could feel the reed matting under us heaving in time with the wooden logs. In addition to the movements of the raft itself, all nine logs moved reciprocally. When one came up, another went down with a gently heaving movement. They did not move much, but it was enough to make one feel as if one was lying on the back of a large breathing animal, and we preferred to lie on a log lengthways.

But the ropes held. A fortnight, the seamen had said. . . . But in spite of this consensus of opinion we had not so far found the smallest sign of wear. Not till we were far out to sea did we find the solution. The balsa wood was so soft that the ropes wore their way slowly into the wood and were protected, instead of the logs wearing the ropes. **9**

Despite these latent fears there was an atmosphere of great tranquillity on board the *Kon-Tiki*:

6 It was as though the fresh salt tang in the air, and all the blue purity that surrounded us, had washed and cleansed both body and soul. To us on the raft the great problems of civilized man appeared false and illusory, mere perverted products of the human mind. Only the elements mattered. And the elements seemed to ignore the little raft. Or perhaps they accepted it as a natural

Torstein Raaby was unexpectedly woken one night by the presence of a snake mackerel, a rare species until then never seen alive, with razor-sharp teeth.

object which did not break the harmony of the sea, but which adapted itself to current and sea like bird and fish. . . . While wind and waves pushed and propelled, the ocean current lay under us and pulled, straight towards our goal. **'**

The inhabitants of the Pacific proved far from shy, as Thor noted in his diary on 24 May.

' Not a day passed but we . . . were visited by inquisitive guests which wriggled and waggled about us, and a few of them, such as dolphins and pilot fish grew so familiar that they . . . kept round us day and night.

When night had fallen, and the stars were twinkling in the dark tropical sky, the phosphorescence flashed around us in rivalry with the stars, and single glowing plankton resembled round live coals so vividly that we involuntarily drew in our bare legs when the glowing pellets were washed up round our feet at the raft's stern. . . . On such nights we were sometimes scared when two round shining eyes suddenly rose out of the sea right alongside the raft and glared at us with an unblinking hypnotic stare – it might have been the Old Man of the Sea himself. These were often big squids which came up and floated on the surface with their devilish green eyes shining in the dark like phosphorus. But sometimes they were the shining eyes of deep water fish which only came out at night and lay staring, fascinated by the glimmer of light before them. **'**

A few days later they encountered a monster from the deep of such strength and size that it spelt great potential danger for the little craft and her crew. It was Knut Haugland who saw it first. He was busy washing his pants off the stern when he looked up for a moment to find himself staring into the face of the ugliest creature he had ever seen.

' The head was broad and flat like a frog's, with two small eyes right at the sides, and a toad-like jaw which was four or five feet wide and had long fringes hanging drooping from the corners of the mouth. Behind the head was an enormous body ending in a long thin tail with a pointed tail fin which stood straight up and showed that this sea monster was not any kind of whale. The body looked brownish under the water, but both head and body were thickly covered with small white spots. The monster came quietly, lazily swimming after us from astern. It grinned like a bulldog and lashed gently with its tail. . . .

It was a whale shark, the largest shark and the largest fish known in the world to-day. It is exceedingly rare, but scattered specimens are observed here and there in the tropical oceans. The whale shark has an average length of fifty feet, and according to zoologists it weighs fifteen tons.

The monster was so large that when it began to swim in circles round us and under the raft its head was visible on one side while the whole of its tail stuck out on the other. And so incredibly grotesque, inert and stupid did it appear when seen full-face that we could not help shouting with laughter, although we realized that it had strength enough in its tail to smash both balsa logs and ropes to pieces if it attacked us. . . .

At last it became too exciting for Erik, who was standing at a corner of the raft with an eight-foot hand harpoon, and, encouraged by ill considered shouts, he raised the harpoon above his head. . . . We heard a swishing noise as the harpoon line rushed over the edge of the raft, and saw a cascade of water as the giant stood on its head and plunged down into the depths. The three men who were standing nearest were flung about the place head over heels and two of them were flayed and burnt by the line as it rushed through the air. The thick line, strong enough to hold a boat, was caught up on the side of the raft but snapped at once like a piece of twine, and a few seconds later a broken-off harpoon shaft came up to the surface two hundred yards away. A shoal of frightened pilot fish shot off through the water in a desperate attempt to keep up with their old lord and master, and we waited a long time for the monster to come racing back like an infuriated submarine; but we never saw anything more of the whale shark. **9**
For all the crew's good intentions to be at peace with the world, sharks appeared to have been cast by nature in the role of the enemy. And this one, they all knew, would have been quite capable of ending the voyage of the *Kon-Tiki* then and there.

10

THE TIMELESS OCEAN

'. . . the trade winds held the orange sail bent
towards Polynesia'.

One by one the weeks glided by, without the
slightest sign that there were any other human
beings on the planet. The rhythm of the ocean
imposed its own pace on their lives. It became more and
more difficult to visualize the seething continents that
waited somewhere beyond. 'With all the gates of the
horizon open,' wrote Thor, 'real peace and freedom
were wafted down from the firmament itself.' The world
seemed empty; and the world was theirs.

If a boat had cruised our way on any average day out
at sea, it would have found us bobbing quietly up and
down over a long rolling swell covered with little white-
crested waves, while the trade winds held the orange
sail bent towards Polynesia.

Those on board would have seen, at the stern of the
raft, a brown bearded man with no clothes on, either
struggling desperately with a long steering oar while he
hauled on a tangled rope, or, in calm weather, just sitting on a box dozing in the hot sun and keeping a
leisurely hold on the steering oar with his toes.

If this man happened not to be Bengt, the latter would
have been found lying on his stomach in the cabin door
with one of his seventy-three sociological books. Bengt
had further been appointed steward and was responsible for fixing the daily rations. Herman might have
been found just anywhere at all times of the day – at the
masthead with meteorological instruments, underneath
the raft with diving-goggles on, checking a centreboard,
or in tow in the rubber dinghy, busy with balloons and

curious measuring apparatus. He was our technical chief and responsible for meteorological and hydrographical observations.

Knut and Torstein were always doing something with their wet dry batteries, soldering irons and circuits. All their war-time training was required to keep the little wireless station going in spray and dew a foot above the surface of the water. Every night they took turns to send our reports and weather observations out into the ether, where they were picked up by casual radio amateurs who passed the reports on to the Meteorological Institute in Washington and other destinations. Erik was usually sitting patching sails and splicing ropes, or carving in wood and drawing sketches of bearded men and odd fish. And at noon every day he took the sextant and mounted a box to look at the sun and find out how far we had moved since the day before. I myself had enough to do with the log-book and reports, and the collecting of plankton, fishing and filming. . . .

All dirty jobs, like steering watch and cooking, were divided equally. Every man had two hours each day and two hours each night at the steering oar. And duty as cook was in accordance with a daily roster. There were few laws and regulations on board, except that the night

The head of Kon-Tiki, *faithfully copied from a statue in Tiahuanaco, had been painted on the sail by Erik Hesselberg.*

'Our proud vessel', wrote Thor,
'made a hopeless, lunatic
impression on us the first time
we saw the whole thing from a
distance, out in the little rubber
boat. . . . The raft looked
exactly like an old Norwegian
hay loft . . . a warped hay loft
full of bearded ruffians.'

119

watch must have a rope round his waist, that the life-saving rope had its regular place, that all meals were consumed outside the cabin wall, and that the 'right place' was only at the farthest end of the logs astern. **,**

Any anxieties they may have had about their food and water supplies running out were allayed by the abundance around them. Heavy rain showers replaced their fresh water rations, which anyway had become brackish after two months. It was not even necessary to fish; bonitos and flying fish propelled themselves on deck, once literally into the frying pan.

By its very existence, the raft was changing the lifestyles of various species. The seaweed hanging from the bottom provided shelter for several varieties of small fish that would otherwise have been easy prey for marauding giants. Others even went so far as to share the crew's living quarters on deck.

' Small crabs were the policemen of the sea's surface, and they were not slow to look after themselves when they saw anything eatable. . . . Aft, in a little hole by the steering block, lived a crab which was called Johannes and was quite tame. . . . While the other small crabs scurried furtively about and pilfered like cockroaches on an ordinary boat, Johannes sat broad and round in his doorway with his eyes wide open, waiting for the change of watch. Every man who came on watch had a scrap of biscuit or a bit of fish for Johannes, and we only needed to stoop down over the hole for him to come right out on his doorstep and stretch out his hands. He took the scraps out of our fingers with his claws and ran back into the hole, where he sat down in the doorway and munched like a schoolboy cramming his food in his mouth. **,**

Whenever the sea was calm enough, they took the little rubber dinghy out to take photographs. But on one occasion they nearly had a disaster.

' The wind and sea were higher than we supposed, and the *Kon-Tiki* was cleaving a path for herself over the swell much more quickly than we realized. We in the dinghy had to row for our lives out in the open sea, in an attempt to regain the unmanageable raft which could not stop and wait, and could not possibly turn round and come back. . . . There was only one thought in the

head of every man – we must not be separated. Those were horrible minutes we spent out on the sea before we got hold of the runaway raft and crawled on board to the others, home again.

From that day it was strictly forbidden to go out in the rubber dinghy without having a long line made fast to the bows, so that those who remained on board could haul the dinghy in if necessary. **9**

Human beings seem to have an in-built dread of certain living creatures which goes far beyond reason. On land, snakes and spiders head the list. At sea, nothing quite matches the reputation of sharks – as the crew had already proved to themselves by attacking the great whale shark. Now, Thor Heyerdahl and his men were presented with the opportunity to observe the behaviour of its smaller cousins from the relative safety of the *Kon-Tiki*'s deck.

6 Generally it is smell more than sight which excites sharks' voracity. We have sat with our legs in the water to test them, and they have swum towards us till they were two or three feet away, only quietly to turn their tails towards us again. But if the water was in the least bloodstained, as it was when we had been cleaning fish, the sharks' fins came to life, and they would suddenly collect like bluebottles from a long way off. . . .

Pulling animals' tails is held to be an inferior form of sport, but that may be because no one has tried it on a

Catching sharks by hand became a favourite sport. A tasty tit-bit was offered, which the shark would leap to snatch. Then, as it turned to dive, its tail flicked above the surface and was easy to grasp.

shark. For it was in truth a lively form of sport.

To get hold of a shark by the tail we first had to give it a real tit-bit. It was ready to stick its head high out of the water to get it. . . . When the shark turned quietly to go under again, its tail flickered up above the surface and was easy to grasp. The shark's skin was just like sand-paper to hold on to, and inside the upper point of its tail there was an indentation which might have been made to allow of a good grip. If we once got a firm grasp there, there was no chance of our grip not holding. Then we had to give a jerk before the shark could collect himself, and get as much as possible of the tail pulled in tight over the logs. For a second or two the shark understood nothing, but then it began to wriggle and struggle in a spiritless manner with the fore part of its body, for without the help of its tail a shark cannot get up any speed. . . . After a few desperate jerks, during which we had to keep a tight hold of the tail, the surprised shark became quite crestfallen and apathetic. . . . When [it] had become quiet and, as it were, hung stiff awaiting developments, it was time for us to haul in with all our might. We seldom got more than half the heavy fish up out of the water, but then the shark woke up and did the rest itself. With violent jerks it swung its head round and up on to the logs, and then we had to tug with all our might and jump well out of the way, and that pretty quickly if we wanted to save our legs. **9**

And it was not just the human crew members who were amused by this sport.

6 The parrot was quite thrilled when we had a shark on deck. It came scurrying out of the bamboo cabin and climbed up the wall at frantic speed till it found itself a good safe look-out post on the palm-leaf roof, and there it sat . . . shrieking with excitement. It had at an early date become an excellent sailor, and was always bubbling over with humour and laughter. . . .

We enjoyed the parrot's humour and brilliant colours for two months, until a big sea came on board from astern while it was on its way down the stay from the masthead. When we discovered that the parrot had gone overboard, it was too late. . . .

The loss of the parrot had a depressing effect on our spirits the first evening; we knew that exactly the same thing would happen to ourselves if we fell overboard on a solitary night watch.

We tightened up all the safety regulations, brought into use new life-lines for the night watch, and frightened one another out of believing that we were safe because things had gone well in the first two months. One careless step, one thoughtless movement, could send us where the green parrot had gone, even in broad daylight. '

At night Thor Heyerdahl and his companions never tired of watching the mighty pageant performed by the heavens.... 'The old Polynesians were great navigators,' he acknowledged.

'Their knowledge of the heavenly bodies was astonishing.... [They] knew five planets, which they called wandering stars, and distinguished them from the fixed stars.... They knew which stars culminated over the different islands, and there were cases in which an island was named after the star which culminated over it night after night and year after year. '

More than half the journey was completed before they encountered their first serious storm at sea. The trade wind, which had blown steadily and reassuringly, day after day, suddenly died away completely and a thick, black cloud bank began to roll up from the south. At first the wind came in gusts from unexpected directions, making the Kon-Tiki impossible to control; but as the clouds rolled nearer and nearer, so the wind from the south began to dominate.

'In the course of an incredibly short time the seas round about us were flung up to a height of fifteen feet, while single crests were hissing twenty and twenty-five feet above the trough of the sea, so that we had them on a level with our masthead when we ourselves were down in the trough. All hands had to scramble about on deck bent double, while the wind shook the bamboo wall and whistled and howled in all the rigging....

When the storm rushed up over the horizon and gathered about us for the first time, strained anticipation and anxiety were discernible in our looks. But when it was upon us in earnest, and the Kon-Tiki took everything that came her way with ease and buoyancy, the storm became an exciting form of sport.... '

There was one storm, however, which brought extreme danger.

❝Herman was out with his anemometer all the time, measuring already fifty feet and more per second [windspeed], when suddenly Torstein's sleeping bag went overboard. And what happened in the next few seconds took a much shorter time than it takes to tell it.

Herman tried to catch the bag as it went, took a rash step and fell overboard. We heard a faint cry for help amid the noise of the waves, and saw Herman's head and a waving arm. . . . He was struggling for life to get back to the raft through the high seas which had lifted him out from the port side. . . . We bellowed 'man overboard!' at the pitch of our lungs as we rushed to the nearest life-saving gear . . . in a trice there was life and bustle on deck. Herman was an excellent swimmer, and though we realized at once that his life was at stake, we had a fair hope that he would manage to crawl back to the edge of the raft before it was too late.

Torstein, who was nearest, seized the bamboo drum round which was the line we used for the lifeboat. . . . Herman was now on a level with the stern of the raft, but a few yards away, and his last hope was to crawl to the blade of the steering oar and hang on to it. As he missed the end of the logs, he reached out for the oar-blade, but it slipped away from him. And there he lay, just where experience had shown we could get nothing back. While Bengt and I launched the dinghy, Knut and Erik threw out the lifebelt. Carrying a long line, it hung ready for use on the corner of the cabin roof, but to-day the wind was so strong that when they threw the lifebelt it was simply blown back to the raft. . . .

Then we suddenly saw Knut take off and plunge head first into the sea. He had the lifebelt in one hand and was heaving himself along. Every time Herman's head appeared on a wave-back Knut was gone, and every time Knut came up Herman was not there. But then we saw both heads at once; they had swum to meet each other and both were hanging on to the lifebelt . . . all four of us took hold of the line of the lifebelt and hauled for dear life. ❞

Only now was the lesson of the green parrot truly learned.

Man overboard! Erik Hesselberg's version of this dramatic incident.

11

LANDFALL

'The whole island looked like a bulging green
basket of flowers, or a little bit of
concentrated paradise.'

On the night of 30 July, after three months at sea,
all attempts at sleep were forestalled by the
sudden deafening clamour of hundreds of sea-
birds sweeping and circling overhead. It could mean
only one thing. There was land not far away.

' . . . over the whole horizon away to the east a ruddy
glow had begun to spread, and far down to the south-
east it gradually formed a blood-red background for a
faint shadow, like a blue pencil line, drawn for a short
way along the edge of the sea.

Land! An island! We devoured it greedily with our
eyes. . . .

Our first thought was that the island did not lie where
it ought to. And as the island could not have drifted, the
raft must have been caught up in a northward current in
the course of the night. We had only to cast one glance
over the sea to perceive at once, from the direction of
the waves, that we had lost our chance in the darkness.
Where we now lay, the wind no longer allowed us to
press the raft on a course towards the island. **'**

There is one golden rule with any form of transport,
be it a horse, a car or a train: 'Learn to stop before you
start!' Now that the islands were all around, Thor was
beginning to realize it was a rule he had failed to
observe.

The islands of Polynesia are of two types. The mountainous ones are volcanic in origin; the others, known as
atolls, are formed by the steady build-up of coral, which
eventually breaks the surface of the water, allowing

plant seeds to settle on it. Both types of island are often protected by reefs which can be lethal to an approaching vessel. Local outrigger canoes can be deftly manoeuvred through natural gaps in the reefs; but the *Kon-Tiki* was another matter – such accurate steering was out of the question.

Two equally unpalatable possibilities loomed over them. The first was that they might very well sail right through the various island groups, unable to bring the raft near enough to attempt a landing. The second was that the force of the current would drive them straight on to a reef, where the raft would very probably be dashed to pieces.

When Thor considered the problem from the point of view of those early mariners who had made the same crossing, it did not bring much comfort. If, as he believed, there were dozens, perhaps hundreds of rafts, it was almost certain that some would get through, while others foundered. But the *Kon-Tiki* was alone. . . . Then he realized his mistake. They were not alone. These islands were no longer uninhabited; and with any luck, help would be at hand.

Erik told them that the second island to appear on the horizon was called Angatau.

❛It happened that this festal day off Angatau was the ninety-seventh day on board. Strangely enough, it was ninety-seven days that we in New York had estimated as the absolute minimum time in which, in theoretically ideal conditions, we could reach the nearest islands of Polynesia. . . .

At half-past five we stood in towards the reef again; we were getting near the west end of the island, and must have a last look round in the hope of finding a passage. The sun now stood so low that it blinded us when we looked ahead, but we saw a little rainbow in the air where the sea broke against the reef a few hundred yards beyond the last point of the island. This now lay as a silhouette ahead of us. And on the beach inside we detected a cluster of motionless black spots. . . . They were people! We steered along the reef as close in as we dared; the wind had died down, so that we felt we were within an ace of getting under the lee of the island. Now we saw a canoe being launched, and two individuals jumped on board and paddled off on the other side of the reef. Farther down they turned the boat's head out, and we saw the canoe lifted high in the air by the seas as it shot through a passage in the reef and came straight out towards us. . . .

The two men in the canoe waved. We waved back eagerly, and they increased their speed. It was a Polynesian outrigger canoe, and two brown figures in singlets sat paddling, facing ahead.

. . . when the canoe bumped against the raft's side and the two men leapt on board, . . . one of them grinned all over his face and held out a brown hand, exclaiming in English:

'Good night!'

'Good night,' I replied in astonishment. . . .

'Angatau?' I asked, pointing towards the island.

'H'angatau,' the man nodded affirmatively.

Erik nodded proudly. He had been right, we were where the sun had told him that we were.

As darkness fell over the island four canoes came dancing out from behind the reef, and soon there was a crowd of Polynesians on board, all wanting to shake hands and get cigarettes. With these fellows on board, who had local knowledge, there was no danger; they would not let us go out to sea again and out of sight; so we should be ashore that evening!

We quickly had ropes made fast from the stern of all the canoes to the bows of the *Kon-Tiki*, and the four sturdy outrigger canoes spread out in fan formation, like a dog team, ahead of the wooden raft. Knut jumped into the dinghy and found a place as draught dog in among the canoes, and we others, with paddles, posted ourselves on the two outside logs of the *Kon-Tiki*. And so began, for the first time, a struggle against the east wind, which had been at our back for so long. **'**

But it was not enough, and Kurt Haugland was the only one who actually landed on Angatau. He decided to row ashore in the dinghy in an effort to get more help, and in so doing became the first of the crew to complete their mission. The islanders whom he met completely failed to grasp that, with no engine, the *Kon-Tiki* could not get any closer. They wanted all these strange white men to pay them a visit, and plied Knut with promises of feasting and beautiful girls. He managed to get back to the raft before temptation got the upper hand.

Their final landfall was as dramatic as Thor had feared it would be. Three days later they found themselves drifting towards the notorious Takume and Raroia reefs, a fifty-mile barrier almost impossible to circumvent.

❦ Everything of value was carried into the cabin and lashed fast. Documents and papers were packed into water-tight bags, along with films and other things which would not stand a dip in the sea. The whole bamboo cabin was covered with canvas, and specially strong ropes were lashed across it. . . . With the centreboards up, the draught of our vessel was no deeper than to the bottom of the timber logs, and we would therefore be more easily washed in over the reef, [but] the raft lay completely sideways on and was entirely at the mercy of wind and sea.

We tied the longest rope we had to the home-made anchor, and made it fast to the step of the port mast, so that the *Kon-Tiki* would go into the surf stern first when the anchor was thrown overboard.

Order number one, which came first and last, was: Hold on to the raft! Whatever happened we must hang on tight on board and let the nine great logs take the pressure from the reef. We ourselves had more than enough to do to withstand the weight of the water. If we jumped overboard we should become helpless victims of the suction which would fling us in and out over the sharp corals. . . .

Next, all hands were told to put on their shoes for the first time in a hundred days, and to have their lifebelts ready. The last-named, however, were not of much value, for if a man fell overboard he would be battered to death, not drowned. We had time too to put our passports, and such few dollars as we had left, into our pockets. . . .

As chance willed, we had on the previous day got into touch with a capable wireless fan who had a set on Rarotonga in the Cook Islands, and the operators . . . had arranged for an extra contact with him early in the morning. And all the time we were drifting closer and closer in to the reef, Torstein was sitting tapping his key and calling Rarotonga.

When we realized that the seas had got hold of us, the anchor rope was cut, and we were off. A sea rose straight up under us, and we felt the *Kon-Tiki* being lifted up in the air. The great moment had come; we were riding on the wave-back at breathless speed, our ramshackle craft creaking and groaning as she quivered under us. . . . On we ran with the seas rushing in behind us; this was the *Kon-Tiki*'s baptism of fire; all must and would go well.

But our elation was soon damped. A new sea rose high up astern of us like a glittering green glass wall; as we sank down it came rolling after us, and in the same second in which I saw it high above me I felt a violent blow and was submerged under floods of water. I felt the suction through my whole body, with such great strength that I had to strain every single muscle in my frame and think of one thing only – hold on, hold on! . . . Then I felt that the mountain of water was passing on and relaxing its devilish grip of my body. When the whole mountain had rushed on, with an earsplitting roaring and crashing, I saw Knut again hanging on beside me, doubled up into a ball. Seen from behind the great sea was almost flat and grey; as it rushed on it swept just over the ridge of the cabin roof which projected from the water, and there hung the three others, pressed against the cabin roof as the water passed over them. . . .

Then I saw the next sea come towering up, higher than all the rest, and again I bellowed a warning aft to the others as I climbed up the stay as high as I could get in a hurry and hung on fast. . . . Then the great wave reached them, and we had all one single thought – hold on, hold on, hold, hold, hold!

We must have hit the reef that time. . . . The sea thundered on, over and past, and as it roared by it revealed a hideous sight. The *Kon-Tiki* was wholly changed, as by the stroke of a magic wand. The vessel we knew from weeks and months at sea was no more; in a few seconds our pleasant world had become a shattered wreck. . . .

Two or three more seas rolled over us with diminishing force, and what happened then I do not remember, except that water foamed in and out, and I myself sank lower and lower towards the red reef over which we were being lifted in. Then only crests of foam full of salt

spray came whirling in, and I was able to work my way in on to the raft, where we all made for the after end of the logs, which was highest up on the reef. . . .

The reef stretched like a half-submerged fortress wall up to the north and down to the south. In the extreme south was a long island densely covered with palm forest. And just above us to the north, only six or seven hundred yards away, lay another but considerably smaller palm island. It lay inside the reef, with palm-tops rising into the sky and snow-white sandy beaches running out into the still lagoon. The whole island looked like a bulging green basket of flowers, or a little bit of concentrated paradise.

This island we chose.

Herman stood beside me beaming all over his bearded face. He did not say a word, only stretched out his hand and laughed quietly. The *Kon-Tiki* still lay far out on the reef with the spray flying over her. She was a wreck, but an honourable wreck. Everything above deck was smashed up, but the nine balsa logs from the Quivedo forest in Ecuador were as intact as ever. They had saved our lives. . . .

I shall never forget that wade across the reef towards the heavenly palm island that grew larger as it came to meet us. When I reached the sunny sand beach, I slipped off my shoes and thrust my bare toes down into the warm, bone-dry sand. . . . Green coconuts hung under the palm-tufts, and some luxuriant bushes were thickly covered with snow-white blossoms, which smelt so sweet and seductive that I felt quite faint. In the interior of the island two quite tame terns flew about my shoulders. They were as white and light as wisps of cloud. . . .

I was completely overwhelmed. I sank down on my knees and thrust my fingers deep down into the dry warm sand.

The voyage was over. We were all alive. . . .

On the reef outside resounded the monotonous drum-beats from the guard at the gates of paradise.

'Purgatory was a bit damp,' said Bengt, 'but heaven more or less as I'd imagined it.'❯

OPPOSITE Kon-Tiki *stranded on the Raroia coral reef, where she was flung by the violence of the surf.*

12

TACKING AGAINST
THE WIND

'A nice adventure, but you don't expect anybody
to call that a scientific expedition.'

There were many misapprehensions, and some downright distortions, about the *Kon-Tiki* expedition. The voyage had set out to demonstrate that the earliest settlers to reach the Polynesian islands could have come from South America; it was never intended to be the final proof that they had come by that route. But inevitably, perhaps, that was how it was interpreted.

In two respects, Thor was taken completely by surprise. The first was the quite extraordinary popular interest that the expedition aroused all over the world. At the end of the Second World War there was a general atmosphere of drabness and flatness everywhere; people needed to rediscover the thrill of peaceful adventure, and this had been an exploit which carried no overtones of violence or political exploitation.

His second surprise was the extraordinarily low level of debate that the voyage engendered in the academic world. A typical comment came from Sir Peter Buck, who, himself half-Maori, was then the leading authority on Polynesia. 'A nice adventure,' was how he described the *Kon-Tiki* voyage, 'but you don't expect anybody to call that a scientific expedition. Now do you?'

❜Those Norwegians want us to believe their pre-Inca Peruvians were doing a bit of coastal fishing and got picked up by the Humboldt Current; and eventually wound up alive and safe somewhere to father the Polynesian race. Well, no fisherman I ever saw had women aboard. And by their own theory the landings

were made on uninhabited islands – so who exactly was going to mother our Polynesian peoples? *'*
But never once had Thor mentioned the possibility of fishermen being inadvertently swept away. And in his reply he pointed out that the Spaniards themselves had reported the interception of rafts with women aboard, a fact of which Sir Peter should have been aware. Other academic reactions were equally discouraging. Professor Karsten from Finland virtually accused him of faking the whole adventure; while from Denmark, Professor Birket-Smith announced that it would be better if the subject were 'killed by silence'.

Thor had made plans to be reunited with Liv in Washington. As soon as she had walked down the steps of the aircraft, a photographer rushed forward to get a picture of the two of them together. Angrily she pushed Thor away, convinced that he had manipulated the scene for the sake of publicity. He never forgot that public, humiliating shove, which was undoubtedly the

Thor with his second wife, Yvonne. After their marriage they rented a secluded cottage on Dartmoor, in the west of England, where Thor began writing about the theory behind the Kon-Tiki *expedition.*

133

single, small event that sealed the fate of their marriage.

There were no rows; everything was decided in an atmosphere of calmness and mutual respect. At one point Liv even said, 'When you find a girl you think you want to marry, bring her to see me. Knowing you so well, I shall be able to tell if she's the right one.' Thor took her at her word. Not long afterwards, he spent a weekend at a skiing hotel. One of the party was a pretty, unattached girl called Yvonne. In Thor's words, 'We immediately made contact' (in fact, he asked her if she would go parachute-jumping with him in Brazil!). But before anything was decided, the girl found herself being taken to Lillehammer and introduced to Liv. The interview proved satisfactory. 'You've found an angel,' was Liv's verdict.

In the meantime Thor was still at the centre of an intellectual tornado. He was not claiming that his theories should be accepted without further debate, but he wanted very much to be taken seriously. There was only one course: to produce an academic work, based on his own research in Canada and Peru, which would deal in detail with all the evidence he could muster. After a brief taste of fame he had a deep yearning to withdraw from the limelight with Yvonne; and in a little stone cottage on the edge of Dartmoor in the west of England, away from the world's press, they settled down to begin work on *American Indians in the Pacific*.

The book is eight hundred pages long, and covers every subject that could possibly have a bearing on Polynesian origins. Thor started by examining the most widely accepted view, that the people of the islands are descendants of the Malays. But as soon as Thor began to study the eye-witness accounts of early travellers, it very quickly became plain that there was no general uniformity of racial type throughout the islands. In 1609 a Spanish expedition made the very first European contact; they were, they said, met by 'four hundred natives, almost white and of very graceful shape . . . many of them are ruddy'. In 1722 a Dutch expedition led by Jacob Roggeveen visited Easter Island; he described the inhabitants like this: 'As for their complexion, they are brownish, about the hue of a Spaniard, yet one finds some of them of a darker shade and others quite white,

OPPOSITE *Thor in his study preparing the manuscript of* American Indians in the Pacific, *his major anthropological work.*

135

and no less also a few of a reddish tint as if somewhat severely tanned by the sun.' A contemporary Spaniard made a similar observation. 'If they wore clothing like ourselves, they might well pass for Europeans . . . being white, swarthy and reddish, not thick-lipped nor flat-nosed, the hair chestnut-coloured and limp. They are tall, well-built and proportioned in all their limbs.' An explorer called Beechey, visiting Polynesia in 1831, made the most telling comments of all: 'There is a great mixture of feature and colour among them. It seems as if several tribes from remote parts of the Pacific had here met and mingled their peculiarities.'

It was clear to Thor that the solution to the mystery was not going to be a simple one. Indeed, there might well have been several waves of migration, from different directions and in different centuries. The more evidence he collected for the book, the more convinced he became that one of those waves, perhaps the earliest one, must have been from the American continent.

American Indians in the Pacific was published in the late summer of 1952. Thor knew that he would be plunged once more into controversy, but now he was ready for it. On the whole, considering its length and complexity, the reviews of the work were favourable. Thor still had his critics, as he was soon to discover at various scientific congresses; but when it came to meeting argument with argument, they tended to fall silent. It was Professor Kristian Gleditsch, president of the Norwegian Geographical Society, who best summed up the prevailing mood:

❛A man who presents a new scientific hypothesis must of course be prepared for criticism and opposition. A man who risks his life to prove his theory must be prepared to call down the special wrath of armchair geographers. A man who, in our age of specialization, combines arguments drawn from at least ten different sciences is inevitably the target of the Olympic thunderbolts of the specialists. More often than not he has even deserved it, for no one can master all the sciences at the same time. And yet from time to time someone must try to combine the results of the different sciences and weigh them one against the other. A young man who, without having passed all the regular examinations, proves that a long list of distinguished professors have been wrong, cannot count on any mercy. No one likes to lose face. **9**

Now an opportunity presented itself for a return visit to the Pacific which he could not ignore. It was an old sparring partner, Dr Alfred Métraux, who started him on a new trail of detection. Métraux claimed to have seen a photograph of a stone statue, or at least the head of a stone statue, which bore a striking resemblance to the famous statues on Easter Island. However, this one had been found two thousand miles further north on the island of Floreana in the Galapagos Group. If the story was true, and the statue of genuine antiquity, then it was a major find: there are only seven islands in the entire Pacific with any sculpture on them of any kind.

Thor went first to the Museum of Natural History in New York, where the photograph had been on display; they told him that it had been taken by a botanist who lived in Boston. A couple of days later the picture was in Thor's hands. Quite clearly he could make out the features of a face, half hidden in the undergrowth. The botanist was absolutely certain that he had seen it; he even drew Thor a sketch map, showing its exact position on the island.

Thor made up his mind immediately that this would be the goal of his next expedition. There were several intriguing possibilities. The first was that sculptors from Easter Island had made their way north to the barren and almost waterless Galapagos. But for what purpose? A second, and much more likely, possibility was that the sculptor had sailed out from the mainland as part of that pre-Incan migration which lay at the heart of Thor's own Polynesian hypothesis; they had passed very close to the Galapagos on the *Kon-Tiki*. If the mysterious statue bore any resemblance to the images of Tiahuanaco, then one more piece of the mosaic would be in place.

Thor decided to take with him two professional archaeologists: Dr Erik Reed from the United States, and Arne Skjolsvold from Oslo University. The skipper of a small merchantman landed the party on the barren coast of Floreana on 8 January 1953. Thor unwrapped the sketch map that the botanist had drawn for him, and boldly set off towards the biggest fiasco of his life.

The camp at James Bay in the Galapagos Islands. Although Thor and his companions had been directed here on false pretences, they found clear evidence that the Galapagos had been visited by Indians from South America long before the Inca period.

The 'statue' was there all right – but it was just a large piece of natural stone lying in the foliage. Someone had scratched two eyes and a mouth on either side of a prominent lump of rock that might have been taken for a nose. At least his two companions managed to laugh with him. Later that day they came across the perpetrator of the 'fraud', a German called Heinz Wittmer. He had carved the face on the stone to amuse his children.

The Galapagos Islands were famous for their wildlife, and nothing else. But since they were there, with some days to kill before the merchantman returned, it seemed worth asking their German hosts whether they had ever seen signs of ancient human habitation. Wittmer's wife smiled and told them they need look no further than her own chicken run. She was right; a combination of soil erosion and the constant activity of the chickens had caused miniature canyons to form in the bare soil. From the sides of these, shards of pottery were protruding. Thor even unearthed a terracotta flute, which closely resembled Incan ones on the mainland.

In the days ahead they travelled from island to island, looking for landing places that would have caught the eye of seafarers. Once ashore, they tried to visualize the most likely campsite, and then started digging. Many hot, fruitless hours were spent in this way, but just occasionally they were lucky and a site would yield a whole variety of potsherds, suggesting that it had been known and used over a long period. But since no evidence was found of any permanent settlement, they came to the conclusion that these visitors were hunters or fishermen. If so, they must have possessed the means to come and go at will. But how? On the *Kon-Tiki* expedition they had travelled four thousand miles, using the prevailing winds and currents; but to travel back to their starting point would have been completely beyond both their skill and the raft's capabilities.

Back in South America, the collection of pottery fragments was despatched to the Smithsonian Institution in Washington to be examined by experts. It was confirmed that they were American Indian, and, as Thor had suspected, some dated back to well before the Incas. Here was irrefutable proof that the Indians had not been content to use their balsa wood rafts for simple coastal journeys; the Galapagos Islands are six hundred miles west of Ecuador.

But this left the central mystery quite unsolved. How had those intrepid mariners succeeded in navigating their rafts, not only through the notorious currents of the 'Enchanted Isles', as the Galapagos were often known, but against wind and current back to South America? All that the local Indians on the coast could tell him was that steering a raft depended on the proper manipulation of the *guaras*, movable centre-boards which could be slipped between the logs. But the secret was now lost.

So with the help of Erik Reed and Arne Skjolsvold, Thor set about building another balsa wood raft – not as

OVERLEAF *The upper slopes of the Galapagos are often shrouded in mist which provides sufficient moisture for cactus plants, the main source of food for the famous giant tortoises.*

An early seventeenth-century drawing of a balsa wood raft off the coast of Peru. Three men could navigate the craft against the wind by raising or lowering the centre-board or guara.

large as *Kon-Tiki*, but on a bigger scale than the little three-log vessels still used by a few Indian fishermen. Aided by local fishermen they carved out several thin planks of curved hardwood with a handle at one end to make traditional *guaras*. But whenever they pushed them through the logs they only succeeded in making the raft spin round and continue on its journey stern first. It seemed hopeless.

Gradually, however, by manipulating the sail and the *guaras* at the same time, they found they could bring the bows closer and closer into the wind. After a few hours of practice the raft was performing almost as well as a modern sailing ship. For the first time in hundreds of years, a balsa wood raft had tacked against the wind.

The experiment was profoundly important. Five years before, it had taken Thor Heyerdahl and his crew three months to demonstrate that a raft was capable of reaching Polynesia, but at the end of that journey they had been quite unable to prevent the *Kon-Tiki* from being hurled on to a reef. Now they knew for certain that the Inca seafarers navigated their craft with far more skill and precision. The Pacific had been theirs to command, and they came and went as they wished.

13

THE NAVEL OF
THE WORLD

'The huge standing figures look down at you
with an enigmatic stare.'

It was the Dutch navigator Jacob Roggeveen who
called it Easter Island when he became the first
European to land there on Easter Sunday 1722. It
was an oddly inappropriate name for a place that had
known nothing of Christianity since it had been thrust
up from the depths of the ocean by volcanic eruptions
long before the appearance of man. On the shore,
Roggeveen's men observed a strange sight. The local
people, some fair-skinned, some dark, had lit fires
before a group of enormous statues high on the cliffs.
Before these the people prostrated themselves; then
they turned to pay homage to the sun as it rose from the
sea in the east.

Later, European visitors were to learn that the
Polynesian name for the island was Te-Pito-o-te-Henua,
which means the Navel of the World. That too may seem
a strange name for the loneliest inhabited place on the
planet, unless the early inhabitants saw it as a kind of
umbilical link between the main Polynesian island
groups and the motherland of South America. But for
that to be true they would have to have known where
they were.

After *Kon-Tiki* and the Galapagos, Thor Heyerdahl
was secretly determined that Easter Island would be the
objective of his next expedition. The reason for secrecy
was simple enough: there were plenty of other archaeologists prepared to jump in first. The origin of the
Easter Island statues was one of the great unsolved
mysteries of the Pacific.

Breakers on the coast of Easter Island. Since the early eighteenth century a number of foreign expeditions had visited this remote spot – few of them, however, had brought anything but fear, disease and death to the islanders themselves.

At some moment, now buried in prehistory, the inhabitants had been gripped by an extraordinary madness. At the expense of all normal activity, they whetted their stone adzes and set about one of the most remarkable engineering projects of ancient times. In a frenzied outpouring of energy they built a series of gigantic stone figures, all in man's likeness and closely resembling each other, tall as houses and heavy as railway engines, which they somehow managed to drag for several miles before setting them up on huge stone terraces at various points round the island, always with their backs to the sea.

Surprisingly, there had been only two previous archaeological expeditions to Easter Island. The first was led by an Englishwoman called Katherine Routledge in 1914. With great thoroughness she surveyed and mapped everything she saw above ground, which included over four hundred of the enormous statues; but she made no attempt at any systematic excavation. Twenty years later, a Franco-Belgian expedition arrived. The Frenchman, Métraux, concentrated mainly on ethnography, while the Belgian, Lavachery, made a detailed study of the rock carvings.

One reason for the comparative neglect of Easter Island was undoubtedly its isolation. Chile, the protecting nation, sent a warship just once a year, which stayed for a week before returning to Valparaiso. For Thor's purposes, a week was far too short and a year was far too long: the expedition would have to acquire its own ship. This would have distinct advantages: they would have the back-up of the ship's crew for heavy work on shore; and at the same time there would be ample fresh water, refrigeration, plenty of storage, a carpenter's shop and a doctor. He finally decided to hire a 150-foot-long Greenland trawler, which seemed ideal for the job.

So in mid-October 1955 she dropped anchor under the protective cliffs of the loneliest island in the world. But Thor himself was far from lonely. Apart from five professional colleagues, this time he was accompanied by his wife Yvonne, his seventeen-year-old son Thor from his first marriage, and his daughter Anette, aged two. Once again he kept a detailed diary which would later be turned into a book, *Aku-Aku: The Secret of Easter*

Island. Their arrival was an emotional moment for him:

❝ What perfect peace. The engine had stopped. The lights had been put out. The whole starry firmament had suddenly escaped from the artificial glare and was swinging to and fro, or in a slow circle, clear and glittering round the masthead. . . . It was as though the plug of an electric line to the mainland had been pulled out. . . . Almost imperceptibly, sight and hearing opened wide again and let a breeze blow right through my soul. . . .

We had stolen up under the land just in time to catch a glimpse of rolling grey-green ridges, steep cliffs along the coast, and, far away in the interior, statues standing scattered up the slope of an extinct volcano like black caraway seeds against the red evening sky. ❞

Thor had read everything he could get his hands

ABOVE *In September 1955 Thor's chartered ship left Europe for the Pacific. Accompanying the expedition were Thor junior, who had taken time off from school to sign on as a deck hand, Yvonne and little Anette.*

OVERLEAF *All along the coast of Easter Island are the gigantic statues known as* moai, *always erected with their backs to the sea.*

147

The head of a moai, *with its distinctive long ears. When the Dutchman Roggeveen first visited the island in 1722 he observed that some of the natives were light-skinned and had elongated ear lobes, which they hooked back over their ears while working.*

on about Easter Island, concentrating particularly on eighteenth-century eye-witness accounts. The Dutch ships were greeted by a 'completely white man', clearly a chief or priest, whose ear lobes had been artificially lengthened down to his shoulders – as had those of many others of the islanders. They lived in low huts made of reeds which resembled an upturned ship, knew nothing of metalworking and generally lived a very primitive, Stone Age existence. Imagine the Dutchmen's amazement, then, to discover gigantic statues larger than anything in Europe. Unable to work out how the natives, who seemed to have no solid wood or thick rope, had erected these giant figures, they solved the question to their own satisfaction by proclaiming that the statues were fashioned from clay and then stuffed with pebbles.

‘ They rowed back to the ships . . . and sailed away from the newly discovered island after a single day's visit. . . . Through a misunderstanding one native visitor was shot on board one of the ships, and a dozen others were shot ashore, while the Europeans got off with the loss of one stolen tablecloth and a few hats which were stolen while they had them on their heads. ’

In 1770 the Spaniards arrived. They solemnly planted three crosses on a piece of high ground on the east coast, and, cheered on by a large crowd of curious natives, declared the island to be Spanish. But when Captain Cook, his men ill with scurvy, came a few years later in search of fresh produce, he found only a few hundred unhealthy-looking natives; the others, he suspected, were hiding underground. When he inspected the stone giants he marvelled at the skill of the ancient carvers who had hewn and raised them up with only the most primitive tools.

Twelve years later, in 1786, the Frenchman La Pérouse made a brief visit. The population were now bolder and showed themselves – probably because, La Pérouse thought, Captain Cook and his crew had not shown them violence.

The next arrival proved disastrous. Seven Peruvian sailing ships anchored in the bay and tricked several hundred natives into coming aboard. Some who tried to escape were shot; the rest were carried away to work as

LEFT *A drawing by the artist who accompanied La Pérouse's expedition in 1786. Though timid at the time of Captain Cook's visit, now the natives were bolder – even, apparently, to the point of stealing the Europeans' fascinating headgear.*

BELOW *A drawing of the Easter Island* moai, *made in 1868 by J. L. Palmer, a doctor on a British warship. He put forward the hypothesis that the island had been colonized by two different peoples, the first of which had carved the statues.*

OVERLEAF *A four-masted school-ship from Chile at anchor off Anakena Bay. In the foreground is a line of re-erected* moai.

151

The Rano Raraku crater, with a line of statues still in place in the foreground.

slave labour on the guano islands off the coast of Peru. After protests had been made on the islanders' behalf the Peruvian authorities ordered their return, but most died of sickness and unfamiliar living conditions and never saw their home again. The few survivors who were landed on Easter Island brought with them small-pox, which practically wiped out the entire population.

The morning after they dropped anchor Thor and his companions took the ship round to the inhabited end of the island at Hangaroa. It seemed as if the entire popula-tion had assembled above the beach as a welcoming party. He had been warned that in the first few days all would depend on one man, Father Sebastian Englert. To any visitor whom he did not trust, all doors would remain closed. But his first words were reassuring: 'Welcome to my island,' he said. It was no less than the truth. In theory political and military power rested with the governor, appointed from Chile; but he had far too much sense to challenge the wisdom and authority of Father Sebastian.

The chief representative of the islanders themselves

was the mayor, Pedro Atan. According to legend there had once been two races sharing the island: the 'long-ears', so called because they extended their ear lobes by hanging weights on them, and the 'short-ears'. The mayor and his brothers were now the last surviving islanders who could claim direct descent on the paternal side from the long-ears. The supposed reason for the disappearance of the long-ears was a notorious massacre hundreds of years before. It was Father Sebastian who told Thor the story, which he firmly believed; certainly it was deeply etched into local folklore.

It seems that the long-ears, though fewer in number, were stronger and more energetic than the short-ears. They were determined to grow crops, and put the short-ears to work clearing rocks and stones. It was hard, back-breaking work in the glaring heat. The short-ears felt they had become slaves and, pushed beyond endurance, they decided to rebel. Surprised and outnumbered, the long-ears retreated to the Poike peninsula at one end of the island, where they dug a huge defensive trench over two miles long and filled it with logs and brushwood. Then they stood ready to set it on fire should the short-ears mount an attack. In honour of their chief they called it Iko's Ditch.

But treachery lay ahead. One of the long-ears had taken a wife from among the short-ears. Her name was Moko Pingei, and she was about to join the ranks of Delilah, Jezebel and other famous traitresses in history. At one end of Iko's Ditch she knew of a weak point. One moonlit night a force of short-ears stole past in single file, while Moko Pingei kept watch from above. When they were safely behind the long-ears' encampment, the short-ears who were still down in the plain made a mock attack. The long-ears rushed towards their ditch and fired it, only to be attacked from behind and driven into a funeral pyre of their own making.

It was said that only three escaped. Two were done to death with sharp stakes. Just one, Ororoina, was allowed to remain alive. In due course he took a wife from among the short-ears; among his descendants was the mayor of Easter Island, Pedro Atan. To be sure, his appearance was different from that of most of the islanders: he looked like a light-skinned Arab with a small

OVERLEAF **Moai** *on the slopes of Rano Raraku. Early observers thought that they comprised only heads and shoulders, but by digging deeper Thor's archaeologists revealed that the figures had bodies and arms as well.*

155

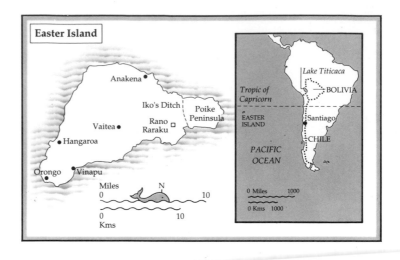

Easter Island

Anakena
Iko's Ditch
Poike Peninsula
Vaitea
Rano Raraku
Hangaroa
Orongo
Vinapu

Miles
0 — 10
N
0 — 10
Kms

Lake Titicaca
Tropic of Capricorn
BOLIVIA
EASTER ISLAND
Santiago
CHILE
PACIFIC OCEAN
0 Miles 1000
0 Kms 1000

moustache. But that, of course, might have been due to any number of causes.

It was Father Sebastian who showed Thor all that remained of Iko's Ditch. Previous archaeologists had dismissed it as a natural fault line in the ground. But the Father was adamant: no legend could be so firmly embedded in oral tradition without some foundation in truth. To his delight, Thor promised that in due course they would try to settle the matter by excavation.

Together with Arne Skjolsvold, who had been with him on the Galapagos expedition and had become a firm friend, Thor decided first to investigate the very source of the island's mysteries – the water-filled volcanic crater of Rano Raraku. This is how he described his first visit to that extraordinary place.

❛Rano Raraku remains one of the greatest and most curious monuments of mankind . . . a warning of the transience of man and civilization. The . . . volcano has been greedily cut up as if it were pastry, although sparks fly when a steel axe is driven against the rock to test its strength. . . . And in the midst of the mountain's gaping wound lie more than a hundred and fifty gigantic stone men, in all stages from the just begun to the just completed. At the foot of the mountain stand finished stone men, side by side like a supernatural army, and you feel miserably small in approaching the place. . . .

Dismounting from your horse in the shadow of a great block of stone, you see that the block had features on its underside: it is the head of a fallen giant. All twenty-three of our expedition could creep under it and find shelter in a rain-storm. And if you try to climb up on

OPPOSITE *Arne Skjolsvold with the exciting discovery he made at the base of one of the excavated* moai: *a carving of a reed ship, which could only mean that the islanders had once seen the real thing.*

The significance of one particular carving from Rano Raraku (ABOVE) *was realized by Arne Skjolsvold. Unlike any other* moai *dug up here, it bore a remarkable resemblance in both posture and detail to the kneeling statues characteristic of ancient Tiahuanaco in Bolivia* (OPPOSITE).

to those which have been flung down flat on their backs, you feel a regular Lilliputian, because often you have the greatest difficulty even in getting up on to their stomachs. And once up on a prostrate Goliath you can walk about freely on his chest and stomach, or stretch yourself out on his nose, which often is as long as an ordinary bed. *'*

Thor noted that many of the figures were about thirty feet in length; the largest, which was unfinished, was a colossal sixty-nine feet – the height of a seven-storey building.

' In Rano Raraku you feel the mystery of Easter Island at close quarters. The air is laden with it; bent on you is the silent gaze of a hundred and fifty eyeless faces. The huge standing figures look down at you with an enigmatic stare; your steps are watched from every single ledge and cave in the mountain, where giants unborn and giants dead and broken lie as in mangers and on sick-beds, lifeless and helpless because the intelligent creative force has left them. Nothing moves except the drifting clouds above you. It was so when the sculptors went, and so it will always be. The oldest figures, those who were completed, stand there proud, arrogant and tight-lipped; as though defiantly conscious that no chisel, no power will ever open their mouths and make them speak.

... Wherever we climbed and wherever we halted, we were surrounded, as in a hall of mirrors, by enormous faces circling about us, seen from in front, in profile and at every angle. All were astonishingly alike. All had the same stoical expression and the most peculiar long ears. ... But the swarm of stone men did not stop even up on the topmost ridge; they went on side by side and above one another in unbroken procession down the inside of the crater. The calvacades of stiff hard-bitten stone men, standing and lying, finished and unfinished, went right down to the lush green reed-bed on the margin of the crater lake, like a people of robots petrified by thirst in a blind search for the water of life. *'*

Only Thor's small daughter Anette failed to be overwhelmed: '"Look at the dolls," she said, enthralled, when I had lifted her down from the pommel at the foot of the volcano.'

Once the statues had been carved, they were some-how moved to the temple sites:

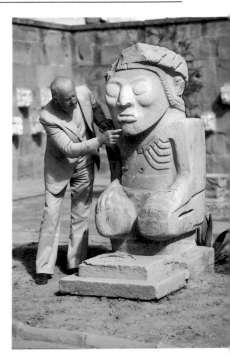

❝ Most of them had actually gone already: only com-paratively few were still on the waiting list for transportation from their holes at the foot of the volcano. All the fully completed giants had moved on, mile by mile over the whole island. . . .

The strangest thing was that the colossi had been moved about not as shapeless lumps which could stand a knock or two, but as perfectly smooth human forms, rubbed and polished front and back, from the lobes of their ears to the roots of their nails. Only the eye-sockets were still missing. . . .

At their destination the blind stone men were not erected just by dropping them down into a hole: on the contrary, they were lifted up and placed on the top of an *ahu*, or temple platform, where they remained standing with their bases a couple of yards above the ground. Now at last holes were chiselled for the eyes; now at last the giants might see where in the world they were. And then came the icing on the cake. They were to have 'hats' put on the tops of their heads – 'hats' which weighed from two to ten tons. ❞

Almost as soon as the team started digging, they uncovered a statue of a quite different type. It had been sculpted in a kneeling position, with a fully developed body and legs that went right down to the toes. Thor immediately recognized a similarity to the kneeling statues of Tiahuanaco, on the shores of Lake Titicaca in the Bolivian Andes. Furthermore, from its position in the quarry it was probably much older than its giant long-eared brethren. If this proved to be the case, then a direct link would be established with the mainland.

No more kneeling statues appeared, which left them free to concentrate on the army of giants. There were three fundamental questions to which they needed to find an answer. First, how had the statues been carved out of the solid rock without the use of metal tools? Secondly, how had they been transported for miles without the use of large numbers of dray animals? Thirdly, how had they been raised into an upright posi-tion, apparently by people who had no understanding of pulleys or block-and-tackle techniques?

14

THE LAST OF THE LONG-EARS

'It was as though we had anchored with a hovering spaceship off the shore of an extinct world.'

At various stages of Thor Heyerdahl's life, when confronted by some seemingly insoluble dilemma, he has tried to find a way forward by practical experiment. To demonstrate that something can be done in a certain way is no proof that it was done; but it destroys the arguments of those who say it could not have been done. Perhaps the time had come to experiment again. Up in the volcanic quarry of Rano Raraku the stone picks still lay where the sculptors had flung them down, and the last of the long-ears still had living descendants in the village. The germ of an idea was stirring in Thor's mind.

In *Aku-Aku* Thor recalled the conversation when he called to see the mayor, Pedro Atan.

❛'Is it true that you're a long-ear too?'

'Yes, Señor,' said the mayor with the utmost gravity. He jumped up and stood at attention like a soldier who had been called out of the ranks. 'I'm a long-ear, a genuine long-ear, and I'm proud of it,' he said dramatically, striking himself on the chest.

'Who made the great statues?'

'The long-ears, Señor,' he replied emphatically.

'I've heard some of the other natives say it was the short-ears.'

'That's an absolute lie, Señor. They're trying to get credit for what my ancestors did. The long-ears made everything. Haven't you seen that the statues have long ears, Señor? You don't think the short-ears made statues of long-ears? The statues are in memory of the long-ears' own chiefs.'

He was so excited that his chest was rising and falling and his thin lips trembling.

'I believe that it was the long-ears who made the statues,' I said. 'Now I myself want a statue made, and I will only have long-ears to do the work. Do you think you can do it?'

The mayor stood motionless for a few moments, with trembling lips; then he drew himself up sharply:

'It shall be done Señor, it shall be done. How big is the statue to be?' he added.

'Oh, medium-size, fifteen to twenty feet.'

'Then there must be six of us. We are only four brothers, but there are several others who are long-ears on their mother's side; will that be all right?'

'Quite all right.' ❜

The night before work was due to begin, Thor and the others were awakened by a strange, rhythmic chant reminiscent of the Pueblo Indians of New Mexico. A bizarre group of figures was sitting in the middle of the camp, hitting the ground with carved paddles and picks. Each wore a crown of leaves, and two of them large paper masks depicting birds' heads.

Next morning the mayor and his five companions arrived early at the quarry and busied themselves collecting up abandoned stone picks and taking measurements with arms and fingers. Then the mayor excused himself, and the six of them held some kind of secret ceremony behind a rock. After that they set to work.

❛ They held their picks in their clenched hands like daggers, and at a sign from the mayor they burst into a stone-cutters' song of the day before, each man lifting his arm and striking against the rock face in time with the rhythm of the tune. . . . And now the singers warmed up, they smiled broadly, they sang and hewed, hewed and sang. One tall old man at the end of the line was so inspired that he danced and swayed his hips as he sang and hewed. Stroke followed stroke; the rock was hard; stone against stone; the little pick was the hardest and the rock must give way. The blows of the picks must have been heard far out over the plain. . . . ❜

To the members of the expedition, inhabitants of the Western world in the mid-twentieth century, it presented an extraordinary sight. 'It was,' wrote Thor, 'as

At Thor's instigation the mayor of Easter Island and some of his relatives, all of whom claimed descent from the long-ears, carried out a demonstration of how their ancestors carved their moai *with stone picks out of the Rano Raraku tufa.*

though we had anchored with a hovering spaceship off the shore of an extinct world.'

❝ On the third day the contours of the giant were clearly visible on the rock wall. The long-ears hacked and cut parallel depressions down the face of the rock, then they cut across the edge left between the furrows, breaking it off in pieces. They cut and cut and flung on water. And continually they changed their picks, for the points soon blunted. . . . When they were worn the mayor grasped one by the end like a little club and struck it against another stone pick on the ground: the splinters flew through the air like sharp flakes and he produced a new point, as easily as a clerk sharpens a pencil. . . . ❞

Widely differing estimates had been put forward in the past as to the time it would take to complete a single statue. Sitting down with the mayor and his brothers after their exertions, they were able to make a more accurate calculation: two teams working on the same statue non-stop would need a full year. Since there were known to be over four hundred statues on the island, the extent of this huge labour of love became apparent.

The mayor and his brothers really did seem to have their roots deep in the oral traditions of the island. If this strange little man with his pale skin, sharp features and wild imagination knew how to carve a statue, a *moai*, perhaps he also knew how to raise one. Thor let a few days pass, then brought the subject up.

❛'Yes, Señor, I do know. There's nothing to it.'

'Nothing to it? It's one of the greatest mysteries of Easter Island!'

'But I know it: I can raise a *moai*.'

'Who taught you?'

The mayor grew solemn and drew himself up in front of me.

'Señor, when I was a very little boy I had to sit on the floor, bolt upright, and my grandfather and his old brother-in-law Porotu sat on the floor in front of me. They taught me many things, just as in school nowadays. I know a lot.'

'If you knew how the statues were raised, why didn't you tell all the people who have been here and asked, long before we came?' I hazarded.

'No one asked me,' the mayor answered proudly. He clearly thought any further information unnecessary.

I did not believe him. I coolly offered him a hundred dollars on the day when the biggest statue at Anakena stood in its place up on the temple wall.

'It's a deal, Señor,' the mayor said quickly, and gave me his hand. . . .❜

The statue Thor had mentioned was nearly ten feet tall and weighed up to thirty tons. There were only twelve men to lift it, and they seemed uncertain. But the mayor exhibited no such doubts. The men gathered up some boulders and large stones, to which he added three wooden poles.

❛The figure had its face buried deep in the earth, but the men got the tips of their poles in underneath it, and while three or four men hung and pulled at the farthest end of each pole, the mayor lay flat on his stomach and pushed small stones under the huge face. . . . As the hours passed, the stones he moved out and shoved in became larger and larger. When the evening came the giant's head had been lifted a good three feet from the ground, while the space beneath was packed tight with stones.

Next day one of the poles was discarded, and five men assembled at each of the others. The mayor set his youngest brother to push the stones in under the statue: he himself stood up on the *ahu* wall with arms outstretched like the conductor of an orchestra, beating the

Having won his trust, Thor persuaded the mayor to show him how the gigantic statues were raised upright. It was simply a matter of small stones and levers, he was told, skilfully applied. It took three weeks to complete the task.

When Thor asked the mayor why he had never before revealed the secret of hauling the moai upright, he replied: 'Nobody asked me.'

air in time as he shouted to the men. . . .

That day they pushed both poles under the right side of the giant. He tilted imperceptibly: but the imperceptible became millemetres and millemetres became inches which became feet. Then the two poles were moved over to the left side of the giant. . . . **9**
They continued in this way, alternating from one side to the next, for about a week. Progress was slow, but clearly the method worked.

6 On the ninth day the huge figure lay stretched on its stomach on the top of an elaborately built tower, the highest side of which was nearly twelve feet above the slope. It was quite uncanny to see this giant of nearly thirty tons lying stretched out up there, a whole man's height above the tops of our heads. The ten men could no longer reach the poles on which they hauled: they just hung dangling from ropes which were made fast to the ends. . . .

This looked deadly dangerous. Anette was no longer allowed to push her doll's pram up to the statue with pebbles for the mayor. Now only the big strong men came staggering along barefoot like Neanderthal men, with heavy boulders in their arms. The mayor was extremely careful, checking the position of every stone: the weight of the colossus was so great that some of the stones cracked under the pressure like lumps of sugar. A single careless placing could mean catastrophe. But it had all been thoroughly thought out, every little move was precisely and logically calculated. . . .

On the tenth day the statue lay at its highest. Imperceptibly the long-ears began to jerk it, feet foremost, in the direction of the *ahu* on which it was to stand.

On the eleventh day they began for the first time to work the giant into a slanting position by building the stones up even higher, but only under the face and chest.

On the seventeenth day a shrivelled old woman suddenly appeared among the long-ears. Together with the mayor she laid a semi-circle of stones as large as eggs at a certain distance in front of the statue's foot, on the great slab on which the giant was now beginning to fumble for a foothold. This was preventive magic. The statue was now leaning at a dangerously sharp angle,

OPPOSITE *Thor on Easter Island at sunset.*

168

and there was imminent danger of its slipping forward of its own weight and rolling down the steep wall of the *ahu* towards the beach. **❯**

When the statue stood on its *ahu*, Don Pedro Atan and his men were justifiably proud of themselves. But Thor wanted more.

❮ I took the mayor away to a quiet spot and stood him up ceremoniously in front of me, with a hand on each of his shoulders. He stood there like a good little school-boy, looking at me eagerly and expectantly.

'Don Pedro, Mayor,' I said, 'now perhaps you can tell me how your ancestors moved the figures from one place to another on the island.'

'They went, they walked,' the mayor replied glibly.

'Rubbish,' I said, disappointed and slightly irritated.

'Take it easy! I believe that they walked, and we must respect our forefathers who have said that they walked.'

A few paces from the camp one of the archaeologists had just dug up a statue which had been completely hidden in the sand. . . . It had no eyes, and consequently had been abandoned before it had been set up at its destination. I pointed to it.

'Can you and your men draw that *moai* across the plain?' **❯**

Again the mayor took up the challenge, but this time he required many more men. A feast was organized to which were invited all the able-bodied from a neighbouring village. After they had eaten their fill, they were called upon to earn their meal. Cheerfully, they took up positions along a rope which had been secured around the neck of one of the fallen statues.

❮ 'One, two, three! One, two, three!'

Pang! The rope broke, and there was wild cheering as men and vahines [young women] rolled over one another on the ground in chaos. The mayor gave an embarrassed laugh, and ordered the rope to be doubled and made fast to the figure. And now the giant began to move – first in short jerks, but then suddenly it seemed to break loose. As it slid away over the plain Lazarus, the mayor's assistant, jumped on to the giant's face and stood waving his arms and cheering like a gladiator in a triumphal procession, while the long lines of toiling natives hauled patiently and yelled at the tops of their voices with enthusiasm. It went as quickly as if each of them had been towing an empty soap box. **,**

Thor called a halt when they were a little way out on to the plain. The point had been made. There was only one question still unaddressed: how did they manage to place the huge topknot on the head of a standing figure? The answer was to use the same tower that had enabled them to raise the colossus on to his legs.

Having satisfied himself that a prone statue could be moved – even if it had not exactly 'walked' – it was now time for Thor to honour his promise to Father Sebastian and excavate the Iko Ditch. Under the supervision of Carl Smith, one of the archaeologists, a team of willing islanders dug holes at intervals along the ditch. Here, for the first time, was their chance to unearth proof of Easter Island's most potent legend.

They were soon to be rewarded. In every hole, at a depth of about six feet, a band of charcoal and ash was revealed in stripes of black and red. Carl was certain that it could only have been caused by a great fire. Next day, he set his diggers the task of carving a cross-section right across the ditch. The truth was revealed. The upper part of the depression had indeed been the work of nature; but the rest was by the hand of man. It was a gigantic artificial moat twelve feet deep and forty feet across, which separated the Poike peninsula from the rest of the island for a distance of two miles. Sling stones and carved slabs were found among the ashes, but no bones. By carbon dating, it was easy enough to date the great fire to between three and four hundred years earlier.

The Iko Ditch raised another important question. If the long-ears had filled it with logs and brushwood, there must have been plenty of trees on the island. If so, where had they gone? Inside the Rano Raraku crater was a lake now partly overgrown with reeds; Thor decided to carry out a series of pollen tests, which revealed that this barren island was once covered by groves of waving palms and a coniferous species known only in South America. It was clear from soot deposits that fire had been the cause of their disappearance. But whether the destruction of Easter Island's trees was caused by an accidental disaster, or systematically carried out by man, remained a mystery.

15

THE SIGHTLESS GIANTS

*The great statue began to waddle forward, rolling
from side to side like some late night reveller
on his way home.*

T hirty years were to pass before Thor Heyerdahl
set foot on Easter Island once more. Following
the logical extension of his theories the path
ahead lay eastwards, first to the Atlantic, and finally to
the Indian Ocean. But whether he knew it or not at the
time, he had already left a part of himself on the island.
For Thor, the place had an attraction and a significance
deeper than anywhere else on earth. Easter Island had
become, and remains, his spiritual home.

Throughout those intervening years, the island, its
people and above all its mysteries were never far from
his thoughts. Wherever he travelled – to the marshlands
of Iraq, to the valley of the Indus, to the Maldive Islands
– he kept finding parallels and strange coincidences.
Were those sightless giants really as blind as they
appeared? What did the local people mean when they
boldly asserted that the statues 'walked'?

During the 1970s Thor visited two museums, one in
the Old World and one in the New; what he saw opened
his own eyes to the first of these questions. In the Syrian
city of Aleppo, once the homeland of the Hittites, he
found himself staring into the face of a statue with one
white, inlaid eye and one empty socket. Later, in Mexico
City, he saw an Aztec statue which still had both its
inlaid eyes. In his book *The Art of Easter Island*, he published photographs of both these statues, speculating on
a possible connection with the sightless giants of Rano
Raraku.

Scholars tended to dismiss the idea on the grounds

that inlaid eyes played no part in Polynesian tradition. But suddenly all their arguments were undermined. Easter Island's first home-grown archaeologist was a young man named Sergio Rapu, and he had made a most important discovery. It was an eye, made from white coral, which fitted perfectly into the socket of one of the statues – one more link between Easter Island and the great landmasses to the east.

Thor felt it was time to turn his attention to the Pacific once more, and his chance came in 1984 when he was invited to attend the first International Science Congress to be held on the island. There had been many changes in the intervening years. A clutch of hotels, two discos and a runway capable of taking the largest jets had turned Easter Island into a modest tourist attraction. But the people were just as Thor remembered them, full of warmth and friendliness, though secretive and superstitious at the same time.

This short visit was enough to rekindle his fascination; within two years he was back as leader of an expedition financed by the Kon-Tiki Museum in Oslo, which had been set up as a permanent record of his scientific work. One member of the team was a young Czech engineer called Pavel Pavel. A few months earlier he had read *Aku-Aku* in translation, and had become so interested in the problem of how the Stone Age sculptors had moved their giant statues that he had conducted his own experiment. In his back yard he had constructed a twenty-ton replica of a *moai*, using cement instead of stone. With the aid of ropes and brawny friends it had

When Thor speculated on a connection between the sightless moai *of Easter Island and Hittite and Aztec statues with inlaid eyes, he was not taken very seriously. But after a large stone and coral eye (BELOW LEFT) was discovered which perfectly fitted one of the* moai's *eye sockets (BELOW), he was vindicated.*

been made to rock back and forth on its pedestal, inching forward at the same time. The statue had 'walked', just as the islanders said it would.

All this he recounted in a letter to Thor. It would have been easy to send a polite reply thanking Pavel Pavel for his amusing story, and wishing him well. But Thor determined to take the young Czech with him to see if he could apply the same techniques to a real Easter Island *moai*.

After establishing a base for his expedition, Thor made a much more thorough examination of the statues than had been possible thirty years before. Very soon he had the evidence he was looking for. The further a statue was located from the Rano Raraku crater, where all of them had been carved, the more rounded were the edges at its base. The statues that had never left the quarry had smooth, flat bases terminating in a sharp edge all round. Furthermore, some of the ones found lying not far from the crater had snapped cleanly in half as if they had fallen from a height. This tended to confirm the theory that they had indeed been moved upright, rather than dragged along the ground and erected on site, as he had previously thought. It seemed therefore that the statues *had* 'walked'.

Pavel's method was simple enough. It had to be, since he spoke no language understood by anyone on the island. But like a conductor with his baton, he knew how to make himself understood. The statue was to wriggle forwards by rocking from side to side. Four ropes were attached, two at the head and two at the base. As soon as Team A tugged at the head, so making the statue lean towards them, Team B had to pull on the base rope on the opposite side, making it take an ambling step forward. To enable it to take a second step – and also to prevent it toppling over altogether – the head now had to be pulled over to the opposite side by Team B. At this point Team A gave a heave on their base rope.

After a little time the two teams learned to co-ordinate their exertions. Then the great statue began to waddle forward, rolling from side to side like some late-night reveller on his way home. Out there on the plain, it looked like Gulliver trussed with ropes in the land of the Lilliputians. For the islanders themselves, the sight must have been truly amazing. The statues that 'walked' had been part of their folklore for centuries; now they saw it actually happening. From first to last, the whole episode had been typical of Thor Heyerdahl: the letter from a complete stranger which he had decided to follow up; his trust in oral tradition; the practical experiment; and finally his natural sense of showmanship which so annoys desk-bound professors while it delights the press.

Now another fragment of evidence fell into place. Thor asked one of the islanders to give him the local word for 'walk'. He was told it was *haere*. But during the demonstration he thought he had heard the islanders chanting another phrase: 'Neke-neke. . . . Neke-neke.' Could there be two words for 'walk' in the Rapa Nui language? In an Easter Island dictionary he looked up the word *neke-neke* and read: 'To inch forward by moving the body, due to disabled legs or the absence thereof.' No other people in the world have ever felt the need for such a word. But then, no other people have felt the need to make giant, legless statues walk.

New excavations will undoubtedly continue for many years; the Navel of the World has not yet yielded up the last of its secrets. But Thor Heyerdahl feels that his own work there has reached a kind of conclusion. He has shown, to his own satisfaction at least, that the earliest settlers were the long-ears, who came from the east – almost certainly from the mainland of South America.

By the time the short-ears arrived, this time from the west, the unique culture of the long-ears, most forcefully represented by the giant statues all over the island, was firmly established. If they were to remain, then the newcomers had little choice but to work within the long-ears' social patterns. However, new waves of migration from the west would eventually put the short-ears in the ascendant. They rose up, and burnt the great majority of the long-ears to death. A unique and extraordinary way of life disappeared in that conflagration. The quarry at Rano Raraku, which for centuries had echoed to the sound of stone ringing against stone, fell silent; and every single monument the length and breadth of the island was hurled to the ground.

Nevertheless, it must be said that there is still a large

Thor with Yvonne and their three daughters, (from the left) Anette, Marian and Bettina, at Colla Micheri on the Italian Riviera.

body of professional opinion that takes a different view. There is no concrete proof that Thor Heyerdahl's long-ears were the first people to settle on Easter Island, and that they came from America. Without it many archaeologists, members of a profession which tends to discount oral evidence and to regard experiments with ropes and rafts as 'publicity stunts', remain sceptical.

Looking at Thor Heyerdahl's life as a whole, it is easy to picture him spending almost as much time on expeditions as in leading a conventional life. In fact there was a gap of fourteen years between the conclusion of his first Easter Island expedition and his next great venture, which was to be the crossing of the Atlantic. They were years which saw the publication of two more books, *Aku-Aku* and *The Archaeology of Easter Island*, the birth of two more daughters, Marian in 1957 and Elizabeth, known as Bettina, in 1959, and a long search for somewhere permanent to settle down. Miraculously, they found it.

A wooded spit of land runs down from the Italian Maritime Alps towards the Mediterranean coast of Liguria, forming a wild headland called Capo Mele that overlooks the resort of Alassio. On a summer's day in 1958, a friendly taxi driver called Gandolfo drove the Heyerdahl family up a steep, winding road to an abandoned medieval village nestling among the pines. Its name was Colla Micheri. Thor knew at once that the search was over. Up there he could build himself a wooden cabin with all the atmosphere of Norway, except for the climate. Up there, with nothing to disturb the peace, he could strike a balance between intellectual and physical labour, and perhaps find the harmony of spirit for which he had been searching so long.

As it happened, when they gave their first party at Colla Micheri Liv and her new husband were in the vicinity. They were duly invited, and the local people were treated to the puzzling spectacle of Thor Heyerdahl opening the dancing, not with his second wife, but with his first.

16

OF MEN AND BOATS

'Easter Island, Peru, Egypt. These strange parallels
could hardly have been found further apart.'

Even today, the birth of civilization in the New
World presents fascinating problems. The Spanish conquistadores found two vast continents
joined by a narrow isthmus. At each extremity, north
and south, they were inhabited by primitive food-
gatherers. But across a broad band in the middle lived
several magnificent and complex civilizations, of which
the most powerful were the Incas, the Aztecs and the
Mayans. Excavation produced no evidence that civilizations in America had evolved over a long period: they
seemed to have sprung into existence fully fledged.
What suddenly inspired these people to establish intri-
cate patterns of social, political and religious behaviour,
to develop scripts and create artefacts of great beauty?
Nowhere else in the world did the mystery present itself
in quite these terms, because no other huge landmass is
quite so isolated. In Europe, Asia and Africa, almost any
idea or tradition could have come from somewhere else.
But the Americas were cut off by two enormous
stretches of ocean.

There was an additional difficulty. Since there were
no apes in the New World from which to evolve, Homo
sapiens must either have had some kind of spontaneous
origin (in defiance of Charles Darwin but no doubt to
the approval of Christian fundamentalists) or migrated
from elsewhere. But from where? Hardly from the
south, from icy Antarctica. The northern route seemed
much more likely. But if people had managed to cross
from Siberia when glacial conditions still permitted it,

why had a highly developed civilization failed to appear in the temperate and fertile lands which now comprise Canada and the United States? There was only one other possibility. In spite of the vastness of the Atlantic and Pacific, the people in that central belt between Mexico and Peru might have had some contact with cultures overseas.

The controversy surrounding these questions has raged for many years. On one side there are the isolationists who do not believe there was any contact between the Old World and the New before 1492. According to this view, man as a species is quite likely to develop along similar lines in widely divergent places. The existence, for instance, of pyramids and hierarchical dynasties in both Mexico and North Africa does not constitute evidence that there was contact between them at some remote time. Indeed, one confirmed isolationist went so far as to argue that, because contact across the ocean had been impossible, then the very large number of cultural similarities between these two areas (he listed over sixty) merely confirmed that Homo sapiens tends to behave in very similar ways wherever he finds himself.

Diffusionists, on the other hand, take the view that close similarities between two or more cultures, whether they take the form of games, fish hooks or burial customs, can be taken as evidence of physical contact, the more so when the evidence is cumulative. The difficulty has always lain in trying to explain how that contact could possibly have been established. There was, of course, only one way – by boat.

Once primitive man had tried to cross calm water by straddling a floating tree trunk, it did not require much ingenuity to deduce that the way to stop it rolling over was to attach another trunk down the side of the first one – the inevitable step towards a crude log raft. It was almost certainly the first form of boat to be devised because it required no tools. All a man would need were some lengths of liana to bind his logs together, and a stick for a paddle.

But then another primitive man in another part of the forest hit on a different use for a tree trunk. Using a stone tool, he scooped out the inside until there was

room to sit or kneel. This form of craft was much more
difficult to keep upright than a raft, but it had other distinct advantages. With less water resistance it was much
faster, especially against the current. It was also more
manoeuvrable along narrow, twisting waterways. What
this primitive man had actually done was create the first
dugout canoe, which depends on the principle of dis-
placing water with air.

So from very early days, boats were constructed
according to two different principles. It did not matter
how much water was shipped aboard a boat made of
logs or bundles of reeds, because it would simply wash
through, leaving the craft afloat. With an air displacement boat, on the other hand, the bottom and sides had
to be completely watertight, and if any rough water was
to be encountered the sides had to be built higher and
higher. But as we know from the metal ships of today,

the material from which the air displacement boat is made does not itself have to be buoyant.

From prehistoric paintings and petroglyphs, it is clear that the first ships of appreciable size were built from bundles of reeds, and not from timber or split planks. Such craft are depicted on the walls of Egyptian tombs, and on the cave paintings at Tassili in what was once the green Sahara. Petroglyphs from before the times of the pharaohs found in dried river beds in the Red Sea show masts, sails and even two cabins on board. A ceramic boat model in the Iraq Museum indicates that in that part of the world the art of sailing goes back at least to 4000 BC.

Yet the first reed boat that Thor Heyerdahl ever saw in practical use was on Lake Titicaca in the Andes. It was relatively small; indeed all the reed boats still in use today – on the Indus, the Nile or the Euphrates – tend to be small and are used mainly for fishing or ferrying. Had the use of larger reed boats, perhaps even capable of making an ocean crossing, died out with the coming of ribbed hulls – or had such craft never existed? Intriguing thoughts presented themselves. Had Cleopatra's barge been a reed boat? Had Noah's Ark? In theory there is virtually no limit to the size a reed boat can be made; but, as with balsa wood, there is a limit to how long it will float.

The more Thor pondered the subject, the more he felt the need to find an answer to just one question that was of enormous consequence to man's understanding of the beginnings of civilization on this planet. Was there a link between the cultures of Central America and those which had developed on the Nile, the Euphrates and, as new excavations were beginning to reveal, in the Indus valley as well? If that could be established, then the link itself could have taken only one form – reed boats, in substantial numbers and of substantial size.

Instinctively, the contemporary mind discards the idea of ocean-going vessels made entirely from reeds. In *The Ra Expeditions*, Thor recalled just such a reaction from an old craftsman on the banks of the Nile.

❛A papyrus reed is a soft, sappy flower stem which a child can bend and crush. When it is dry it snaps like a matchstick and burns like paper. On the ground in front of me lay a tinder-dry papyrus reed, savagely screwed and fractured into a zigzag tangle. It had been thrown there in the morning by an indignant old Arab who mangled it between his fingers before flinging it away from him on the sand, spitting after it and pointing scornfully. 'That thing,' he said, 'that wouldn't even hold a nail; and how could you fix masts to a thing like that?' The old man was a canny boat-builder who had taken the bus up from Port Said to conclude a contract for masts and rigging for the vessel we were building. He was so outraged that he took the next bus back to the coast. Were we trying to make fun of an honest craftsman . . . ? It was no good explaining to him that similar boats were painted in large numbers on the walls of the burial chambers of the ancient pyramid-builders out here in the desert. After all, these tombs also contain paintings of men with the heads of birds and serpents with wings. Anyone could see that a reed was a soft stalk in which neither nails nor screws could find a grip. Material for a haystack. A paper boat. **'**

Could the first crossing of the Atlantic have been made in a wooden boat, as opposed to a reed one? Speculation on the subject was renewed in the late 1960s when four great funeral ships were discovered, buried on either side of the great pyramid of Cheops at Giza, outside Cairo. The cedarwood from which they were constructed had been imported from the Lebanon. One of them has now been reassembled, and at first glance appears to have been designed to survive in heavy seas. But the wooden planks were merely sewn together with hemp, so the ship would almost certainly have disintegrated at its first encounter with a heavy swell.

Evidence of chafing on the woodwork suggests that this was a working vessel before it carried the pharaoh on one last ceremonial journey. It was probably a royal barge. But if it never ventured beyond the placid waters of the Nile, why had the ancient shipwrights incorporated an exaggerated prow and stern? It may simply have been a form of flattery – but they must have copied the design from somewhere, and they knew what they were doing. To judge from the wall paintings in the burial chambers, the most obvious source of inspiration would have been the robust papyrus vessels still plying their trade on the Nile, but undoubtedly capable of venturing out into the open sea. It seems reasonable to assume that a fleet of reed boats was sent to bring back a cargo of cedarwood from the Lebanon.

Nevertheless the possibility remains that it was a wooden ship that made the first crossing of the Atlantic. But, as Thor Heyerdahl was to point out, if this had been the case it seems very strange that the American Indians made no attempt to copy it. If there had been a crossing before 1492, it seemed to Thor that a reed boat would have been a much more likely, and much safer, form of conveyance.

But he had no evidence. Indeed, this time he had no particular theory about how or when some aspects of Egyptian civilization might have been carried to the New World. However, having satisfied himself that the Pacific Ocean was the main highway of communication

OVERLEAF *An Aymara Indian manipulating a reed boat on Lake Titicaca, twelve thousand feet up in the Bolivian Andes. In the pre-Inca period, huge slabs of stone were ferried across the lake in larger craft than this to build the ancient capital of Tiahuanaco.*

183

Figures of bird men carved into the Orongo rocks at the southern tip of Easter Island.

between the American mainland and the nearest islands to the west, he was bound to ask himself whether that conclusion had wider implications. If it was true for the Pacific, then why not for the Atlantic, where the flow of the currents was, if anything, even more favourable?

Four years earlier, in 1965, Thor had paid a visit to Egypt. In the Valley of the Kings he was immediately struck by the similarity between the reed boats depicted on the wall paintings and others that he had seen on ceramic pots in northern Peru, which he was later to write about in *The Ra Expeditions*:

❜The largest reed boats in Peru were depicted as two-deckers. Quantities of water jars and other cargo were painted in on the lower deck, as well as rows of little people, and on the upper deck usually stood the earthly representative of the sun-god, the priest-king, larger than all his companions, surrounded by bird-headed men who were often hauling on ropes to help the reed boat through the water. The tomb paintings in Egypt also portrayed the sun-god's earthly representative, the priest-king known as the pharaoh, like an imposing giant on his reed boat, surrounded by miniature people, while the same mythical men with bird heads towed the reed boat through the water.

Reed boats and bird-headed men seemed to go together, for some inexplicable reason. For we had found them far out in the Pacific Ocean too, on Easter Island, where the sun-god's mask, the reed boats with sails, and the men with bird heads formed an inseparable trio among the wall-paintings and reliefs in the ancient ceremonial village of Orongo, with its solar observatory. Easter Island, Peru, Egypt. These strange parallels could hardly have been found farther apart. . . . But what was even more strange was that the aboriginal people of Easter Island called the sun *ra*. *Ra* was the name for the sun on all the hundreds of Polynesian islands, so it could be no mere accident. *Ra* was also the name for the sun in ancient Egypt. . . . Giant monolithic statues as high as houses had been erected in honour of the sun-god's earthly priest-kings on Easter Island, in Peru and in ancient Egypt. And in all three places, solid rock had been sliced up like cheese into blocks as big as railway trucks and fitted together in stepped pyramids designed on an astronomical basis according to the movements of the sun. . . . Was there some connection, or was it just coincidence? **9**

17

REEDS IN THE WIND

'On a floating reed boat there was room only for
people who could shake each other by the hand.'

Throughout what might be called his *Kon-Tiki* years Thor had taken a passing interest in reed boats, but more as evidence of cultural links than as a form of transport to which one day he might entrust himself and his companions. Now he began to look more closely. He started by retracing earlier journeys to Lake Titicaca and Mexico. Then he turned his attention to Africa. One place, he knew, where reed boats were still in regular daily use was Lake Chad, south of the Sahara. It is a vast inland sea, sometimes spreading over an area of ten thousand square miles, and sometimes evaporating in the burning heat to less than half that size. The surface is dotted with thousands of floating islands that collide and drift apart like stately dodgem cars. In that watery landscape, devoid of trees, reed boats are the essential form of transport.

In 1969 Thor decided to go and see for himself, as he subsequently recounted in *The Ra Expeditions*:

❛That day I saw my first papyrus boat. It came drifting silently past over the glassy water on that enchanted lake, which had completely changed its appearance from the day before. When we arrived, one large, low island had been lying straight in front of our hut, but now it had disappeared without trace and three other islands had loomed up in quite different places in its stead. The smallest of them moved slowly as I watched it, drifting off to the right, leaving a faint hint of a wake behind it on the left. It looked like a big, well-arranged flower basket, a thick bouquet of bristly golden papyrus

flowers. . . . The papyrus boat glided smoothly and surely past the floating flower basket. On board stood two tall Africans, dressed in white and erect as toy soldiers, punting the boat along with long poles. The yellow boat and the straight black bodies were also mirrored in the lake and the reflection, sailing upside down, reminded me of those other reed boats which now actually were sailing upside down in relation to us, because they were on the other side of the globe, in South America. The boats on Lake Titicaca were so strikingly like the boat we were looking at now that they could easily have replaced the mirror image. **'**

The first task was to learn how to build a papyrus boat. The tall, dignified Omar M'Bulu of the Buduma tribe, helped by his half-brother, Mussa, began by cutting large piles of reeds from the borders of the lake.

' The papyrus reed was at least six feet long and about two inches thick at the root, with a tricorn-shaped cross-section. It was not jointed and hollow like bamboo but compact and spongy throughout its length, like a sort of stiff white foam-rubber covered with a thin, smooth sheath. Omar began by taking a single reed and splitting it part way lengthwise into four strips, still joined at the thicker end. In the forks he stuck four whole stems, root first, and tied them with a loop so tight that the spongy

Reed boats on Lake Chad, on the southern edge of the Sahara Desert.

189

ends were pressed together as compactly as possible. Between them again he inserted a steadily increasing number of reeds, which he lashed fast all the time with loops of rope so that the bundle gradually increased in thickness like the head of a projectile. Mussa joined him and the two boat-builders each took an end of cord in their mouths and tightened the knots with all their combined strength. . . . The point was apparently to squeeze the cut end of the spongy reeds together until the pores closed. When the bundle increased to a thickness of about eighteen inches, it was continued lengthwise, keeping the same diameter, like a giant pencil. Finally the pointed end was lifted on to a sturdy tree stump and the boat-builders began to jump and trample on the reed bundle until it curved like a huge elephant tusk.

The problem of shaping the stern was solved by Omar and Mussa in the simplest way. They took the longest machete and cut all the superfluous reed straight across as if slicing the end of a sausage. Then the papyrus boat was ready for launching, with pointed upswept prow and thick, flat, sawn-off stern. The work was completed in a day.

'*Kaday*,' said Mussa, patting his finished product with a grin. That was the Buduma word for the reed boat on which the whole of their lakeside existence had depended since the morning of time. . . . No one knows who were their teachers. Perhaps they developed the craft themselves. More probably the Buduma tribe had distant ancestors who had travelled the caravan route from the Nile valley. **9**

Thor was just about to try out his new *kaday* when a new friend entered his life.

6 '*Bonjour, monsieur*,' he said simply. 'My name is Abdullah and I speak French and Arabic. Do you need an interpreter?'

That was just what I did need. How else was I to learn anything from Omar and Mussa when the three of us were out on the lake in the little vegetable boat?

Abdullah, swathed in an ankle-length white robe and with a bearing like a Caesar, behaved with all the confidence of a gentleman. His face was blacker than night, his head smooth-shaven like Omar's and Mussa's, with a long scar running centrally down his forehead and over the bridge of his nose. . . . Abdullah Djibrine was a true, full-blooded child of nature, an alert assistant, a really merry companion. . . .

The boat was so narrow that if I wanted to sit I could only ride astride it, yet there we were, all standing on it together and swaying, and the papyrus gave no hint of a bend or a wobble. The water, so blue at a distance, was far from limpid and I was not anxious to capsize into the worm-soup. Here in the sedge it was especially perilous, for the little [bilharzia-carrying] worms come swimming out of a snail which lives on the reed itself. **❯**

Thor understood his own nature well enough by now to know that his imagination, propelled by considerable willpower, was capable of leaping ahead of day-to-day practicalities. His heart was already set on building a reed boat capable of sailing across the Atlantic from east to west, but such were the difficulties that he hardly dared admit the ambition to himself.

To build his boat on the shores of Lake Chad was out of the question: there was no way of transporting it anywhere. To build it on Lake Tana in Ethiopia, the source of the Blue Nile, was a glamorous idea and would give him an ample source of papyrus. But the difficulties of transportation were just as great: the Titisat Falls downstream from the lake are impassable; and below them the Nile passes through a perilous, crocodile-infested gorge for several hundred miles. The obvious place was Egypt. There was only one serious disadvantage. In the delta area, where once papyrus reeds had grown in abundance, there were now none at all. Even the ancient craft of making paper from the stems had been lost (although it has since been rediscovered in the laboratories of the Papyrus Institute and is now mass-produced). Nevertheless, if Egypt proved to be right in every other respect, the raw material would have to be imported from either Lake Tana or Lake Chad. Thor decided to investigate Lake Tana.

❮ The lake itself was the home of the black monks. They lived on luxuriant jungle islands a long way out, and for centuries the papyrus boats had been their only link with the outside world. . . . While the papyrus boats on Lake Chad were sliced straight across behind . . . this type, which had survived at the Nile's own source, had

A relief from an Egyptian burial chamber. Whenever a pharaoh ordered a new ship, the building materials were close at hand: once the papyrus marshes stretched for miles along the banks of the Nile, but they have long since been replaced by more lucrative crops.

kept the ancient Egyptian form. Both prow and stern curved up above the waterline and the stern was bent in the peculiar ancient Egyptian curl over the boat itself. . . .

. . . Although huge jungle trees grew on their islands, the monks had never taken to building canoes or plank boats. Their predecessors had paddled the papyrus boat from antiquity into the Middle Ages and now they were calmly continuing to paddle it into the nuclear age. . . . **9** One thing Thor had observed here rather worried him. The monks never left a reed boat in the water for a minute longer than was necessary, but pulled them ashore to dry out – not something that could readily be achieved in mid-Atlantic.

Lake Tana was clearly the best source of papyrus: the reeds could be transported by lorry down to the Red Sea, then shipped up to Suez before completing the journey to Cairo by road. But although the Ethiopian reed boats resembled the blueprints he proposed to use, taken straight from the walls of Egyptian tombs, he did not trust them. With their thin, undulating hulls they looked as if they would become water-logged in a couple of weeks. He decided to bring in boat-builders from Lake Chad, with their much more robust techniques. As for a shipyard, why should he not build his boat at Giza, in the shadow of the great pyramids themselves?

Getting permission to rope off an area of sand on the south side of the pyramids proved relatively easy; as the Deputy Minister of Tourism said, 'It's a good thing to remind the world that Egypt does not only make war.' The Six-Day War was still fresh in people's minds, and sporadic hostilities in the hot-spots of the Middle East were commonplace. But none of the experts whom Thor consulted expected his craft to float for more than a few weeks. Even the ebullient and optimistic Hassan Ragab, the head of the Papyrus Institute, said so.

At last everything seemed to be in place. But Thor knew that, once started, there could be no going back. Expenses would mount and eventually have to be repaid from royalties on a book. It was a daunting decision. No expedition – no book. Then, out of the blue, a letter arrived, and from that moment the matter was decided.

❛I unfolded the scrap of paper. The cramped and childish handwriting on it read:

Dear Thor in Italy,

Do you remember Abdullah in Chad? I am ready to come to you and build a big *kaday* with Omar and Mussa. We are waiting for orders and I am carpenter with Pastor Eyer in Fort Lamy.

Greetings, Abdoulaye Djibrine

. . . It was a marvellous thing that this illiterate in the heart of Central Africa had had the initiative to take my address to a scribe in Fort Lamy and rouse me to action. Why did I hesitate? Abdullah was ready and Omar and

One of the world's leading experts on ancient Egyptian boat construction, Björn Landström, drew a design for Thor and his team to work from.

Mussa were prepared to come with him. They built larger reed boats to freight their cattle on Lake Chad than those used by the Christians to escape alone and take refuge on Ethiopian islands, and they knew more about the floating capacity of papyrus than all the scholars in the world put together. They believed in their *kaday*. They were willing to build one big enough to float for months, and they were willing to come on board themselves and sail to distant lands which I could only describe to them in terms of the number of days and moons it took to reach them because they had not the faintest notion of geography. **9**

Once the decision was made, a crucial timetable had to be observed to avoid the hurricane season. The voyage had to start in May – less than six months away. Thor sent urgent instructions to Ethiopia for the cutting of the reeds to begin; then they would have to be dried out to prevent them from rotting on the long journey to Cairo.

Nothing was to prove quite so frustrating, and in retrospect quite so hilarious, as Thor's attempts to get Abdullah, Omar and Mussa out of Chad and into Egypt. The saga began when Yvonne cabled to say that

Abdullah had been arrested; she had no idea why. There was only one way to find out, and that was for Thor to go to Chad himself. There he discovered that Abdullah was suspected of slave trading; the authorities thought he was about to smuggle Omar and Mussa out of the country and sell them to Heyerdahl. In Africa, tribal memories die hard.

Negotiations went on for days. In the end Thor decided to gamble on something that had worked for him once before, when he was trying to get himself out of the Norwegian armed forces after the war – if a document looked imposing enough, he reasoned, no one would notice whether it had been signed by the right people. He succeeded, and brought the three Buduma tribesmen back with him by plane to Egypt.

In Cairo he had a lucky break. A Swedish historian, Björn Landström, the world's leading authority on ancient Egyptian boat design, happened to be there. He was sceptical about the seaworthiness of papyrus boats, but readily agreed to make a drawing incorporating all the features he had seen on tomb paintings along the Nile; Thor used it like a yacht designer's plan. Others were less impressed.

❛On the third day the clash between tradition and scholarship began. The reed roll was now so long that it was time to narrow it off into a point behind, but this the Buduma brothers flatly refused to do. They wanted to extend it without altering the diameter and then slice it off like a sausage, as they had always done on their own lake. No *kaday* could have a bow at both ends! With Abdullah as interpreter, Landström . . . and I tried to explain that this was to be a papyrus boat of the special design which the ancient Egyptians used, and their boats were pointed at both ends. But the generally cheerful Mussa turned and went off to bed. . . .

Before the sun rose next morning the two brothers slipped down to the building site. . . . Landström had made a construction drawing which showed seven separate rolls curved to a point front and back and then lashed side by side to give the boat width. But the two brothers had already begun the second roll by weaving it directly into and together with the first in a compact, firm whole. Not only were the ropes woven together in

Ra took shape in the shadow of the pyramids, with close access to tomb paintings and reliefs of ancient reed-ship rigging.

parallel chains across the boat, but a handful of papyrus reed from one roll was regularly woven diagonally into the rope rings of the neighbouring roll, so that they formed an inseparable whole. The technique was so superior to anything a non-initiate could have thought out that the scholars could only capitulate. A thousand years of practice swept away the theories of a single lifetime. . . . 〉

Gradually the work continued, but not without its hazards. A sandstorm ripped through the camp, driving them all into their tents for three days. As soon as the boat began to take on a recognizable shape, they were plagued by tourists who thought nothing of breaking off a reed here and there as a souvenir. Camels edged up for a nibble. The biggest danger of all was fire: one match dropped by a careless visitor, and all their work would be reduced to ashes in seconds. The disadvantages of choosing one of the Seven Wonders of the World as a construction site were becoming all too apparent.

Meanwhile, Thor continued to visit the tombs to study the frescoes, partly for inspiration and partly to make sure that no vital detail had been overlooked.

❛ The pictures of long wooden ships always showed a thick cable running from bow to stern high above the deck. It was kept up by two forked posts located fore and aft. The purpose of this arrangement was to keep both boat ends tensioned and thereby prevent the vessel from collapsing fore or aft and thus breaking amidships. Evidently the papyrus boats could be allowed more flexibility lengthwise, because they lacked this tension cable. On the other hand, they had a short cable running diagonally from the in-curled tip of the stern down to the after-deck, making the stern look like a harp with a single string. I spent hours pondering the function of this harp-string, convinced that it must have a practical purpose, though all the scholars and even the practical men from Chad said that its only function was to preserve the in-curved shape of the stern. Of course. But why, why this in-turned arc? Just a matter of beauty, everyone said. None of us could work out a better reason, but that was reason enough for us to copy the old pictures on this point as well. The harp-string stayed there for many days, but one fine morning it had gone. Our friends from Chad had removed it: it hampered them in their work and was not needed any more because the curl on the stern now stayed immovably in place by itself. We asked them to tie the rope on again at once, but yielded to the logical argument that if the curl began to straighten out we could simply tie the harp-string on again ourselves whenever it was needed. It was not needed now.

Whereas the wooden boats had their giant cable strung between two forked posts, the paintings and reliefs of papyrus boats showed that they had a thick twisted cable made fast round the edge of the whole deck to hold the vessel together lengthwise, increase rigidity and provide a hold for the mast stays, which of course could not be lashed directly to the thin reeds. ❜ In due course they would discover the purpose of the mysterious harp-string.

On 28 April *Ra* was finished. By coincidence it was the anniversary of the start of the *Kon-Tiki* voyage, twenty-

The finished vessel. Two hundred and eighty thousand reeds, each approximately ten feet long, had had to be brought from Lake Tana in the Ethiopian highlands to the coast and then up the Red Sea.

two years before – it is easy to forget how long the gaps were between Thor's various expeditions. On that occasion there had been nine sturdy logs to sustain the crew; this time there would be nothing but paper.

❝ Broad-chested and squat, with upstretched neck and curved tail, *Ra* looked like a big, golden hen brooding on round logs in the sand in front of the pyramids. We had built it lying free on top of a large wooden sledge, and four long cables were stretched out in the sand in front of this support. Busy men were laying out a slipway of telegraph poles on which the sledge could be towed over the sand-dunes. For assistance in this task the President of the Papyrus Institute in Cairo had taken me to the Egyptian Institute of Gymnastics. . . .

The school could bring five hundred physical training students, and here they were, arrayed in white shorts, with their gymnastics instructor organizing them in long rows along the ropes. Two men stood on the boat issuing directions, and one stood in front on the sledge, giving start and stop signals with a conductor's baton. There was something biblical about the scene. Perhaps it was because the old-fashioned boat, lying there, solid and home-made, with the basket cabin on its deck and the pyramids in the background, made one think of

Noah's Ark lying abandoned in a desolated world after all the animals had left it. Or perhaps it was because Moses had come here to the pyramids, he who had begun his days drifting alone in a papyrus basket by the banks of the Nile. But what is certain is that, when the man on the sledge raised his stick and five hundred young Egyptians threw themselves into the traces until the desert resounded with rhythmic roars, when the timber began to creak and the big papyrus ship moved slowly forward against the still background of the timeless pyramids, there were not a few of the onlookers who shivered, suddenly aware of ghosts walking under the broiling sun. **'**

What a contrast to this splendid scene was the trip to her port of departure. Rather ignominiously, *Ra* had to travel from Egypt to the Atlantic coast of Morocco on the deck of a Swedish cargo ship. There was no time even for a short trial on the calm waters of the Nile. Another

In a scene more befitting some Hollywood epic, five hundred students from the Cairo Institute of Gymnastics hauled Ra *across the sands towards her destiny.*

factor in Thor's choice of transport was his reluctance to use up even a few hours of her potential 'floating time' before launching her into the Atlantic itself.

The ancient port of Safi had been selected as the point from which the voyage would begin. Phoenicians, Berbers, Arabs and Portuguese had all left their mark on the place. Once reed boats would have been a familiar sight, but now the vision of *Ra* trundling through the narrow streets caused almost as much excitement as she had done in Egypt. With his usual sensitivity towards local feelings Thor had asked not Yvonne, but the wife of the ruling Pasha, Aicha, to perform the launching ceremony.

❛She arrived in her long Berber robe with a brightly coloured ceramic pitcher in her hand and we rose from our camel-skin pouffes to go down to the port.

'Since I, a Berber, am to baptize the boat, I think goat's milk would be most suitable,' she said. . . . 'Goat's milk is Morocco's ancient symbol of hospitality and good wishes!'

Our golden boat was decked out festively, with the flags of all the participant countries [in the crew] fluttering in the wind. Aicha smashed the fine pitcher into a thousand fragments against the wooden cradle, so that goat's milk and potsherds sprayed over papyrus and distinguished guests alike.

'I name you *Ra* in honour of the sun-god!'

Chains and cogwheels began to screech at once. The crowd pressed back. As the papyrus boat began to glide down the slipway towards the water I exchanged looks with the loyal friend of the expedition, [Norwegian] Ambassador Anker, who stood straight and smiling, with milk-spots on the lapels of his dark suit. ❜

Following the principle that had worked well on the *Kon-Tiki*, the crew would only have a couple of weeks to get to know each other on shore before setting out. There might be friction later, but Thor was much more worried about the effects of tedium.

One by one the members, selected according to the international criteria Thor had devised, now began to arrive in Safi.

❛On the *Kon-Tiki* we had been five Norwegians and one Swede – six Scandinavians. But this time I felt

tempted to assemble on the little reed boat as many nations as space would allow. . . . Since I myself came from the northernmost country in Europe, the southernmost part of Europe should provide a contrast, so Italy would be the obvious answer. Since we Europeans were 'white' we ought to have a 'coloured' man with us . . . so it would be logical to take one of the papyrus experts with us. Since the experiment was meant to demonstrate the possibility of contact between the ancient civilizations of Africa and America, it would be symbolic to take an Egyptian and a Mexican on the voyage. And, in order to have contrasting ideologies . . . , it was an appealing idea to take one representative from the USA and one from the Soviet Union. All the other nations . . . could be symbolized by the flag of the United Nations, if we could get permission to fly it.

The times called for every sort of effort to build bridges between nations. Military jets thundered over Sphinx and pyramids, and cannons boomed along the closed Suez Canal. Soldiers from the five continents of

The truly international crew of Ra. From the left: Abdullah Djibrine, from Chad; Yuri Senkevich, from the USSR; Norman Baker, from the USA; Santiago Genovese, from Mexico; Thor Heyerdahl, from Norway; Georges Sourial, from Egypt; and Carlo Mauri, from Italy.

the world were at war in one foreign land or another. Where there was no war, men sat poised behind atomic buttons, warheads primed, for fear of other nations. On a floating reed boat there was room only for people who could shake each other by the hand. The voyage itself was intended as an experiment, a study trip into the dawn of civilization. But there was room for an experiment within the experiment. . . .

A papyrus boat sailing along in the grip of the elements could be a micro-world, a practical attempt to prove that men can work together in peace regardless of country, religion, colour or political background if they can only see as a matter of self-interest that it is necessary to fight for a common cause. **,**

18

WESTWARD WITH SUN AND MOON

'The Egyptian sail was drawing as never before and once again we seemed to be riding on the back of a wild beast.'

The day of departure was set for 25 May 1969. If anything, the scene was even more frenetic than it had been at the start of the *Kon-Tiki* voyage. On that occasion a last-minute recruit had joined the ship's company in the form of a green parrot. This time it was a monkey, produced by the Pasha's wife Aicha, and appropriately named Safi. Thor himself, he wrote later, was the last to jump aboard.

❛All the fishing boats in the harbour had started up their piercing sirens, accompanied by deep blasts from factory hooters, silos and warehouses on land. Ships' bells were rung, the crowd cheered, and a cargo-ship lying at anchor outside the harbour began to send up crackling signal rockets which burst in a shower of stars and slowly settled on the water ahead of us in a blood-red carpet of smoke. It was a royal farewell which almost scared us. ❜

Ra was about to face her first big test. They had copied the steering mechanism from ancient wall paintings without really understanding how it would work. It consisted of two oars, each twenty-five feet long, lashed fast on either side of the upturned stern. Two strong wooden cross-pieces, one just above the waterline and another, which served as a kind of ship's rail behind the bridge, supported the steering oars in such a way that both of them could be twisted at the same time – but they could not be moved from side to side, like the free-swinging steering oars on the *Kon-Tiki*. They were more like slanting rudders than punting poles. Tentatively,

Thor manipulated the thin rod joining them together. Beneath his feet he felt the ship respond. The system worked.

But only seven hours later both oars snapped at the junction between shaft and blade. The voyage had hardly begun, and already *Ra's* steering mechanism looked shattered beyond repair. Thor knew the underlying reason: in Egypt he had been unable to obtain cedarwood and had settled for local iroco. The timber merchant's assurances that it would prove just as strong were obviously worthless.

With the sail flapping uselessly above them, it looked as if the voyage would have to be abandoned. But at that moment *Ra* herself seemed to take charge. Very slowly she came about, until the bows were pointing westward once again. As she did so, the sail billowed out, and she set her own course like a proud and elegant swan.

Remembering his experiments off the coast of Peru, it only took a few seconds for Thor to realize what had happened. With no competition from the stern, the two perpendicular lee boards mounted forward of the mast had come into their own. This was the way the Incas used to steer their rafts, using lee boards or *guaras* instead of a rudder.

Euphoria, however, was short-lived. On the second day, fierce winds began to blow them back towards Africa. In their efforts to lower the sail it blew over the

*In mid-Atlantic, Thor leans out
from* Ra *to adjust the ropes.*

side and was nearly lost. Gradually they managed to haul it back aboard, to be stored along the length of the deck. For Carlo Mauri, by profession a mountaineer, this was a matter for relief. 'There's nothing left on this craft to obey human orders any more,' he said. 'Nature is in command now. We can relax and enjoy ourselves.' They made one further attempt to get the sail up, this time reefed to a third of its full size. But even so the strain was too great for the yardarm, which snapped in two. Thor watched in despair as the sail shrank inwards, like a huge bat folding its wings.

Throughout all these struggles, and more that still lay ahead, the lack of a common language added to their predicament. They understood each other well enough when all was quiet, but when the wind got up all was confusion, with shouted orders lost or misunderstood in the teeth of the gale. There were cultural misunderstandings, too. The ration of drinking water was one litre per man per day, but Abdullah insisted he must have at least five times as much as that. As a good Moslem, it was necessary to wash his body in pure water every time he prayed. The wisdom of Solomon was required. 'Have you ever thought how many monkeys and dogs live round all the water sources in Chad?' Thor asked him. 'Out here in the ocean, the water is the purest in the world.' Abdullah was convinced; and Allah, it seems, was not offended.

Thor seldom gave way to anger, and when he did it was usually the madness of mankind as a whole that provoked him, rather than that of a single individual. One morning he could hardly contain his rage when he woke up to find the sea so polluted that, as he later wrote, he could find no place clean enough to dip his toothbrush.

❛ The Atlantic was no longer blue but grey-green and opaque, covered with clots of oil ranging from pin-head size to the dimensions of the average sandwich. Plastic bottles floated among the waste. We might have been in a squalid city port. I had seen nothing like this when I spent 101 days with my nose at water level on board the *Kon-Tiki*. It became clear to all of us that mankind really was in the process of polluting its most vital well-spring, our planet's indispensable filtration plant, the ocean. . . .

The strange thing is that when you are bobbing over the wave-crests on a few papyrus bundles, aware at the same time that whole continents are gliding past, you realize that the sea is not so limitless after all; the water which rounds the African coast in May passes along the American coast some weeks later with all the floating muck which will neither sink nor be eaten by the inhabitants of the sea. **❯**

The days began to slip by with no further mishaps; and *Ra*'s papyrus hull continued to perform splendidly. For the crew it was like living on the back of a sea-serpent, undulating through the waves. Abdullah managed to repair the broken yardarm and they tried the sail once more – this time with better results. In case the mast itself broke, they had also brought a sturdy length of timber as a replacement. But since the mast had held, even in the roughest conditions, Thor decided that it would be quite safe to use the spare as an alternative to one of the broken steering oars. For a while at least, their troubles were behind them. It was time to enjoy the voyage.

❮ Sun and moon rolled westward in turn to show us the way. The lonely night watches gave us in full measure that timeless perception of eternity I had experienced on *Kon-Tiki*. Starry sky and night-black water. The immutable constellations sparkled above us, and just as brightly beneath us the shining phosphorescence glittered: the living plankton glowed like sparks of neon on the soft dark carpet on which we were floating. . . . The only thing that was firm and near in these omnipresent stellar heavens was the supple bundle of golden reeds on which we rode, and the big, square sail which stood like a shadow against the stars, broader above, by the yardarm, than across the bottom, near the deck. . . .

Stiff, but fitter from the struggle which now lay behind us, we changed watches by the meagre light of paraffin lamps swaying above our undulating vegetable deck. It was unspeakably good to crawl to rest in a warm sleeping-bag. You woke up with such an infernally good appetite. You felt an extraordinary physical well-being. Small pleasures grew big; big problems felt small. . . .

Westward progress of over one hundred kilometres (or nearly sixty nautical miles) could be plotted on the chart every day, even though the horizon never changed. . . . The Canary current was a fast-moving, salt-water river flowing towards the setting sun, keeping eternal company with the trade-wind, westward, westward, air and water and all that floats and blows. Westward with sun and moon. **?**

Day by day the ship told them more about itself, and about ancient navigation.

' The slanted rudder-oars had been the first to disclose their secrets, showing themselves to be a missing link in the evolution of man's earliest steering mechanism from oar to rudder. Next the wash-through bundle-body of the raft-ship itself began to reveal its true qualities. In addition to an almost unbelievable loading capacity the papyrus reeds possessed both a toughness in rough seas and an enduring buoyancy which quite contradicted the preconceived verdict of modern man. Yet it was the rigging that revealed the most significant secrets about this ancient vessel's forgotten history, showing that it had been originally developed as something more than a mere river craft.

In the design we followed, Landström had copied all the details of mast and rigging from the ancient Egyptian wall paintings. A strong rope ran from the masthead to the bow of the boat. But no corresponding rope ran from masthead to stern, although one rope forward and one aft would have been all that was needed to hold the straddled mast erect on a river boat in calm waters. Therefore it seemed very strange that the designers of the ancient Egyptian ships had, for some unknown reason, carefully avoided running any rope from the masthead all the way aft. Instead they secured five or six ropes at different heights on each leg of the straddled mast, and these ropes were stretched diagonally down in parallel lines to either side of the vessel a little aft of midships. In this way the whole sternmost part of the boat was free of mast stays and could rise and fall on the waves with no attachment to the mast.

No sooner had *Ra* begun to pitch on high seas than we realized how vital this special system was. The stern hung behind the rest of the boat like a trailer which was allowed to ride up and down freely over all the bumps. Had it also been secured by a stay to the masthead, then the mast would have broken as the first big ocean rollers surged beneath us. In our dance over the high wave-crests the middle section of *Ra* was rhythmically thrust upwards while the full weight of bow and stern sagged simultaneously in the wave-troughs on either side. Had both ends of the hull been attached to the mast, it would have snapped under the burden. As things were, the mast supported the curved bow while holding the central part of the soft deck suspended in a straight line. The aft third of the boat was allowed to follow the motion of the sea.

Daily we all praised this ingenious arrangement and special function of the rigging. Norman, the naval expert, immediately realized what [it] indicated. . . . After the third day at sea I was already writing in the expedition journal: 'This rigging is the result of long experience in navigation on the open sea; it was not born on the calm Nile.' **❯**

But in one vital respect they had failed to copy the ancient tomb paintings. During *Ra*'s construction period no one had been able to think of a use for the 'harp-string' rope, stretching from the tip of the curved stern down to the deck; consequently there was little concern when Abdullah failed to attach it. Now they were beginning to wonder. The vessel was still in perfect shape from the bows as far back as the point where the last pair of stays came down from the mast to be firmly secured on either side of the hull. But aft of that point her tail was drooping.

Thor pondered on that missing rope. Then, in a flash, he thought he had the answer. The mysterious rope was not there to hold the tail in position; the opposite was the case. It was there to hold up the weakest part of the hull, the section just aft of the last pair of stays. If he was right, then the high curve of the stern, higher even than the roof of the cabin, was not decorative at all but served a vital purpose. It was like a gantry, poised over the ship's stern, from which a rope could be suspended to give extra support.

It was one thing to solve the mystery; quite another to do anything about it in mid-Atlantic. In a matter of minutes, Abdullah had fixed up a rope in the harp-string position. But he was three weeks too late, and it would

TOP OF PAGE *As on* Kon-Tiki, *the tiny cabin allowed the men little elbow room. Here Norman Baker operates the radio while Thor dictates his daily report into a microphone. Outside, Yuri Senkevich entertains Safi, the monkey.*

ABOVE *Georges Sourial acts as Santiago Genovese's barber.*

only be a matter of time before the whole stern section was sagging into the water. Would it pull the rest of the ship down with it?

Surprisingly, the condition of the ship itself concerned Thor less than the condition of his crew. He had deliberately chosen them from the most disparate backgrounds to demonstrate that international co-operation was the only way forward. But it was never going to be easy, as he recalled in *The Ra Expeditions*:

❛Everyone was within speaking and touching distance of everyone else, day and night. . . . We were not only black and white, from communist and capitalist countries, we also represented the extremes of educational levels and living standards. When I visited one of our two Africans in his home in Fort Lamy, he was sitting on a fibre mat on the earth floor with no other chattels than a paraffin lamp. . . . With the other African, in Cairo, I was ushered in by bowing oriental servants between the pillars of a rich man's home. . . . One crew member could not read or write; another was a university professor. One was an active pacifist; another a naval officer. . . . Norman was a Jew. Georges was Egyptian. Their distant relatives were shooting at each other from opposite sides of the Suez Canal, while they themselves lay side by side in a wickerwork cabin, afloat on the Atlantic. Abdullah . . . was completely bewildered because Yuri and Norman, who were both white, represented two countries which were hostile but wanted peace and therefore helped the yellow-skinned men in Vietnam to kill one another. . . . Our paper boat was loaded with psychological petrol and the heat generated by friction in the little basket capsule could only be extinguished by the ubiquitous waves.

The most insidious danger on any expedition where men have to rub shoulders for weeks is a mental sickness which might be called 'expedition fever' – a psychological condition which makes even the most peaceful person irritable, angry, furious, absolutely desperate, because his perceptive capacity gradually shrinks until he sees only his companions' faults, while their good qualities are no longer recorded by his grey matter. The first duty of an expedition leader at any time is to be on guard against this lurking menace. *

Meanwhile, their floating home was becoming less and less secure. As every storm took its toll, *Ra* became, in Thor's phrase, a little bit more 'loose-jointed'. She was far from shaking to pieces, but the sagging tail was now acting as a brake on their progress. Something had to be done.

The remedy they chose had the look of desperation about it – even of madness. The idea came from Santiago, the Mexican professor; he suggested that, since they had no more papyrus to strengthen the stern, they should cut up the foam rubber life-raft and use that instead. Abdullah set to work with a saw. Strips of foam rubber were tied into bundles and lashed to the sunken part of the deck. For a time it worked. The level of the stern was raised appreciably, and *Ra* began to run more smoothly before the wind. But gradually the sea gnawed away at the foam rubber until there was none left. The stern drooped lower than ever, and now they were without any means of escape, entombed in a floating haystack which each morning felt a little more 'loose-jointed' than it had the day before.

They continued, nevertheless, to make remarkable progress. The islands of the West Indies were now much closer than the coast of Africa, and if they could only avoid a really serious storm there was still a chance. But Thor was much more worried than he was prepared to admit. He had sent a radio message to Yvonne to send out a photographer in a motor vessel in order to take some shots of *Ra* at sea. In his heart, he confided to his diary and later recorded in *The Ra Expeditions*, he knew that this might turn into a rescue mission, for the hurricane season was beginning.

❝ *8 July.*

. . . the wind began to rise and the waves piled up as if a big storm had taken place beyond the horizon. . . . At about six o'clock the following morning I was standing on the bridge . . . when the sea quite unexpectedly rose about me and engulfed everything. A shining stretch of water moved slowly up to my waist and without any appreciable noise the cabin roof in front of my chest was submerged. Some seconds later *Ra* began to quake violently while at the same time the whole vessel lay hard over into the wind, so hard that I had to hang on to the tiller of the rudder-bar in order not to skid down the slope and overboard with the water. At every moment I expected the heavy straddled mast to tear the papyrus bundles under it to shreds and topple into the sea. But *Ra*, shivering, simply rolled on to her beam ends to empty out the water, then righted herself, though never again as fully as before.

9 July.

. . . we had just discovered that the sea which had gone over the cabin roof had also forced its way through the lid of a cask containing almost two hundred pounds of salted meat, which soon rotted. It was during this morning inspection that an agitated Georges came to report something much worse. All the main ropes which secured the outermost papyrus roll on the windward side to the rest of *Ra* had been chafed through as the floor of the cabin shifted to and fro under the onslaught of the waves. . . . The boat was split in two lengthwise. The big starboard bundle, supporting one mast, was moving slowing in and out from the rest of the boat down its entire length. The roll was attached to *Ra* only at bow and stern. Every time the waves lifted the big papyrus roll away from the rest of the boat we stared straight down into the clear blue depths. . . . With stoic calm, and without a tremor in his voice, Abdullah said coolly that this was the end. The ropes had worn away. The chain was broken. The rope links would unravel

OPPOSITE *Despite all the crew's efforts, the after-deck of* Ra *sank lower and lower into the water. Eventually it began to act like a huge sea anchor, drastically reducing their speed.*

themselves one by one and in an hour or two the papyrus reeds would be drifting away from each other in all
directions. . . . Then Norman was suddenly standing
beside us, glaring like a tiger about to spring.

'Let's not give up, boys,' he said through clenched
teeth.

Next moment we were all on the go. Carlo and Santiago pulled out coils of rope and measured and chopped
up lengths of our thickest cordage. Georges plunged
into the waves and swam crosswise under *Ra* with a
thick rope end. Norman and I crawled all over the boat
examining the chafed lashings to find out how long it
would be before we fell apart. . . . Abdullah stood with
the sledge-hammer, driving in *Ra*'s huge sewing needle,
a thin iron spike with an eye at the bottom, large enough
to take a rope one quarter of an inch thick. With this needle we were going to try to sew the 'paper boat' together.
Yuri stood the gruelling turn at the rudder-oar alone,
hour after hour. First Georges swam crosswise under
the boat four times with our thickest rope, which we
cinched up on deck like four big barrel hoops, in the
hope of holding the bundles together so that the straddled mast would not burst open at the top. Then he
ducked under the papyrus bundles to the spot where
Abdullah's big sewing needle had been pushed
through. In the depths Georges had to pull the thin rope
out of the needle's eye and re-thread it a moment later
when Abdullah pushed the needle down again empty in
another place. In this way we got the fatal gap 'sewn' up
again to some extent, but we had lost a lot of papyrus on
the starboard side and were consequently lying harder
to windward than ever before.

10 July.

Norman heard that two American photographers were
expected on the island of Martinique and that a little
motor-yacht called *Shenandoah* was on her way there to
pick them up. But Italian television had announced that
we were disabled and had taken to the rubber boat. We
thought with sardonic humour of the day when we had
carved it up. But no one missed it. No one would have
boarded the lifeboat if we had had it. We had more than
enough papyrus left to float on. . . . Georges suddenly
appeared with a dripping red object which he had

fished up out of knee-deep water.

'Do we need this, or can I heave it overboard?'

It was a little fire-extinguisher from the days when smoking on the starboard side was forbidden.

11 July.

In the middle of the night some big seas poured in over the submerged starboard beam and drove right through the wickerwork of the cabin wall, so hard that the one case on which Norman had been sleeping until then was splintered to matchwood. . . . *Ra* had begun to make some particularly disagreeable noises on the side where the papyrus rolls had been stitched on, and that night no one heard Safi's cries for help when her perforated sleeping suitcase was knocked off the wall by the next wave. She sailed about, imprisoned, among the splintered fragments of Norman's case until, incredibly, she managed to open the lid and release herself. Santiago was awakened by her sitting, dripping wet, by his cheek, screeching to be admitted into his warm sleeping bag.

12 July.

As night began to advance over a pallid wet, overcast sky, we saw real storm-clouds rolling up like a herd of angry black cattle over the horizon to the east and stampeding thunderously after us. We made ready to weather the full storm which was tearing along, lightning flashing, in fiercer and fiercer squalls. . . . The Egyptian sail was drawing as never before and once again we seemed to be riding on the back of a wild beast. The scene had a savage, barbaric beauty. Black seas grew whiter, boiling, streaked with foam; more showers came from the sea than from the clouds.

13 July.

The watch aft had a hard stint and we tried to change shifts as often as possible. The stilts under the starboard side of the bridge had sunk with the bending papyrus rolls and the platform on which the helmsman stood had become as steep as the sloping roof of a house. We could no longer reach down to the tiller of the starboard rudder oar. We had to cling to the port corner, where the bridge was highest, and had therefore worked out a system as laborious as it was ingenious. With one rope tied to a foot and another held in the hand we swung to and fro on the starboard rudder-oar, but only when we

Ra continued to float, with her port side undamaged. But her starboard side had lost so much papyrus that it was no longer able to support the double mast with its heavy sail.

could not hold the course with the port oar alone. For brief seconds at a time we made fast all the ropes we could in order not to be completely exhausted.

14 July.

... we made radio contact with *Shenandoah*, now heading east from Barbados. They reported that the storm had reached them too, with waves breaking over the yacht's twenty-foot-high wheelhouse.... Only the thought that we were lying still further out under the same conditions made them sail on eastward into the storm. The captain gave the maximum speed he could allow as eight knots ... at best it might reach us in a day or two, if we were heading straight towards each other on opposite courses.

15 July.

. . . the storm reached a climax. The sail could no longer stand up to the strain, and in squalls which flung us so hard over that an ordinary boat would have capsized, we lowered the sail, whose frenetic flapping sounded like thunderclaps. Lightning flashed, rain fell. With the sail gone, the masts, with their gaping ladder bars, stood swaying naked in the lightning flashes like a skeleton. There was a ghastly sense of emptiness and apathy without the sail. The waves seemed to pluck up more courage to attack us as our speed slackened.

16 July.

. . . we regained radio contact with *Shenandoah*. . . . The captain asked us to send up signal rockets after dark. The wind had dropped. . . . Norman looked out the signal rockets we had kept when we cut up the life-raft. They were so sodden with water that we could not even light the fuse with a match. . . . We asked *Shenandoah* to send up her own rockets. Shortly afterwards, the captain replied that they could not light theirs, either. Neither of us had a completely accurate position after the storm, but as far as we could judge we were travelling in precisely opposite directions on the same latitude.

Late on the afternoon of [this day] the weather was fine again. . . . Norman, who was sitting immovably in the cabin doorway, turning [radio] knobs with both hands, suddenly stared strangely straight ahead without looking at any of us and said in a voice full of emotion:

'I see you, I see you; can't you see us?'

A dramatic moment passed for the rest of us, sitting speechlessly round him, before we realized that he was talking to the radio operator on the *Shenandoah*. . . .

And there she was! She came into view at brief intervals, like a white grain of sand on top of the distant crests. As she came closer we saw that she was rolling wildly. What was left of *Ra* took the seas with far more stoic calm. How we found each other is still a miracle to us, but here we were, leaping in turn, up and down, at sea off the West Indies. . . .

The weather reports on *Shenandoah* were ominous and the captain had good reason to urge our return to

Abandon ship! Everything of value was removed from Ra, *now wallowing mastless in the surf like a drifting heap of vegetation. The rescue launch's rubber dinghy had to make several journeys, while seventeen sharks watched and waited.*

harbour. [But] the entire crew of *Ra* agreed that if another gale blew up we would be safer on board our own wreck. True, our papyrus boat was no longer navigable, with rudder-oars broken and a sloping steering bridge on which we could scarcely keep our feet, but the remaining bundles were afloat and would continue to drift westward like a giant lifebuoy until they were washed ashore. On the other hand, *Shenandoah* was navigable, even if both pumps and one of the two diesel engines had been put out of operation by the storm. But both her captain and crew were fully aware that in a hurricane, however small, she could spring a leak or capsize, and then the whole metal craft would go straight to the bottom.

I summoned all the men of *Ra* to the first really serious 'pow-wow' since we had sawn up the rubber raft off the African coast. I explained that it seemed to me right to end the experiment now. We had lived on board the papyrus rolls for two months; they were still afloat, and we had sailed almost exactly five thousand kilometres – over three thousand miles – even without taking our zigzag course into account. This was equal to the distance across the North Atlantic from Africa to Canada. We now knew that a papyrus boat was seaworthy. We had the answer. There was no reason to risk human lives pointlessly.

All the men, bearded and weather-beaten, with palms calloused from pulling cords and tillers, sat listening gravely. I asked each of them to say what he thought.

'I think we should go on in *Ra*,' said Norman. 'We have enough food and water. . . . It will be tough, but in a week's time we shall be at the islands, even with the little scrap of sail we have set now.'

'I agree with Norman,' said Santiago. 'If we give up now, no one will believe that papyrus boat sailors could have reached America. . . . We must get all the way from coast to coast.'. . .

'We must go on,' said Georges. 'Even if the rest of you give up, Abdullah and I will go on. Right, Abdullah?'. . .

Yuri had been sitting, staring in front of him, for some time.

'We are seven friends who have shared everything,' he said at last. 'Either we should all go on, or we should all stop. I am dead against our splitting up.'❯

But then Thor thought of their families, all of whom he knew personally. Perhaps it was better to stop while the going was good. And so he reached his decision, and reached it alone.

Safely aboard Shenandoah. *The decision to end the voyage was made by Thor alone. The others were for going on, but Thor felt he had a responsibility to their families: the risks were too great.*

19

THE VOYAGE OF *RA II*

'Morale on board will collapse if we begin to live like pigs.'

Thor Heyerdahl today is mild-mannered, court-eous and amusing. He is interested in everyone and treats them just the same whether they are ambassadors or taxi drivers. He gives very little thought to fame, or the advancing years. But you cannot be with him for any length of time without being aware of an underlying tenacity, a steely determination to overcome any obstacle in pursuit of an objective. Nothing in his life illustrates this better than his decision to start all over again – with the building of *Ra II*. He told his crew that he was satisfied with the first voyage. Together they had proved beyond question that the Atlantic could be crossed in a reed boat, even if they themselves had not quite succeeded in doing it. However *Ra I*, as she must now be called, had been unsatisfactory in many small but cumulative ways. Much might be said for the voy-age, but they could never claim that they had reached the New World in a seaworthy vessel. By the end, she was little more than a floating heap of drifting wreckage. Now Thor had a difficult choice. He could write a scien-tific paper based on their experiences, outlining the changes he would recommend to anyone else venturing out into the Atlantic in a reed boat; or he could start again.

Most men would have stopped after *Kon-Tiki*, yet here was Thor, soaked, battered and almost drowned by the mighty Atlantic, actually contemplating a return fixture. The logistics alone were daunting enough. Fresh reeds would have to be cut and transported. New boat-builders would have to be found, new funds raised, and all within the space of ten months. Thor's response was: 'There's no time to lose.'

Such was the spirit and cohesion of the crew by the end of the first voyage that there was not one member whom Thor wanted to be rid of for the second. Even more surprising perhaps, after the drubbing they had taken from the Atlantic, to a man they wanted to try again. In the event only Abdullah, who had complicated family arrangements, felt that he could not spare a further year away from his native Chad.

Sad to lose Abdullah, Thor replaced him with another African, a full-blooded Berber called Madani Ait Ouhanni. Thor also decided to increase the ship's company to eight by adding a Japanese film photographer, Kei Ohara. Neither of them had any experience of the sea, but as Thor pointed out to a complaining Norman, 'Practised ski jumpers seldom make the best parachutists.' There were other important changes. The reeds were to be cut on Lake Tana as before, but this time he decided to build the vessel in secret on the Moroccan coast, rather than suffer the gaze of thousands of tourists in Egypt. Also this time, because of war in the Red Sea the reeds for *Ra II* had to be transported round the Cape of Good Hope. For his expert builders, he turned to the Aymara Indians from Lake Titicaca. Thor was convinced they were the best reed boat-builders in the world, as they were used to big waves on their stormy mountain lake.

❝ The four taciturn Indians, Demetrio, José, Juan and Paulino, and their equally calm Bolivian interpreter, Señor Zeballos, a museum curator from La Paz, organized the building of *Ra II* in masterly fashion with a handful of Moroccan helpers. . . .

The Indians first stacked up two huge untidy rolls of loose papyrus stalks, each elegantly wrapped in a thin papyrus mat . . . woven so that all the ends [of its reeds] turned inward and were squashed flat. Before the ropes were drawn tight, these two thirty-foot cylinders were so thick that no one could get on top without the help of scaffolding. In the open passageway between these two big rolls a much thinner roll of the same length was now made, to which both the large

Kei Ohara, the Japanese cameraman who joined Ra II.

ones were to be bound. This was done by first winding a rope, several hundred yards long, in a continuous spiral which at the same time encircled both the thin central roll and one of the thick outer rolls. A second rope was then run, without touching the first, in a complementary spiral round the thin roll and the other thick outer roll. So when these two independent spiral ropes were drawn tight by the united strength of the Indians, each of the big rolls was forced closer and closer to the little one in the middle, until it was jammed between them and ended up squeezed right into them, forming a completely invisible core. Thus only the two big rolls remained visible, pressed tightly together all along their centre line. This resulted in an unshakeably compact, double-cylinder hull, with no knots or criss-cross ropes; and all that remained was to extend the hull on the same principle, to produce the elegant upswept peaks at bow and stern. A sausage-shaped bundle was finally bound on either side of the deck to give it breadth and to break the waves. **"**

At forty feet, the finished vessel proved to be about ten feet shorter than *Ra I*, but she was much firmer and more tightly packed. At its widest point the hull measured sixteen feet.

There was one alarming difference between the Aymara Indian and African methods of binding the reeds together. The men from Lake Chad tied the bundles with dozens of short rope lengths, so that if one broke the reeds would still be held by those on either side. But the men from Lake Titicaca took a single long length of rope and bound it round the reeds in one continuous spiral. They insisted that, even if the rope broke, it would never unwind. There were some anxious faces among the crew. After all, these Aymara Indians knew nothing of conditions on the high seas. But Thor maintained that it was pointless to hire men for their expertise and then ignore it.

On 17 May 1970 the crew and Safi the monkey, who had cheerfully signed on for a second journey, were ready to depart. Immediately they all noticed the difference. Whereas *Ra I* had sat rather heavily in the water, undulating like a serpent, *Ra II* pitched and rolled much more violently. It was almost impossible to move about

without holding on to something. A greater cause for alarm was the speed with which the hull seemed to be absorbing water. After just four days, they were all convinced that she was sinking. No one could explain it. Perhaps the reeds were inferior to the ones they had used the year before. Perhaps she was carrying too much cargo. There was only one course of action – to throw overboard everything that was not absolutely essential (except Safi). In *The Ra Expeditions* Thor recorded the sad disposal of so much that would have been useful or pleasurable:

❛ . . . a big sack of potatoes went overboard. . . . Then two whole jars of rice. Flour. Maize. Two sacks, contents unknown. A wicker basket. Better to starve than sink. Then most of the grain for the chickens went. A big beam, planks and hardwood boards for splicing and repairs. . . . A heavy coil of rope plunged overboard. A whetstone. A hammer. Georges's heavy iron spike for repairing the boat vanished for ever in the depths. Books and magazines floated about us in the calm water.

. . . the chickens began to flutter overboard. Two of the men took hatchets and knives and were about to cut the whole chicken coop loose so that it could be heaved out to sea. Without a proper primus stove we could not eat poultry. Then it was time to halt the frenzy. The chickens' days were ended, but Georges pleaded for the

To avoid the pressures and dangers of public scrutiny that they had endured while Ra *was being built in the shadow of the pyramids,* Ra II *was built in secret and then unveiled in the port of Safi.*

Shorter, and much more rigid in her construction, Ra II proved to be more seaworthy than her predecessor, but a much less comfortable ride.

single duck, which to Safi the monkey's indignation was allowed to strut freely about the deck and nip her tailless bottom. . . . The empty hencoop on the foredeck I myself broke up and turned into a light dining table, though there were some who wanted to get rid of both this and the crude benches, arguing that we could eat with plates and cups in our hands. But this brought a unanimous protest from the two of us who regarded a meal as a real high point in the day's programme.

'In any case, morale on board will collapse if we begin to live like pigs,' stated Norman, as an experienced naval officer.

Our minds were at peace. The air had been cleared, as though by a lightning conductor, and for once there was really room to move about on board without mountaineering. **9**

The rest of the voyage can be briefly recounted. In some respects, their experience was much the same. Once again it was the solid wooden steering oar, not the supple reeds, that broke in a storm. Once again they were enraged by the sight of so much oil pollution in mid-ocean. They had their moments of friction, and their moments of peril, in seas even bigger than they had encountered the year before. But as the days passed, it became more and more obvious that *Ra II* was a far better vessel than her predecessor. With wind and currents propelling them on, they made some of their best average speeds in the final days of the voyage.

When they were within two hundred miles of Barbados the island authorities sent the *Culpepper*, a small but nippy little boat, to meet them. However, the weather was such that it took three days to locate each other on the stormy seas. Aboard was Thor's wife Yvonne and their eldest daughter Anette. Next day there were four aircraft circling round their mast, one bearing the Prime Minister of Barbados. A host of speedboats raced towards them, carrying Thor's two younger daughters, Marian and Bettina, and other families. Finally, some fifty vessels accompanied their triumphant arrival at Bridgetown, which was packed with excited people wanting to congratulate them. It was enough to make them long for the peace of the sea again.

They had completed the crossing in fifty-seven days.

20

THE CRADLE
OF CULTURE

'I sensed that I was travelling back through time, not into
savagery and insecurity, but into a culture as remote from
barbarism as ours and yet incredibly simple and
uncomplicated.'

6 The beginning. The real beginning.
This was the place.
This was where written history began. This
was where mythology began. This was the source of
three of the mightiest religions in human history. Two
billion Christians, Jews and Moslems all over the world
are taught by their sacred books that this was the spot
chosen by God to give life to mankind.

Here two large rivers, the Euphrates and Tigris, drift
slowly together. . . . Silent as the rivers when they meet
are the narrow rows of date palms lining the banks,
while sun and moon, passing over the barren desert, are
reflected day and night on the calm waters. A rare canoe
glides by, with men casting nets.

This, most of mankind believes, was the cradle of
Homo sapiens, paradise lost. 9
So wrote Thor Heyerdahl in *The Tigris Expedition*, his
account of the next quest on which he embarked.

By 1977, Thor was turning his attention to a question
which has absorbed archaeologists for centuries. Did
the world's oldest civilizations have a common source,
and if so, where was it to be found? The evidence
seemed widely scattered. It was as if some great
upheaval had destroyed a beautiful floor mosaic, leaving the pieces spread over a vast area; sometimes as
small fragments unrecognizable as part of a larger pattern, but sometimes as considerable sections with a
meaning and symmetry of their own.

It is only comparatively recently that scientists

OVERLEAF *The confluence of
the Tigris and Euphrates
rivers.*

229

learned of the existence of such people as the Hittites in the Old World, and the Olmecs in the New. Who can say when some fresh discovery will turn all the existing theories on their heads? It has been a matter of decades only since the ruins of Mohenjo Daro in the valley of the Indus were unearthed. They had lain unknown and undisturbed for two millennia.

Nevertheless, enough is known to pose some intriguing questions. Could it possibly have been mere coincidence that, after about two million years of living as a simple hunter-gatherer, man should suddenly develop fully fledged cultures in three different areas, all at the same time? Around 3000 BC civilizations sprang into existence around the estuaries of the Nile, the Euphrates and the Indus. Had men and women in all three areas spontaneously felt an overpowering need for written languages, elaborate social and religious rituals, temples and fine art? Was it really conceivable that each had developed without any knowledge of the other two?

That was certainly the prevailing opinion. But to Thor it seemed even less plausible than the isolationist theories about the New World. This time there were land links, arid and dangerous, but capable of sustaining caravan routes. And, of course, there was the sea. In Thor's view, there was another symbol of civilization common to all three areas – the reed boat. Between expeditions he always spent time researching in libraries, looking at museum collections and visiting archaeological sites. Now he felt ready to apply the theories he had developed and refined in the Pacific and Atlantic to a still older and greater problem. Where did civilized man have his beginnings?

Traditionally the cradle of civilization lay somewhere in Mesopotamia, in the land of the Sumerians. But they themselves had left written records testifying that they came by ship from a mysterious land called Dilmun. But where was Dilmun? Each clue led backwards to another clue, but never to the true beginning. As Thor wrote at the time:

❛The real puzzle is that human history has no known beginning. As it stands it begins with civilized mariners coming in by sea. This is no real beginning. This is the continuation of something lost somewhere in the mist. Is it still hidden under desert sand, as was Sumerian civilization itself, remaining unknown to science until discovered and excavated in southern Iraq in the last century? Was it buried by volcanic eruption, as was the great Mediterranean civilization on the island of Santorini, unknown until discovered in our own time under fifty feet of ashes? Or could it possibly be submerged in the ocean that covers two-thirds of our restless planet, as suggested by the hard-dying legend of Atlantis? *9*

There were those who thought that the world had nothing more to learn from Thor Heyerdahl about the construction and navigation of reed boats. He was aware that the public reaction might well be to stifle a yawn at the thought of one more reconstruction of a prehistoric voyage. But the Indian Ocean was different. There were no constant currents, 'conveyor belts' as Thor calls them, to carry craft in a given direction. What he needed now was a reed ship that could be navigated, in the fullest sense of the word.

So Thor took up residence in the Garden of Eden Resthouse near the banks of the Tigris in Iraq. Within walking distance lies the eastern boundary of one of the strangest human habitations in the world. This is the land of the Marsh Arabs – six thousand square miles of channels and floating islands, stretching westwards in a giant watery maze towards the Euphrates. Thor boarded a shallow boat propelled by tall marshmen wielding long poles, and almost immediately they left the modern world behind, as he wrote later in *The Tigris Expedition*:

*6*The water was crystal clear; plants grew on the bottom; I saw fishes and there were long garlands of watercrowfoot floating on the surface. We slid silently away from the green turf and slipped in between two high walls of canes and bulrushes. As these tall water plants closed in about us and shut the green door behind us we left the bustling, rumbling modern world and felt as if transported with the speed of spacecraft into the past. With each calm punt-stroke by the two silent marshmen I sensed that I was travelling back through time, not into savagery and insecurity, but into a culture as remote

OVERLEAF *The homeland of the Marsh Arabs, considered by Jews, Christians and Arabs alike to be the site of the biblical Garden of Eden. 'As these tall water plants closed in about us . . .', wrote Thor of his first visit, 'we left the bustling, rumbling modern world and felt as if transported with the speed of spacecraft into the past.'*

from barbarism as ours and yet incredibly simple and uncomplicated. . . .

In its elegant perfection, the architecture is as impressive as the result is astonishingly beautiful, each dwelling recalling a little temple with its golden-grey vault outlined majestically against a perpetually cloudless sky extending from the surrounding desert. Some are mirrored in the water together with the blue sky.

This was pure Sumerian architecture. The industrious people who first handed the art of writing down to our ancestors had lived in such houses. In their regular cities they had built walls from enduring bricks, but in the marshes they had constructed their houses entirely from reeds. They are realistically illustrated in Sumerian art five thousand years old, carved in stone and incised on seals, just as their present boats are identical in line to the small models in silver or asphalt-covered reeds, found as Sumerian temple offerings. Both have proved themselves perfectly adapted to the environment and to local needs. 〉

Just as he had on Lake Titicaca, Lake Chad and Lake Tana, Thor was embarking on the kind of research that cannot be gleaned from books. The type of reed that grows in the marshes of Iraq is called *berdi* locally, and the marsh people were unanimous: it had to be harvested in August if it were to float for any length of time. This information had not been available to Thor on the *Ra* trips, when the reeds were cut in December; his local informants only used their boats one day at a time. As was the case with balsa wood and papyrus reeds, the European authorities on Mesopotamian boat-building insisted that *berdi* would float for only two weeks.

For more detailed information Thor was directed to the house of a bearded sage, said to be at least a hundred years old. His name was Hagi Suelem. From him Thor learned that there had once been three different styles of boat on the rivers and among the marshes. The most common, a *jillabie*, was a light, slender reed canoe. The second, a *guffa*, was circular in shape like a coracle, and very difficult to capsize. Both of these types could still occasionally be seen on the upper Euphrates, beyond Babylon.

But the third type had disappeared. These had been

The tranquil way of life of the Marsh Arabs has remained unchanged over the centuries, and they still build reed houses similar to those depicted in ancient Sumerian art.

similar to the *jillabie*, but much bigger; and they had probably been capable of tackling the open waters of the Persian Gulf. They were made from many bundles of *berdi*, lashed together and tapering at both ends. The secret, the old man said, was to bind the reeds together so tightly that they became almost as hard as logs. Such boats, Thor was assured, were capable of staying afloat for many months, perhaps years.

Listening to the old man, Thor was reminded of the Hebrew legend of Noah and the Flood. It seemed much more likely that the Ark was not a wooden houseboat, as it is usually depicted, but a reed ship of the sort that old Hagi was describing. The instruction to Noah in the Bible reads, 'Make yourself an ark with ribs of cypress, cover it with reeds, and cover it inside and out with pitch.' The biblical story of the Flood was by no means the only one; the Assyrians had their own legend of a deluge. In their version it was the king Uta-nipishtim who built a ship to save his family, his household and his livestock. When the waters subsided, the ocean god who had spared him gave him instructions to start a new life 'at the mouth of the rivers'.

Here was a possible origin of the widespread belief that the estuary of the Tigris and Euphrates was the first area to be resettled after some global catastrophe had buried the first cradle of civilization. There is an even older Sumerian account of the story, from which the Assyrian one has been derived. In this version, after the flood the survivors settled in Dilmun, across the sea in the direction of the rising sun. Later they were led by the gods to their present home at the mouth of the rivers. Thor noted that all three accounts contained references to big reed ships, capable of saving their occupants from some appalling disaster. Myths are not history; but at the very least Thor must have felt that he was about to build his own 'ark' in a most appropriate place.

❛August is the hottest month in southern Iraq. The thermometer wavered between 40° and 50°C (105°–120°F) in the shade, but there was no shade anywhere in the open swamp-land where we cut the reeds. The Marsh Arabs advanced with curved machetes into the reed thickets with the speed and energy of a band of warriors and the long green stalks fell like slaughtered troops. The heat was so great that I soon became exhausted merely watching the battle from the canoe, and as my marshman interpreter, with a vocabulary of a few dozen English words, assured me that there were no longer any bilharzia in the water, I jumped into the canal and joined the [native] Madans, who were waist deep and fully dressed. From Lake Chad and the Nile I had learnt to dread the little bilharzia worm that lives on snails in the reeds and drills its way through the human skin in a few seconds to multiply inside the body. I enjoyed the slowly running water until a beautiful snail shell came floating by. I picked it up and hesitantly showed it to my reed-cutting informant. 'That?' he said. 'That is only the *house* of the bilharzia.' **"**

This was Thor in his element. In spite of the heat and the threat of disease, he was doing what he does best, working side by side with the sort of people he instinctively knows and understands, and by doing so winning their friendship and loyalty. But there is another side to the planning of expeditions; and the bigger they are, the more burdensome it becomes. They need constant backing, both financial and political; and people with power and influence in those fields have the knack of taking the fun out of things.

Filming arrangements provide a good example. Thor is well aware of the need for this; in fact he encourages it. But the logistics have a tendency to escalate. On the *Kon-Tiki* he took with him a single lightweight 16mm Bolex camera which, for the most part, he operated himself. With no professional training, he and his crew still managed to produce a ninety-minute Oscar-winning film. For the *Ra* voyages it was thought necessary to have one member of the crew whose prime responsibility was to make a film record of day-to-day events. On *Ra II* they actually took a professional cameraman – but he was still a fully integrated member of the team, taking his turn at the chores or the tiller as required. This film, too, was nominated for an Oscar.

For the voyage of the *Tigris* it was all to be very different. Thor found himself confronted by an international consortium of television networks, representing six different countries. Lawyers were called in to draw up contracts; each of the countries involved had varying

The Tigris *voyage would be Thor's fourth expedition in ancient craft across the world's oceans. Now he was about to explore the relationship between the three early civilizations which bordered the Indian Ocean – Egypt, Mesopotamia and the Indus valley.*

requirements which had to be included in a document running to over thirty pages. All this was, as Thor wryly pointed out, 'for a journey which had not yet started, in a boat which was not yet built'. Fame can sometimes feel like wearing a winter overcoat on a hot summer's day.

The serried ranks of negotiators wanted to know when the voyage would start, where it would go and for how long, so that all this could be pinned down in small print. With the best will in the world, Thor couldn't give firm answers to any of their points. In the end he agreed to provide four hours of television or refund the money in proportion to the missing television time if the vessel failed to function. This was taking an enormous risk. After all, *Tigris* might sink as soon as she left the river.

The first hint of the political squalls that lay ahead came with a visit to Broadlands, home of Earl Mountbatten of Burma, then President of the United World Colleges, some of whose members were to sail with *Tigris*.

❛'Thor, would you believe that you have got me into international trouble?' Lord Mountbatten looked at me sternly as we took our seats at table in the company of his adjutant and were served melon by a butler in a naval uniform. **,**

Thor thought it was just a joke, and his host realized that some proof was required.

' He sent his adjutant to fetch a letter from the Imperial Court in Teheran. It was a long and sharp protest against the wording of the circular from the United World Colleges concerning my planned reed-ship expedition. . . . I was quoted as planning to sail down the river Shatt-al-Arab into the 'Arabian Gulf'. How could an international college institution headed by the Admiral of the Fleet use such a fictitious geographical term? Was this the result of the growing tendency to flatter the Arabs? The true and only name for this body of water was the 'Persian Gulf', and it was indeed the British Admiralty that had originally given the gulf this proper name.

I was sorry. This was an unforeseen problem for a reed-boat voyager who had to test an ancient vessel in a modern world. I explained to Lord Mountbatten that I had indeed originally used the name the 'Persian Gulf', which I had learnt in school. But officials in Baghdad had corrected me and my message and made it abundantly clear that if I wanted to sail anywhere from Iraq it had to be into the 'Arabian Gulf'. **,**

Thor had no wish to cause offence, so he consulted the Norwegian Foreign Office, who told him that they normally spoke of the 'Persian Gulf' when referring to a port on the Iranian side, and vice versa. But the expedition was to sail in open water, so he asked a PR officer at the United Nations for advice. Alas, there was no easy answer. 'It is a considerable problem,' the man admitted. 'All the nations around the gulf you are sailing into are to have a meeting against pollution of their common waters, but we cannot agree on a word to explain where it is!'

Excellent though the Marsh Arabs were at handling their own local *berdi* reeds, they had nevertheless lost the art of building ships of any size. To supervise the actual construction, Thor decided to bring over to the Garden of Eden Resthouse the same group of Aymara Indians who had helped him construct *Ra II* in Africa.

Their arrival was not propitious. They took one look at the *berdi* and pronounced it quite unsuitable; then they disappeared into their quarters. With great patience, Thor coaxed them out again. Of course totora and even papyrus were superior to *berdi*. Who could think otherwise? But in this region there was nothing but *berdi* to be obtained; they must all learn to work with it. He explained that it would be the responsibility of the Marsh Arabs to construct suitable bundles. The responsibility of the Aymaras, who had come so far, was of course much greater. They would build the ship. Thor's subtle persuasiveness worked, as he later recalled in *The Tigris Expedition*:

❛Nothing on the whole expedition was more pleasing to observe than the spontaneous friendship and mutual respect between the Indians and the Marsh Arabs as they sat down together and began handling the reeds. The eyes of Señor Zeballos and the four Aymaras reflected astonishment and approbation the moment they saw the marshmen select the best reeds and throw them together with loops around until they became bundles as compact and smooth as if made of the best totora. The Aymaras concluded that the Arabs of Iraq were superior to the Arabs of Morocco, who could not work reeds like this. Obviously the Arabs here descended from Adam. ❜

The boat-building proceeded at a good pace. Meanwhile the crew began to assemble; this time the number would be increased to eleven. Thor had long ago decided to give priority to any member of the *Ra* expeditions who wanted to join him again. Three of them took up the invitation: Norman Baker, the experienced American navigator; the Russian doctor, Yuri Senkevich; and Carlo Mauri, the mountaineer from northern Italy. Not only were these three tried and trusted companions, but it also meant that Thor had the nucleus of another truly international crew.

The new recruits were to arrive later, one of them on special conditions that Thor had already been forced to accept in his contract. Norris Brock, a photographer/cameraman hired by the National Geographical Society of America, was to have no extra duties beyond his photographic ones, and these were to take priority even if

the vessel were in danger of sinking. They were strange terms for a leader to have to accept, but part of the price of international funding. Nor was it a very auspicious way for Brock to strike up a good working relationship with the rest of the team.

Thor's previous experience had not equipped him for conditions in the Indian Ocean, where the traditional sailing vessel is the dhow, with its triangular sail; so he had asked if some proficient dhow handlers could be found, who were accustomed to the vagaries of the monsoon. In due course three 'experts' arrived from Bombay. The first thing they pointed out was that the *Tigris* had no engine. Certainly not, explained Thor; she would sail just like a traditional dhow. Their expressions told him that something was amiss. The men were dhow seamen all right; but sailors they were not. In a vessel without mechanical power they would be lost. Someone in Bombay had bungled.

A few days later all three 'experts' were slightly injured in a car accident. They now wanted only to return home, and Thor was happy enough to comply.

ABOVE *Once the bundles of reeds were ready it would be the job of the Aymara Indians, brought over again from Bolivia, to construct the vessel. After Thor had exercised his diplomatic skills on them they developed an excellent working relationship with the Arabs.*

OVERLEAF *The largest reed ship the world had seen for thousands of years gradually began to take shape on the banks of the Tigris.*

243

But from this misfortune, there immediately sprang another. If there were to be no dhow sail on the *Tigris*, Norman decided he wanted the extra canvas to enlarge the existing mainsail. To preserve the reinforced edges he had it cut in half, with the intention of adding an extra section in the middle. But at this stage he discovered that they lacked strong enough needles and thread to finish the job. This was a self-inflicted wound if ever there was one. Even before the launch they had cut up their main means of propulsion, and had no way of putting it together again. All that was left was a thin, downwind sail that might get them to Bahrain on the prevailing wind, but not much further. The auguries were not good for the voyage of the *Tigris*; and worse was to come.

Next day, it began to rain; and the next, and the next. It rained so heavily that Thor was afraid the nearly completed vessel would become water-logged even before she was put into the river. The encampment became a sea of mud. From the north came stories of a cholera epidemic. Then, one by one, the team took to their beds with a high fever which sapped everyone's morale. If this was the Garden of Eden, someone had some explaining to do.

Finally, despite all the problems, the moment of launching arrived.

❝Zero hour. All flags up. . . .

We had invited no one, but the Garden of Eden was packed with spectators who seemed as curious as we were to see the reed ship enter the river. . . .

The silence was broken by the roar of thousands of jubilant voices as the lofty reed colossus began to move and then to slide along the metal rails. Slower than a turtle, she moved in jerks towards the gap in the broken wall, with the flowing river below. . . .

It was a great relief to see the monster moving out of our own home-made wooden jig and on to the improvized steel beams which an engineer from the upstream paper-mill had kindly welded together as rails to the water's edge. The corn-coloured vessel still carried blood marks on the bow that rose proudly like a swan's neck, but covered by red human handprints after the recent naming ceremony. ❞

OPPOSITE *The crew of* Tigris. *On the deck are the four veterans of the* Ra *expeditions; left to right: Norman Baker, Thor, Yuri Senkevich and Carlo Mauri.*

This had been the cause of some problems. The Marsh Arabs had wanted to sacrifice six sheep, and Thor was then supposed to hand-print their blood on the bow. Although opposed to such a barbaric custom, he realized he could not run the risk of insulting the Arabs, for whom this was a tradition dating from the days of Abraham. A compromise was reached: they would carry out their ritual alone (and enjoy the subsequent feast of roast lamb, by no means the least important part of the ceremony), but the actual naming would be done Thor's way by the grand-daughter of the Arabs' leader, Gatae.

6 Gatae stepped up from the river's edge leading this tiny black-haired lady in colourful costume by the hand. Little Sekneh struggled to carry a traditional Marsh Arab bottle-gourd dripping full of river water that was to give the ship its name. With sparkling eyes she splashed it successfully on the reed bow, forgot all her lessons, and only those who stood close could hear her mumble 'Dídglé', the local name for Tigris. Her grandfather never let go her hand as he took over and declared with loud voice in Arabic:

'This ship is to enter the water with the permission of God and the blessing of the Prophet, and will be called *Dídglé Tigris.'* 9

But neither God's permission nor the Prophet's blessing proved quite enough. The bow section of *Tigris* duly hit the water with a satisfying splash. The onlookers roared, but too soon. The stern section, 'like a rebellious hippopotamus', stuck firmly in the mud, refusing to be budged by muscle power alone. Finally a passing Russian truck gave *Tigris* an unceremonious shove into the murky waters of the river. But by that time it was dark, and the crowds had vanished.

Two more chaotic weeks were to pass before Thor and his crew were able to begin their journey down to the open sea, but at last *Tigris* was able to slip her moorings. Larger and stronger than either *Ra I* or *Ra II*, she was a fine sight as the current swept her towards the Gulf, pursued by running boys who vainly tried to keep pace with her along the banks of the river.

A few days after the River Tigris joined the Euphrates to form the Shatt-al-Arab, they felt as if they were being sluiced down a huge drain; for that is what has become of the mouth of those two wondrous rivers. Slabs of white and yellow chemical waste from a nearby paper factory covered the surface of the water and piled up against the sides of the ship. When they reached the huge industrial complexes of Basra and Abadan, they were confronted by the worst pollution Thor had ever experienced. An unbroken layer of crude oil and human refuse made it impossible to see the water beneath. The high-water level was visible as a stark tidal mark of tar along the line of reeds on the opposite bank. Whichever way they turned, there was nothing to see but ugliness; and nothing to smell but filth. If this place, Thor thought, had seen the birthplace of one civilization, it must surely be witnessing the decline of another.

However, their spirits rose when salt water began to replace fresh (if fresh is the word), and the water turned from black to brown. At last they were entering the Gulf.

❝ By leaving the mouth of the outer channel I felt as if I were once more about to break a scientific taboo. Vessels like *Tigris* were not supposed to go any further. We were trespassing beyond the limits of what competent scholars had set for the range of a Mesopotamian vessel of *berdi* reeds. . . .

We were about to violate a well-established time barrier. Zero hour for marine history and cultural contact by sea were both tied to the change from compact bundle-craft to the hollow hull. So important was this transition that we were led to take it for granted that if there was an open stretch of water between them cultures and civilizations arose independently before that time.

I knew as we hoisted sail beyond the Shatt-al-Arab that to scientists in many fields this would seem as a vote of no confidence in long-accepted teachings in anthropology. Perhaps it was. But it was fair play. To those who really believed in the old doctrine we should now be about to prove that they were right, and I wrong. But with all respect for my own colleagues among the scholars, none of them had ever seen a *berdi* ship nor were they able to quote anyone who had. Nor was I. ❞

But the reed ships of Sumeria had never been obliged to run the gauntlet of that polluted river. The old hands, Thor, Yuri, Carlo and Norman, were seriously worried that the acids and other chemicals which now disfigured

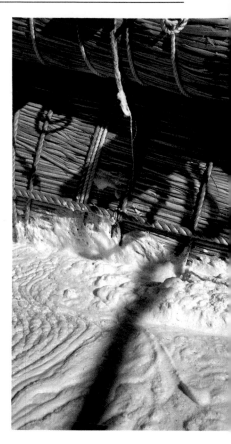

Chemicals from a paper mill polluted the Shatt-al-Arab river, covering it with a thick white soup. Used in the process of converting berdi *reeds to paper, nothing could have been more deadly to the precious fibres of* Tigris.

the sides of *Tigris* might have eaten away at the *berdi* reeds, greatly reducing their resistance to water. Even though the vessel was almost twice the size of *Ra II*, they were now carrying a crew of eleven instead of eight. Thor decided to take no chances: everything that was not absolutely essential must be carried ashore. Compressed air bottles, underwater lighting equipment, spare timber, batteries and other heavy items were all off-loaded at the port of Fao. The task completed, they felt in a better state to face the overcrowded shipping lanes that would take them, wind permitting, towards the island of Bahrain.

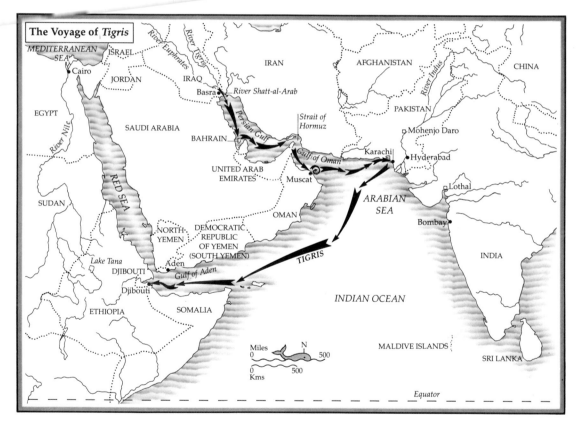

The Voyage of *Tigris*

21

THE GRAVEYARD
IN THE GULF

'Civilizations spread like seeds with the wind and the currents once the tree is grown and in bloom.'

'WHY did the chicken cross the road?' runs the old, familiar Christmas cracker joke. 'To get to the other side,' might flippantly be said of the voyages of *Kon-Tiki* and *Ra*; but never to that of *Tigris*. This time there was no question of crossing an ocean – the motives for the voyage were more complex, and at the same time more intangible. Thor was a man with a half-formed theory in his head which he was not yet ready to articulate. There were mysteries to unravel, of huge significance for mankind. But the flash of inspiration was still missing. He could not even tell the world whether he intended to sail east, south or west when he and his crew reached the mouth of the Gulf. For the moment it must be one step at a time, and the first of these was Bahrain. But at least the firmament above their heads was unpolluted.

❜This was 5 December; the sky was clear and the evening stars just began to sparkle in the firmament when I climbed up on the bridge platform to relieve the steering watch. Rashad and Asbjörn were up there and jokingly asked if I had seen how the new moon looked like our ship. At that very moment it certainly did. As always in southern latitudes, the new moon hung like a hammock in the sky instead of standing on end as in northern countries, but just then it rested with its bottom on the black waters of the horizon, precisely like a golden, sickle-shaped reed ship. We were really looking at a true god-ship sailing parallel to us on the horizon. . . .

The sight had made on me a deep impression. For

years I had followed this as a basic motif in prehistoric art. I was back in the days when the great reed ship-builders of Sumer, pre-Inca Peru and lonely Easter Island shared the tradition that the new moon was a god-ship, on which the sun-god and the primeval ancestor-kings travelled across the night sky. The ancient Sumerians and Peruvians expressed this belief both in words and in art. The Easter Islanders of our own days had forgotten the original symbolism, but the traditional badge of sovereignty, hanging at the chest of all their divine kings, was a sickle-shaped wooden pectoral which was known by two names: *rei-miro*, meaning 'ship-pectoral', and *rei-marama*, meaning 'moon-pectoral'. **'**

Tigris was the first vessel to enter the brand-new dockyard in Bahrain, the world's largest. It had been built to handle supertankers of 450,000 tons, but its first customer was a floating haystack.

Thor was dumbfounded to discover that there was not one single remaining sailmaker in Bahrain capable of repairing that mainsail. In desperation he decided that Detlef Soitzeg, the merchant seaman member of the crew, would have to fly to Hamburg and have the job done there. The round trip would take three weeks, but at least it would give Thor the time he needed to investigate whether Bahrain island was indeed the legendary Dilmun.

The greatest expert on the archaeology of the area was an English scholar named Geoffrey Bibby, who had flown in to Bahrain a few days earlier to greet the expedition. First he took Thor to see the oldest prehistoric burial ground in the world, comprising over a hundred thousand mounds each of which had once been a tomb, dating back over five thousand years. There appeared to be no signs of ordinary habitation near the burial ground itself, which suggested to Thor that men had possibly travelled great distances to bury their dead in this sacred place.

' We first came to an area named Ali, where a large cluster of them exceeded the pyramids of Egypt in number and compared favourably in size with a medium-large Mesopotamian pyramid. . . . The colossi of Ali were amply spaced and majestically located closer to the sea,

whereas the adjacent cemetery of smaller, dome-shaped hills continued inland and across the naked landscape, so closely packed that there was barely room to walk between them. I could not help feeling that the colossi, with all the space between them, antedated the closely packed fry. The big ones seemed to have been built while there was still room to spare in this locality, and the multitude of smaller mausolea was packed close to them in a desire to be their neighbours.

It is usually taken for granted that things begin small and afterwards grow into more impressive proportions. But not always so with civilizations. There may be two reasons. Cultural growth ends in most known cases with stagnation and cultural decadence. The reasons for this might be anything from over-affluence to war, pestilence or natural catastrophe. But in addition, at the peak of evolution most civilizations tend to possess ships and be involved in some kind of seafaring. At this advanced stage they may suddenly escape invaders or

At Bahrain the world's largest dockyard had just been opened, built to handle the supertankers of the Gulf. Yet their first customer was a 'floating haystack'.

travel in search of a better land. Families or entire organized colonies may settle with an advanced cultural level in areas previously uninhabited or occupied by some primitive society. We should not be surprised then to find that most ancient civilizations seem to appear without local background and often to disappear again without a trace. We dig in search of the roots, and expect every civilization to have grown like a tree in the place we find it. But civilizations spread like seeds with the wind and the current once the tree is grown and in bloom. . . . The pyramids of Egypt did not grow with time; the biggest were built by the first Pharaohs; later they got smaller. The same happened in Mesopotamia. And in Peru. . . . the famous Inca culture never attained the height of its Tiahuanaco or Mochica predecessors, either in art or in magnitude of architecture. And now one was left with a similar impression on visiting the Ali cemetery.

I had seen groups of burial mounds and prehistoric cemeteries in many parts of the world, but nothing like this. There was just nothing like it. And from now on

Not far from Bahrain is the world's largest prehistoric graveyard, containing over ten thousand burial mounds. Its sheer size has led archaeologists to conjecture that this may be the Dilmun of Sumerian legend.

Bibby did not have to argue to convince me that Bahrain was Dilmun. 〝

But if it were indeed Dilmun, the place from which the Sumerians came before they settled on the fertile banks of the Euphrates, then it must surely have been more than a city of the dead. Where was the evidence for a city of the living? Bibby next led Thor to a site on the northern side of the island dominated by the ruins of an old Arab fort, which had been captured and rebuilt by the Portuguese in the sixteenth century. A team of Danish archaeologists, of which Bibby was a member, had excavated the dunes at the base of the fort. Hidden beneath the shifting sand they found what they were looking for – the remains not just of one city, but of a city beneath a city, the oldest of them dating from the same period as the cemetery.

Here they found objects made of copper, ivory and carnelian beads, which could only have reached the island from far-off lands. All the evidence suggested that Dilmun – if Dilmun this was – had been an important trading port, a vital link between the burgeoning

The British archaeologist Geoffrey Bibby (centre) shows Thor a local fishing boat made from palm fronds.

new civilizations of Africa, India and Mesopotamia. There was another strong reason for the supposition that this had been no isolated community. The area round Bahrain has always had ample fresh water. Rain falling in the distant mountains of the Arabian peninsula follows underground channels and comes up as artesian wells in Bahrain. It would have been the ideal staging post for vessels passing up and down the Gulf, as it still is today.

Gazing once more over the vast burial ground, another thought came to Thor.

❝Dilmun . . . was the land recorded by the Sumerians as the one-time abode of their early ancestors, the home of Ziusudra, the venerated priest-king praised as the one who by his ship had given eternal life to mankind. . . . The same important personage who finally found his way into the teachings of Hebrews, Christians and Moslems as Noah.

. . . According to Sumerian texts Ziusudra never left Dilmun, *alias* Bahrain. It was his descendants that finally came to Sumer. If he ever existed, he would probably be buried in one of these giant mounds. . . . Perhaps I was really sitting on the tomb of Noah. . . .

It would be foolish of us today to underestimate the early Sumerians just because they lived five thousand years before our time, when the world at large was peopled by savages. They were not illiterate. From them we learnt to write. . . . From them we got the wheel, the art of forging metals, of building arches, of weaving cloth, of hoisting sail, of sowing our fields and baking our bread. They gave us our domesticated animals. They invented units for weight, length, area, volume, and instruments to measure it all. They initiated real mathematics, made exact astronomical observations, kept track of time, devised a calendar system and recorded genealogies. . . . Noah is a legend to us, but Ziusudra was history to them. Dilmun may seem a castle in the air to us, but to them it was a trading centre. . . . ❞

Finally, a little further along the coast, Geoffrey Bibby pointed out the site where the team had discovered the remains of a temple. Remarkable as it was in itself, for Thor it was a revelation of another kind. For here was the same beautifully dressed stonework that he had seen on the West African coast, in the Bolivian Andes and on remote Easter Island. It seemed to occur wherever reed boats had been in use, and always in that band encircling the earth which today we call the Tropics.

It was time for *Tigris* to move on. The hole in the bows had been successfully patched with palm stems, and Detlef Soitzeg was back from Hamburg with the mainsail in one piece. Before leaving Bahrain Thor got into conversation with a Norwegian tanker skipper, who told him an alarming tale. He had taken his ship by night through the Strait of Hormuz – probably the busiest shipping lane in the world. At first light one of the crew had reported finding the remains of a dhow sail caught on the tanker's bow. He told Thor that from the moment you slam a supertanker into 'Hard Astern' it takes about two miles to arrest her momentum. It was a daunting thought for the crew of the little *Tigris*, which could easily slip unnoticed under one of those massive hulls. But they had to pass through the narrow Strait of Hormuz if they were to reach the open waters of the Indian Ocean.

However, further enquiries revealed the existence of a narrow passage, sheltered from the main shipping lane in the Strait by some outlying rocks, which was regularly used by smaller vessels. One of the dhow captains who was about to make the return journey to Oman offered to act as their guide. Thor readily agreed. He longed for the open ocean; but there was no point in being squashed like a beetle in the world's mad scramble for fossil fuels.

As they weighed anchor from Bahrain next morning, they saw their pilot ship for the first time. It was battered and leaking, without mast or sail, and they could hear the crew working the pump full-time to keep the weatherbeaten craft afloat at all. Not for the first time, the crew of *Tigris* felt a great deal safer where they were. Nevertheless, for communication purposes one of them would have to go aboard the dhow, and young Rashad from Iraq volunteered. For the rest of them there was the sheer exhilaration of sailing for the very first time with a proper mainsail, and free of towlines. Norman Baker, the navigator, was astonished at their progress. He logged a speed of nearly five knots, which had never

257

After making the hazardous passage through the Strait of Hormuz, Tigris set a course along the rocky coast of Oman towards Muscat.

been achieved before on any of Thor Heyerdahl's voyages.

In retrospect, the decision seems a harsh one. The unwritten lore of the sea requires mariners to come to each other's assistance, whatever the circumstances. But in Thor's defence it must be remembered that there were two voices aboard the dhow to which he could listen. There was the frantic captain and there was his own man, Rashad, who took a much more sanguine view of the dhow's condition and was happy to remain where he was.

With the wind freshening all the time they set a north-easterly course, aware that the man-made obstacles in their path were likely to prove just as hazardous as any natural ones. All the paraphernalia of the oil boom lay spread out before them like a watery maze, and they were being pitched into the very midst of it at an alarming speed. Then the elements appeared to turn against them.

❛Just before sunrise the wind went mad. It turned more westerly, with violent gusts, and the sea was as chaotic as one would normally expect it to be only where there is interference from reefs or currents. . . . A sudden treacherous gust . . ., helped by a twisting wave, unexpectedly threw us side on to the weather and before the sail could be adjusted or the unfortunate helmsman could get us back on course, all the devils in the universe seemed to thunder down upon us. . . . The thick sail battered with a force that would lift any man off the deck, and loops and rope-ends from sheets, braces and leach-lines whipped left and right and struck at everything on board. Like savages we clung to the canvas and ropes, and in the mad fight that followed the wooden block that held the port side topping lift split asunder and the yardarm with the sail sagged to port. The flapping and slashing sail had to come down quickly before all the rigging broke. . . .

At this time two gigantic tankers crossed in front of us, and a third passed along our side. Too big to roll like us, they split the swelling seas into white geysers that rose high up their bows. We had no such geysers striking our bundles, otherwise cabins and all would have been washed overboard. But we danced about like a duck,

preventing the seas from getting any sort of grip on us. Our only dangers were land or ships. . . .

By midday we found ourselves for the first time in a terribly polluted area. Small clots and large slices of solidified black oil or asphalt floated closely packed everywhere in a manner that clearly testified to recent tanker washings. But the black tar soup was all mixed with bobbing cans, bottles and other refuse, and an incredible quantity of solid, usable wood: logs, planks, boards, cases, grids and large sheets of plywood. One such sheet carried a deadly yellow snake as passenger. All the wood was smeared and clotted with oil from the seas that tossed it about. None of us had ever seen pollution this thick out of sight of land. **9**

No sooner were they through the worst of it than they found themselves confronted by an awe-inspiring sight. Nothing on their sea charts had prepared them for the huge mountain escarpment rising ahead of them above the clouds. They were already far too close to these mighty cliffs, which appeared to drop straight into the sea from a height of nearly seven thousand feet; and the

The polluted waters of the Indian Ocean off the coast of Pakistan.

gap was closing at an alarming rate. It was clear that they had been blown towards the base of the Hormuz peninsula instead of the tip. Throwing over the rudder oars, Thor set a new course heading north-north-east, parallel to the mountain range. It was going to be a test of nerve, and the sailing qualities of *Tigris*, to see if they could round the cape before being dashed against that fearsome coast. And there was another worry. The dhow, with Rashad aboard, had disappeared from sight when the storm broke, and was still nowhere to be seen.

Up to this point it could be argued that the voyage had been something of a disappointment, at times verging on downright failure. They had been beset by delays and frustrations at almost every stage. But after everything has been taken into consideration – the weather, the natural and man-made hazards of the route and, above all perhaps, the ship's primitive steering mechanism – the passage of *Tigris* through the Strait of Hormuz deserves to stand as one of the most remarkable feats of seamanship in modern times. Certainly, on *Kon-Tiki, Ra I* and *Ra II* there had been nothing to approach it. Thor wrote of it later:

Never on any sea had we seen so many brilliantly lit ships in motion at the same time as appeared around us at the moment when Detlef ordered a sharp, 90° turn to starboard and the men on the bridge sent us into the main traffic lane of the Hormuz Strait. We immediately received a violent air stream straight at our back and were pressed into a wind funnel between two opposed capes of the same continent, a sort of Asiatic Straits of Gibraltar. The current must also at this time have run like a river out of the gulf. Our speed past the tip of the Arabian dagger was the fastest we had ever experienced with a reed ship, and the black mountain silhouettes at our side were changing from one minute to the next. With this speed Tigris responded to the slightest touch on the tillers and we raced in between the superships which thundered around us as if we were all of a kind.

Things went almost ridiculously well, and with double steering watch and both navigators alert on the roof Carlo and I could steal a few minutes' snooze before we were back at the steering oars for our next turn at 2 a.m. . . .

OPPOSITE Tigris, *a 'paper boat', in the vastness of the Indian Ocean. En route to the ocean she had already coped with the tricky sea and weather conditions better than the leaky dhow that had been towing her.*

I was awakened by Detlef crawling over my legs heading for his own berth. 'We've made it,' he said. 'We're outside.' It was half-past midnight and the night was at its darkest, still young. We were outside? I crawled to the starboard door opening and lifted the canvas cover. . . . It was an unforgettable change of scene. Beautiful. Impressive. The rolling had ceased and the sky was full of stars over vaguely moonlit rocks and hillocks. These were at the foot of tall, wild peaks and mountain ridges, which together formed a fabulous landscape just beside our ship.

At noon the next day a small miracle occurred. Heading towards them they saw a tiny speck on the horizon. Through binoculars they recognized it as a dhow, with a figure in the bows waving frantically. It was Rashad. No one was ever more pleased to make the leap back from the tattered technology of the twentieth century to the warmth and serenity of 3000 BC; from gasoline to grass. Now, from a cache beneath the cabin floor, Yuri produced champagne and caviar. It was New Year's Eve – and the hazards of the Persian Gulf were behind them.

Thor Heyerdahl had no fixed itinerary for the *Tigris* voyage; and, once out of the Gulf, he invited the crew to vote on which way they should go. It was almost as if he wanted fate to impose its own pattern and meaning on their activities, not the other way around. Carlo voted for the open ocean while the winds were still favourable: he had had enough of being the salami, sandwiched between giant supertankers. The rest were divided between the Iranian coast to the north of them, which offered some spectacular scenery, and a course to the south towards Muscat, the capital of Oman.

Thor himself was in two minds, but eventually cast his vote with the latter group. An intriguing message had reached him just before *Tigris* left Bahrain, that a temple pyramid in the stepped ziggurat style had been discovered in Oman. If this proved to be true, it would be the only one in the Old World outside Egypt and Mesopotamia.

Even with the Gulf behind them, the passage to Muscat was by no means easy. The waters off the coast of Oman at that time were notorious for pirates; and the oil traffic was as thick as ever. Their position became even less comfortable when waves of suspicion began to emanate from the shore. Radio messages reached them warning *Tigris* to keep well clear of land until permission was granted to approach Oman. To his fury, Norman was even forbidden to use his own radio to keep in touch with the outside world. So much for their United Nations flag, flying bravely at the masthead. Worse was to come. A further message was received forbidding them to enter the port of Muscat at all. The reason, Thor discovered later, was because they had a Russian on board.

Thor decided the time had come to lend a deaf ear. Stealing into the inner harbour under cover of night, they anchored in the midst of a cluster of dhows from many lands to await developments. Several days later, and after innumerable visits from the security services, the Sultan of Oman himself finally signed an order permitting the crew to go ashore.

By great good fortune, on their first evening Thor was invited to a party where he met a distinguished Italian archaeologist named Paolo Costa, who was working for the Sultan as Director of Antiquities. Intrigued by the concept behind the *Tigris* voyage, he immediately offered to act as guide on the following day. They drove north, past the old capital of Sohar, then inland between burial mounds which seemed identical to those on Bahrain island, though not in such profusion. Bumping along dry river beds, they suddenly rounded a black conical peak and saw what they were looking for.

❢ Norman and I . . . swallowed the big mound with our eyes as Costa took us to the side where a long, narrow ramp led from the ground up to the top terrace. Gherman was almost beside himself with excitement; this was a stepped pyramid of the type we had so often seen together among pre-Columbian ruins in Mexico. At the same time, the whole concept was that of a Mesopotamian ziggurat. As Costa emphasized, nothing like it was known in any other part of Oman or the entire Arabian peninsula. Huge natural boulders had been used to wall in a rectangular structure that rose above the plain in compact, superimposed terraces, four of which were seen above ground. The four corners pointed in cardinal directions, and the well-preserved, stone-lined ramp led centrally up one side in the fashion characteristic of the temple-pyramids of the sun-worshippers of Mesopotamia and pre-Columbian America. Whoever might have built it did not follow Moslem norms, but it struck me that the concept was also the same as that of the Dilmun temple Geoffrey Bibby had excavated on Bahrain and described as a mini-ziggurat. 9

Within sight of this temple, Thor saw the remains of prehistoric copper mining in Oman. Then Costa drove them to another site further inland where a whole mountain had been excavated, leaving an estimated hundred thousand tons of multi-coloured slag, still glinting in the sun and heaped in piles around the quarries. Thousands of labourers must have been employed in the enterprise; now it all lay abandoned, but still majestic in that parched landscape beneath the fierce Arabian sun.

Copper and tin are the two vital ingredients needed to sustain a Bronze Age culture like that of the Sumerians. Thor knew that there was no copper nearer to Mesopotamia than this. He also knew of two tablets that had been found in the ancient city of Ur, in the heart of Sumeria. They were records, or perhaps receipts, itemizing an exchange of goods: wool, clothing, animal skins, sesame oil and other prized items. The tablets were over four thousand years old, and in each case the imported commodity was the same – 'copper from Makan'. He turned to Paolo Costa, who might have been reading his mind. 'Yes,' said the archaeologist, 'this may well be the legendary copper mountain of Makan.'

The clues in the treasure hunt were leading further and further eastward. But that had been the story of Thor's life. It is nearly a thousand miles from Oman to the heart of Sumeria, with the Persian Gulf as the only sea route between them. If this were indeed Makan, then instead of supertankers awash with oil the Strait of Hormuz must have been witness to an equally spectacular sight five thousand years ago – dozens of reed ships laden with copper, and proceeding in the opposite direction.

There was, of course, no time for original archaeological research on the *Tigris* expedition. The voyage had a

value of a different sort. As it progressed it became a thread on which necklace beads of research could be assembled one by one, creating a new pattern and a new order.

Nor can it be denied that chance played its part. On leaving Oman it had originally been Thor's intention to set a course for Africa; but various circumstances intervened. Norris Brock was now plunged into a deep depression. His sound camera, the only one aboard, had been irrevocably damaged by the rough journeys overland in Oman. Without it he could not work, and the greatest assignment of his life seemed to be in jeopardy. Two strong wills clashed, but eventually Thor agreed to return to Muscat where a new camera would be waiting.

Several days were lost there, but this unexpected delay gave Thor time to revise his plans. With a new topsail fitted by Norman Baker, they now had greater speed and manoeuvrability. Why not try for the Indus valley, third and most easterly of the great civilizations that had sprung up around 3000 BC? They did; and in so doing found the jewel which was to become the centrepiece for the whole necklace, giving meaning and purpose to all the other stones.

Once the site of mining on a vast scale, this extraordinary landscape inland from Muscat was almost certainly the legendary copper mountain of Makan. In ancient times reed ships plied the Persian Gulf, carrying their cargo of valuable metal to Mesopotamia.

22

THE MYSTERY OF
THE INDUS VALLEY

'The citizens of Mohenjo Daro and their uncivilized contemporaries would have learnt to drive a car, turn on a television set and knot a neck-tie as easily as any African or European today.'

For 3,500 years, the oldest civilization in the Indus valley vanished from human sight. The conquering armies of Alexander the Great and Genghiz Khan came and went, without ever suspecting that beneath their feet lay the remains of a culture as great as any of theirs. True, there were no monuments to compare with the Egypt of the pharaohs, but the Indus valley civilization had been much more than a widely scattered collection of villages, individually supporting themselves in that fertile region.

It was not until 1922 that an English archaeologist, Sir John Marshall, first led an expedition to the Indus. Under a huge mound of sand three hundred miles from the Indian Ocean, and no longer even on the banks of the great river (which frequently changes course when the floods come), his team began to uncover the remains of a city. Locally, it acquired the name of Mohenjo Daro, which means 'Mound of the Dead'. What the name might have been at the time of the city's heyday, no one knew.

This was the place, now in Pakistan, that Thor Heyerdahl was determined to visit; not with *Tigris*, which would have been virtually impossible at that time of year, but overland. As well as containing references to Dilmun and Makan, Sumerian and Assyrian tablets sometimes mentioned the mysterious place known as Meluhha. It might have been anywhere, but all the evidence Thor had been accumulating seemed to point to the east. Not that the name itself was of paramount

importance: what he was really seeking was evidence of contact between the earliest inhabitants of the Indus valley and those in Egypt and Sumeria to the west.

To reach Mohenjo Daro today you take the Great Trunk Road which follows the river north past the city of Hyderabad. Gaily painted buses and lorries jostle their way through many villages, where today Islam has imposed its own demanding culture. The women, when seen at all, are completely veiled from head to foot. If the little bronze figurine of a naked dancing girl found in the ruins is any guide, then life in ancient Mohenjo Daro would never have earned the approval of the Prophet.

The remains of a Buddhist temple dominate the excavated part of the city. This, a much later addition, was built on top of a pyramid made from large bricks which was undoubtedly the central feature of the original city. The layout of the streets below followed a highly sophisticated plan, beyond the reach of any Stone Age culture and solar-oriented.

The ruins of Mohenjo Daro, probably the most important city of the Indus valley civilization, were not discovered until 1922. The circular structure at the top is a Buddhist stupa from a later period, built on top of an adobe-brick pyramid.

ABOVE *A soapstone seal depicting a reed boat, found at Mohenjo Daro in Pakistan. It is thought to be at least four thousand years old.*

OPPOSITE *Thor walking with Christopher Ralling through the public bath in Mohenjo Daro. This structure was made watertight with asphalt, a substance which could only have come from Mesopotamia.*

How and why did Mohenjo Daro spring so suddenly into existence? And how and why, just fifteen hundred years later, did it so suddenly vanish? Clues lie all around. There is evidence, for instance, that the city was partially destroyed and rebuilt no less than seven times, following disastrous floods. After such a history, one would think it might have dawned on the inhabitants that their city was in the wrong place. But Thor has never been one to make such glib assumptions, nor to underestimate the ability and inventiveness of early man.

❛Take away our hundreds of generations of accumulated inheritance, and then compare what is left of our abilities with those of the founders of the Indus civilization. . . . The citizens of Mohenjo Daro and their uncivilized contemporaries would have learnt to drive a car, turn on a television set and knot a neck-tie as easily as any African or European today. In reasoning and inventiveness little has been gained or lost in the build-up of the human species during the last five millennia. With this in mind a visitor to Mohenjo Daro will be left with the impression that the creators of this city . . . had either . . . surpassed all other human generations in inventiveness, or that . . . they were immigrants bringing with them centuries of cultural inheritance.

There is only one opinion among scholars: the city of Mohenjo Daro was built by expert city architects within a rigidly organized society. The planning of the city was one adhered to, but never surpassed, by subsequent town planners in Central and West Africa for four thousand years. Even at the beginning of our own century few of the lesser towns maintained an equally high cultural standard. . . .

There were also fresh-water conduits among the houses, and a big public bath or swimming-pool, possibly built for cleansing rituals. It measures thirty-eight feet by twenty-two feet, is eight feet deep and it was waterproofed by a double wall of bricks set in asphalt, with another layer of asphalt one inch thick between the walls. ❜

This public bath was to prove of major significance. The nearest readily obtainable source of asphalt was in far-off Mesopotamia. It was just conceivable that some

of the first inhabitants of Mohenjo Daro had originally come from there, and had brought the substance with them. If not, it must have been obtained by trade across the Indian Ocean.

Thor was in no doubt that these early inhabitants of the Indus valley had boats capable of reaching the sea, and very probably of crossing it. *Berdi* reeds grew in abundance nearby; and as if to clinch the point, a stone seal had recently been found in the old city, depicting a reed boat with high prow and stern of the same design as the ones on the walls of Egyptian tombs.

Following the excavation of Mohenjo Daro, and another equally important city called Harappa five hundred miles further inland, archaeologists began to search for ports which might have served these communities. Several were found along a thousand-mile stretch of seaboard on both sides of the vast Indus delta. The best-preserved was Lothal, just across the Indian border – the oldest man-made harbour ever discovered. It was designed for vessels considerably longer and wider than *Tigris*, and therefore just as capable of making similar ocean voyages.

What, then, did they export from the huge Indus hinterland? Thor found a list compiled by an Indian archaeologist, Dr S. R. Rao, most illuminating. In Lothal itself there was evidence of a flourishing community of craftsmen working in ivory, carnelian and soapstone. Artefacts made from all these materials were highly prized in Sumeria. And as proof of trade in the other direction, Dr Rao had found 'eight gold pendants similar to those found in the Royal Cemetery at Ur'.

The main crops in the Indus valley at that time were almost certainly wheat and cotton. Whether it was their failure, or a sudden lack of demand in the outside world, which caused the collapse of civilization throughout the region is still a mystery. There are other theories. Many of the skeletons found at Mohenjo Daro appeared to have suffered a violent death: perhaps an invading horde from Asia or the flood waters from the Himalayas were responsible. With no certain proof, but convinced in his own mind that the legendary land of Meluhha was indeed located in the Indus valley, Thor retraced his steps. It was time for *Tigris* to move on.

OPPOSITE *A ferry on the Indus. Throughout history the Himalayan floodwaters have constantly changed the river's course, and may have been the reason for the sudden abandonment of Mohenjo Daro.*

272

It was February 1978, and they were leaving Asia with the ship in better condition than the day she first entered the Persian Gulf. Thor considered their situation:

❛ At one time I had seen the main purpose of the experiment as to test the buoyancy of a Sumerian *ma-gur* built from *berdi* cut at the correct time. I had visualized sailing with no predetermined goal as long as the *berdi* kept afloat. If it did not sink we could cross the Indian Ocean with the monsoon at our back. . . . But instead we had followed the trade routes of Sumerian merchants. We had spent so much time visiting prehistoric remains in Bahrain, Oman and Pakistan that my finances had started to run low. . . . We had so far voyaged between the legendary Dilmun, Makan and Meluhha of the Sumerian merchant mariners. Across the Indian Ocean lay the Horn of Africa, Somalia, considered by all scientists to be the legendary Punt of the Egyptian voyagers. If we could reach that coast also, then we would have closed the ring. Then we would have tied all the three great civilizations of the Old World together with the very kind of ship all three had in common. We had linked Africa with the New World before, with the same kind of ship, and the New World had in turn been shown to have access to the mid-Pacific, where Easter Island was the nearest speck of land, with its stone statues and vestiges of an undeciphered script which some scientists claim has a strong resemblance to the Indus Valley writing. ❜

OPPOSITE Tigris *bound for Africa on the final leg of her journey.*

23

SHE WAS A FINE SHIP

'Tigris will have a proud end, as a torch that will call
men to reason. . . .'

According to his usual custom, Thor gave each
member of the crew a chance to air his views as to
their next destination. It was a democratic ges-
ture, sincerely undertaken and excellent for morale. But
it would be wrong to conclude that if, for instance, the
younger members had all opted for Bali with its beautiful women, they would have carried the day. It was
much more a question of bringing the whole crew
round to a consensus after free discussion.

The reasons behind this process lie deeply embedded
in Thor Heyerdahl's character. He is a man who knows
what he wants, and if it is sufficiently important he will
stop at nothing to get it. Yet at the same time he hates the
distinction between the commander and the commanded; on expeditions he never claims the small privi-
leges, like occasional privacy, to which most leaders feel
entitled. He is a man apart, who craves the common
touch.

The ritual completed, Africa was chosen as their next
destination. But almost immediately they were hit by a
violent storm.

❛The wind howled and whistled in the empty rigging
and the canvas-covered cabin. Like Noah we waited
inside cover for the weather to abate. The rudder-oars
were abandoned, lashed on. . . . It was an incredible
comfort to all of us to know we were on a compact bundle-boat and not inside a fragile plank hull . . . breaking
seas [came] tumbling on board by the tens of tons, up on
the benches, everywhere. But next moment all the froth-

ing water whirling around the cabins was gone, dropping straight down through the sieve-like bottom. And the bundle-boat rose from the sea like a surfacing submarine, glitteringly wet in the lamp-light, and sparkling intensely with the phosphorescent plankton trapped on board. **❯**

In warmer seas and kinder weather, the rest of the crossing was relaxed and pleasurable. Once or twice the more intrepid (and foolhardy) members of the crew almost pushed their luck too far while sharing the ocean with sharks, but that was all. *Tigris* performed splendidly, and the approach to Africa was achieved without mishaps or accidents. The troubles that lay ahead were of a different kind.

The Gulf of Aden is like a giant funnel. To the south lies the Horn of Africa; to the north the Arabian peninsula. Little did the crew of *Tigris* realize it, but they were sailing into a trap. Thor had already been warned that a landing in Somalia was out of the question because of the continuing war with Ethiopia. But now came equally bad news from the northern side of the Gulf. The two Yemens, North and South, were also at each other's throats. This meant that the whole of Somalia, the entire southern coastline of Arabia and the first three hundred miles of coast bordering on the Red Sea were effectively barred to them.

The expedition's London backers were becoming alarmed. A message came crackling over Norman's radio: 'DO YOU ACTUALLY INTEND TO NAVIGATE INTO THE GULF OF ADEN AND FROM THERE INTO THE RED SEA? ARE YOU ABLE TO SAIL AND NAVIGATE THIS COURSE? PLEASE BEWARE OF THE POLITICAL SITUATION IN THIS AREA AS PREVIOUSLY ADVISED. WE HAVE HAD NO CO-OPERATION FROM EITHER THE SOUTH YEMEN OR SOMALIAN GOVERNMENTS STOP.'

At the narrowest part of the funnel they were now entering lies the tiny African republic of Djibouti. Having recently been granted independence by France, it was now staunchly maintaining its neutrality in the wars raging on all sides. It was a triumph of *Tigris*'s navigational ability that they were able to sail precisely to the tiny spot of land that makes up this mini-republic. Here, at last, *Tigris* obtained permission to land. No one on board knew it, but this was to be her final port of call.

TOP OF PAGE *The route and progress of* Tigris *were subjects of constant discussion.*

ABOVE *Thor and Detlef Soitzeg take their turn at rowing during a flat calm. Old pictures sometimes show reed boats with as many as twenty oars in the water.*

Tigris *lying becalmed in the Gulf of Aden.*

On 28 March 1978 they dropped anchor in Djibouti harbour. For a few hours, Thor's hopes were raised: a friendly letter was waiting from the North Yemen ambassador in London, offering every co-operation. But even this ray of light was quickly extinguished. A second message reached him, banning *Tigris* from Yemeni coastal waters 'for security reasons'. Apparently their frail little reed boat had taken on the semblance of an armed warship. It might have been amusing, if it were not so dispiriting. Nevertheless, in his hotel Thor had time to reflect on their five-month journey, and on his own enlarged perceptions about the early civilizations bordering on the Indian Ocean.

❝The greatest discovery of recent years is how incredibly little we yet know of man's past, of the beginning. In the first decades after Darwin and the discovery of the unknown Sumerian civilization, we thought we had all the answers: the jungle gave birth to man and two large and fertile river valleys gave birth to twin civilizations. Egypt and Mesopotamia. That made sense.

That two amazing civilizations suddenly arose side by side in the Middle East about 3000 BC was not surprising. The Garden of Eden was there, and Adam and Eve were born only a few millennia earlier. Then came the discoveries in the Indus valley. . . . But then field archaeologists found the ruins of the first civilized city builders here too, which dated roughly from 3000 BC as well. . . . The definite impression is as if related priest-kings at that time came from elsewhere with their respective entourages, and imposed their dynasties on areas formerly occupied by more primitive or at least culturally far less advanced tribes.

Why this impressive, seemingly overnight blossoming in three places simultaneously . . . ? How can we assume that three reed boat-building people began to travel in search of tin and copper at the same time, the two metals they needed to mix for shaping bronze in their wax-filled moulds? Nor is there any natural tie between bronze moulding and, say, the invention of script or the use of wheeled carts; yet these three civilizations suddenly shared all of man's major inventions and beliefs, as if they had inspired each other or suddenly had drawn from a common pool.❞

Thor at the helm as Tigris *enters Djibouti, her final port of call.*

But now the twentieth century had put a clamp around the voyage like a steel trap designed to catch poachers. In that politically polluted atmosphere, even the United Nations flag seemed to have lost all meaning.

Stealing away from the hotel, Thor spent what he alone knew would be one last night under the stars on the deck of *Tigris*. The voyage was over, and her captain had decided on a fiery climax. In his mind he composed her epitaph: '*Tigris* will have a proud end, as a torch that will call men to reason, so that they might resume the cause of peace in a corner of the world where civilization first found a foothold.'

Next morning Thor outlined his plan to the crew, who gave him their unanimous approval. In strictest confidence, he also informed the local harbourmaster. He was determined that these symbolic flames should not be doused by the fire-fighting services before they had a chance to take hold.

Thor the meticulous planner, Thor the showman, Thor the crusader were all on display on that momentous day. At a given signal, *Tigris* was towed to a safe anchorage outside the harbour, but well within sight of the town. Before lowering the United Nations flag, a telegram was despatched to the Secretary General, Kurt Waldheim, setting out the reasons for their action. Then the entire crew sat down on board to eat a last meal together.

❦ Yuri's dried rainbow-runner; Rashad's pickled flying-fish; biscuits. We had great memories from around this table. . . .

The sun was getting low. It would soon set behind the blue mountains of Africa, which fell off in a blunt cape at the entrance to the Red Sea. . . . It was zero hour for *Tigris*. . . . I looked at the empty table as I jumped into the dinghy after the others. Nobody had troubled to clean the table tonight. Provisions for eleven men for another month, blankets and everything else serviceable had been carried ashore to the refugees.

We lined up ashore and none of us could say much. 'Take off your hats,' I said at last as the flames licked out of the main cabin door. The sail caught fire in a rain of sparks, accompanied by sharp shotlike reports of splitting bamboo and the crackling of burning reeds.

OPPOSITE *The symbolic end of* Tigris. *In a message to the UN Secretary General, Thor signalled: 'Today we are burning our proud ship with full sails, and the rigging and hull in perfect condition, as a protest against the inhuman elements of this 1978 world of ours. Our planet is larger than the bundles of reeds that bore us across the sea, but still small enough to risk the same threats, unless those of us living acknowledge that there is a desperate need for intelligent co-operation if we are to save ourselves and our common civilization from what we are turning into a sinking ship.'*

280

Nobody else spoke, and I barely heard myself mumble:
'She was a fine ship.' **9**

The *Tigris* conflagration appeared to mark the end of
Thor Heyerdahl's experiments with reed boat navigation; but even in his seventies he is still seriously considering invitations to take part in further voyages.
Whether he does or not, there is a satisfying complete-
ness about his ocean expeditions. They will surely stand
the test of time, not only as great journeys in themselves, but as a contribution to our knowledge of the
remote past.

There are sections of the scientific establishment
worldwide that have never really approved of Thor
Heyerdahl. It is said that he attempts to embrace far too
many disciplines; that he reaches conclusions and then
sets about finding highly selective evidence to prove
them; that he pays too much attention to myth and oral
history; and, most infuriating of all, that he is forever
away on expeditions instead of sitting behind a profes-
sorial desk, as most of his critics have to.

It is quite true that his methods are unorthodox. Bengt
Danielsson, the only Swedish member of the original
Kon-Tiki crew, expressed it graphically when he said:
'Thor builds his pyramids upside down.' It is also true that
he does have a high public profile, which has enabled
him to raise money and arouse media interest for new
ventures, an advantage often denied to others. But he
has fought hard for his reputation over many years.

In the end he will be judged, as he would wish to be,
by his achievements. Anyone with visionary ideas must
expect to see them refined and modified by succeeding
generations. The theories of Pasteur, Freud and Darwin
have all undergone that process. Not for a moment
would Thor expect his own life's work to be compared
with scientific giants like these. But in one respect it
already deserves to be. Like them, he has permanently
changed our perception of the planet on which we all
live. Never again will it be possible to think of the
oceans as barriers to early man in his search for enlight-
enment. On the contrary, Thor has demonstrated that
they were highways providing a means of contact
between widely separated peoples, from the very birth
of civilization.

24

THE UNCOUNTED ISLANDS

'Whatever might be the answer, we are back with boats
marking the beginnings.'

T hor Heyerdahl was far from finished with the
Indian Ocean. The very next year after the *Tigris*
voyage, 1979, he was back on the Indian sub-
continent, this time to visit the prehistoric port of Lothal
some two hundred miles north of the modern city of
Bombay.

Today the water level has changed, with the result
that the harbour area is high and dry; you have to walk
across wide mud flats to reach it. Thor was convinced
that Lothal, as the main outlet for the Indus valley civilization, had once been the most important trading port
for the entire area. He himself had demonstrated that
a reed ship could reach the Indus valley from
Mesopotamia and even continue on to the Red Sea.
Now he pondered on what other destinations might
have been within reach of those intrepid seamen of long
ago.

To the south-west of India and Sri Lanka a huge archipelago of tiny islands lies on the surface of the ocean,
stretching for over a thousand miles right down to the
Equator and beyond. These are the Maldives. Unlike the
islands of the Pacific they have not attracted much scientific attention; indeed before the 1980s not a single
archaeological expedition had ever been there. Then a
mysterious photograph arrived in Thor's mail. It came
from a fellow Norwegian, Björn Bye, who had just
returned from the islands where he had established a
branch of the Worldview International Foundation, of
which Thor was a member.

'One thing was certain,' wrote Thor, 'the Maldives adorned the earth. Spread out over a blue velvet carpet, each little island was an inlaid jewel in a ring of bottle green. On a map, the islands looked like peppercorns. No one knows exactly how many there are. New islands emerge from underwater reefs, while others are ground to pieces by the sea, and disappear.'

Sent by a stranger, this is the photograph of a totally unexpected Buddha-like image which first drew Thor to the Maldives, a stronghold of Islam. He was particularly intrigued by the figure's similarities to the ones on Easter Island.

The picture showed a half-buried statue found on one of the islands. Its mere existence was interesting enough since the Maldives had been Moslem for eight centuries, and Islamic law expressly forbids representation of the human figure. But Thor noticed features about it which immediately brought to mind the statues of Easter Island on the opposite side of the globe. On the crown of the head there was a topknot, and the ears were extended right down to the shoulders. Buddha had long ears. Could the Buddhists have been here before Islam was imposed throughout the archipelago in 1153? In *The Maldive Mystery* Thor wrote:

❛Buddha was born in the sixth century BC. Ear extension did not start with him, however. . . . Buddha was a title adopted by an historical person, Siddhartha Gautama, who was born a Hindu prince. It was as a Hindu prince that he had had his ear lobes perforated and extended with large plugs, because it was a very old Hindu custom in noble families. But ear extension did not begin with Hindu nobles either. Big ear plugs, just

like those used by the Inca nobles and the long-ears on Easter Island, had recently been excavated in large numbers at Lothal. . . .

Was it pure coincidence that remote oceanic islands like the Maldives and Easter Island had been found and settled by navigators whose gods and nobles were supposed to wear big discs in their ear lobes? Perhaps yes. Perhaps no, because we were dealing with people, and migrating families, whose remote island discoveries had proved them to be skilled, long-range ocean explorers. **)**

Thor and Björn Bye made a preliminary visit to Male, the capital island, which contained the only town of any size in the archipelago. He soon discovered problems. The Maldive islanders are such devout Moslems that they would never break the law of the Prophet by making human figures, and when they found any such sculptures made by their predecessors they were in the habit of destroying them.

Thor learned that since the photograph had been

Local legend had it that a fearsome demon claimed the regular sacrifice of a virgin. Grotesque masks like this were found on the island of Male near the site of a temple where the offerings were said to have been made.

taken the body of the statue had been smashed to pieces. Only the head remained, and this was now locked away in the national museum where it would not offend local religious susceptibilities. As soon as he saw it, Thor was convinced that it was indeed the head of a Buddha. But then he caught sight of some of the other objects on the shelves. The serene features of the Buddha were flanked on both sides by ferocious-looking demons, carved in wood and stone.

As images they had no place in either Moslem or Buddhist teaching, which suggested to Thor that they might be earlier than both. Every one had large discs inserted into extended ear lobes. If he was right, then the islands must have experienced several migrations stretching back into the mists of time. He learned that most of the demon images had been found on Male itself.

There are some twelve hundred islands in the Maldives archipelago, forming a marine barrier which blocks all navigation around the southern tip of India. Travellers from east to west can find a passage through in only two areas: either exactly on the Equator or at 1° north. All other ways are blocked by perilous reefs. After studying a detailed map, Thor immediately decided to head for the Equatorial Channel. The peoples of all early civilizations were sun worshippers who would find it natural to follow the route of the sun along the Equator and erect monuments in its honour on any islands they found in the Channel.

Fua Mulaku, reputed to be the most beautiful island in the whole Maldive chain, was situated right in the middle of the Equatorial Channel. There were many things of interest on it, among them a large mound, obviously built by ancient man and once covered by beautifully dressed limestone slabs now scattered about. There was also a delightful freshwater lake, the only one of its kind that Thor had ever seen on a coral island. It was here, too, that he first began to hear about a mysterious people called the Redin. Putting his faith in oral tradition, as so often in the past, Thor had approached some of the older inhabitants and found one forthcoming old fellow:

❛'Who were the Redin?'

The old man shrugged his shoulders. They might have been Singalese, at least they spoke a language different from the Divehi of the Maldivians. The Redin were on these islands first and the Maldivians came later. The Redin were white people. The colour of their hair was brown. Our informant touched Björn's chestnut-coloured hair to emphasize what he meant. They had big hooked noses and blue eyes. A tall people, with long faces. They made statues and worshipped them. . . .

Legendary references to seafaring people with fair skin and brown hair are well known from pre-Columbian Mexico and Peru, and even on Easter Island. Certainly these early seafaring stone-masons in the leg-

A stairway leading down to a public bath excavated on the island of Nilandu.

Thor had already seen examples of this sophisticated 'fingerprint masonry' on Easter Island, in South America, North Africa and the Middle East. Here it was again on these islands far out in the Indian Ocean. Who had introduced it, and what was the connection between the places?

ends had not come from Europe. But people fitting this description had also existed outside Europe. There were brown-haired people with fair skin in the Middle East and western Asia. The only thing we could deduce with certainty . . . was that the present population on Fua Mulaku did not believe that the big mounds had been left by their own ancestors, but by an earlier people who looked to them like foreigners. **9**

References like this can be found in all Thor Heyerdahl's writings, dating right back to *Fatu Hiva*. Always the legends speak of tall, fair-skinned, red-haired people who came from the east, following the path of the sun. But to date, Thor has never attempted to draw these many threads together into a single theory. Oral history, by its very nature, can never be proved; and on this subject he could so easily be misquoted. If such a mythical race of wanderers ever existed, they were certainly not Europeans; Thor is convinced of that. But if he were to theorize any further, the implication would still be there that it took men with red hair and fair skins to make the first crossing of the world's oceans. And of that there is no proof whatever.

Thor's next discovery confirmed his suspicion that there might be interesting remains left in the Equatorial Channel. When the bases of some of the mosques on the island were examined, it was found that they had been built on much older foundations oriented towards the movements of the sun; the Moslem worshippers inside had to line up obliquely to the walls to face Mecca. In addition, it was found that original sections of the stone walls had been built using an extremely sophisticated construction technique which Thor considered a sort of 'fingerprint masonry'.

6 These walls carried my thoughts back to distant places I had visited in my efforts to trace early human migration routes by sea. They had been typical for people with notedly maritime cultures, in fact for ocean navigators. The first time I saw such walls was on the world's loneliest speck of land, Easter Island. Next time, it was in the former Inca territory of South America. Then on the Atlantic coast of North Africa, in Asia Minor, and lastly on the island of Bahrain in the Persian Gulf. Each time I saw them, these walls were associated with reed ships, and each time they came closer to the Indian Ocean. Here I had finally seen them on an island far out in the Indian Ocean. Thus they were spread around half the world's circumference, with Easter Island and the Maldives representing antipodes. Contact would seem impossible. But no. When I came to think of it I had covered all these same ocean gaps myself in prehistoric types of vessels. **9**

Statues of long-ears, fingerprint masonry, fair-skinned people with red hair; the coincidences were piling up at such a rate that it was hardly surprising that Thor should permit himself a few wild speculations.

6I had long suspected that Middle East culture had reached tropical America by sea centuries before Columbus, but direct from Africa, not from distant Asia. . . .

Nobody seemed to realize that America lay much closer to India westwards by way of the Atlantic Ocean; nor that this course would, furthermore, be favoured by the elements.

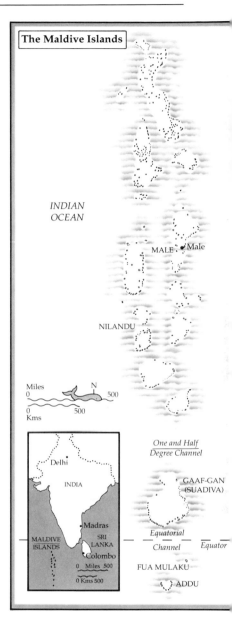

The Maldive Islands

INDIAN OCEAN

MALE · Male

NILANDU

Miles 0 — 500
0 — 500
Kms

One and Half Degree Channel

GAAF-GAN (SUADIVA)

Equatorial Channel — Equator

FUA MULAKU

ADDU

Delhi
INDIA
Madras
SRI LANKA
MALDIVE ISLANDS
Colombo
0 Miles 500
0 Kms 500

Now, as we had discovered that prehistoric seafarers had established a foothold on the Maldive Islands, we could see that they had been in a good position to sail on even to America. The winter monsoon from the northeast would give Maldive sailors a fair wind for the southern Cape of Africa and there the Atlantic Ocean begins. At any time of the year the South Atlantic Current and the south-east trade winds would carry them straight on to the Gulf of Mexico. . . . With the reed ship *Ra II* we had come from North Africa with the North Equatorial Current and the north-east trade winds. We could have come as easily from South Africa by the South Equatorial Current and the south-east trade winds. These two mighty Atlantic Ocean rivers converge off the coast of Brazil and flow together into the Gulf of Mexico. . . .

But what really made me scratch my head and wonder what might have happened were the long-eared images that had lured me to the Maldives in the first place. We had now linked them with the builders of the fingerprint masonry. Together with the fingerprint masonry and reed boats we had traced the custom of ear extension back from Easter Island to Peru and Mexico, but so far no further. The custom of elongating the ear lobes until they hung to the shoulders was still in use on Easter Island when Captain Cook arrived. . . . The Inca nobility also extended their ear lobes with the same kind of discs until the Spaniards arrived, and claimed that they had been told to do so by their legendary sun-king, Con-Tici Viracocha. According to Inca history he ruled a long-eared people who lived in Peru until he sailed away into the open Pacific. . . .

I had been looking in vain for the custom of ear extension among the pyramid builders in Mesopotamia and Egypt, among the early mariners who had settled Cyprus, Crete and Malta, among the remains of the Phoenician seafarers, and the founders of Lixus [a Phoenician port on the Atlantic coast of Morocco]. None of them seemed to have practised it. I had a list of well over one hundred culture traits peculiar to pre-Columbian Mexico and Peru, and so special that they were unknown elsewhere in America. Yet all of them reappeared within the restricted territories of the earliest Middle East civilizations. The only item missing from that list was ear extension. Although it was shared by the earliest civilizations in Mexico and Peru, I could not locate it among seafaring civilizations on the other side of the Atlantic. **9**

But at Lothal in India archaeologists from the University of Baroda provided him with the missing link.

6 There was a drawer full of round discs with grooved rims, like colossal vertebrae made from ceramic. They looked precisely like the ceramic ear plugs of prehistoric Mexico and Peru. In Inca times they were made from pure gold. We had excavated them ourselves on Easter Island, carved from thick shell. I was in not a moment's doubt as to what these archaeologists had dug up at the Lothal port, but asked them just the same.

'Ear plugs,' was the answer. 'You see, these ancient mariners pierced their ears and expanded their ear lobes to insert these large plugs.'

So the Indus valley mariners were long-ears! **9**

While Thor and Björn Bye were still in the Equatorial Channel they also visited the largest island in the archipelago, Gaaf-Gan. Uninhabited and covered by luxuriant jungle, it is visited only by people who harvest its coconuts and root crops. From them Thor learnt that

there was a huge mound, larger than the one on Fua Mulaku, hidden in the interior. It proved to be completely covered by ferns and great jungle trees, some so large that three men with linked arms could not encircle them. The mound itself was built from loose coral rubble, but on the ground lay large numbers of beautifully squared limestone blocks, many decorated with sculptured reliefs.

In November 1982, Thor had to return to Europe. But by that time the government had overcome their phobias about anything to do with the islands' pre-Moslem past. In fact it was the President himself who invited Thor to return with a full team of experts at the earliest opportunity. Over the next fifteen months he made three visits, accompanied by specialist archaeologists from Norway. Chief among these was Arne Skjolsvold, the old and trusted friend and collaborator who had been with Thor to the Galapagos, Easter Island and South America.

The first block Thor and Björn had found under the foliage was carved with a high relief of the ancient

A hawitta, or pyramid-shaped mound, was uncovered on the island of Gaaf-Gan on the edge of the Equatorial Channel. At each corner the archaeologists found sun symbols, dating from before the arrival of Buddhists, Hindus or Moslems.

RIGHT *A sun symbol from Gaaf-Gan, with a central 'eye' surrounded by concentric circles. The limestone plaster covering the lower half suggests that later arrivals tried to obliterate it – perhaps because they found it blasphemous.*

ABOVE *Thor points to a sun symbol on the walls of the former sultan's palace in Aden – yet another link in the chain, which he would soon investigate.*

symbol of the sun, a round disc surrounded by concentric circles. Later excavations proved that this large structure was precisely solar-oriented with a square base, and walls built in steps like a Mesopotamian ziggurat. Ramps ran up the centre of each of the four walls of the pyramid to the truncated summit which must once have held a temple, to judge from the remains of carved stones fallen down along the steep slopes. Among the most exciting finds were three different sculptures of lion heads and one block with a bull emerging in high relief.

Throughout the archipelago they gradually discovered a large number of mounds and temple ruins, clearly of Buddhist origin. On Isdu, the easternmost island, they photographed the remains of a stupa so large that it could be seen far out at sea. It must have been observed countless times from passing ships, yet no one suspected that the remains of an ancient culture might exist so far out into the Indian Ocean.

On the island of Kondai they found a large sculptured head of a typical Makara, the Hindu water god. On Kuru Huradu they found fingerprint masonry of such quality that it compared with the best Inca work in Peru. As more and more islands were examined, a list of symbols began to accumulate which could not possibly have had their origins in the Maldives. Lions, bulls, lotus flowers, sun-wheels and swastikas were unearthed, all carved on fragments of stone. There were tiny beads of agate almost certainly from the Indus valley, pottery from China and phalloid sculpture echoing that of Kerala in southern India. All pointed to the conclusion that the Maldives were at the very hub of busy ancient maritime trade routes: east to China and Indonesia; west to Africa and the unique culture of Zimbabwe; north to India, Mesopotamia and the Mediterranean.

They were known as the 'Money Islands' since they possessed a virtual monopoly of much-prized cowrie shells, used as currency throughout the Indian Ocean – and, as Thor was soon to discover, far beyond. Astonishingly, cowrie shells had been found in tombs in Finland and northern Norway dating from AD 600, long before Viking times. On such evidence there must have been a trade route, by sea and land, all the way from the Maldives to the Arctic Circle eight hundred years before Columbus crossed the Atlantic.

By the end of his expeditions, and after further visits to Sri Lanka and the Indus valley, Thor was convinced that both these areas had played a substantial part in populating the Maldives long before the mass conversion to Islam. There are parallels in plenty to suggest that the Buddhist connection originated among the Singalese, living in the southern part of Sri Lanka. The Tamils to the north of them were, and are, Hindu. But Thor found evidence to suggest that this earlier migration began in north-west India, after the collapse of the Indus valley civilization around 1500 BC. It is generally accepted that this had been the cradle of all the cultures and kingdoms that gradually spread down to the southern tip of India, then eastwards to Java and other distant lands.

But what of the Redin, the mythical Redin with their wild music and abandoned dancing, whose potent image is still imprinted in the minds of the people today? Oral history awards to them the earliest occupation of the islands. But where did they come from? And where did they go?

Ever since his earliest Pacific journey, to Fatu Hiva in the Marquesas group, Thor Heyerdahl has been steadily amassing a bewildering array of evidence from textual references, oral recollections, statues, artefacts, even drawings by ships' artists, which all relate to an elusive

Also found on Gaaf-Gan was the figure of a lion, an unlikely animal ever to have established a habitat on the island. This and many other archaeological discoveries suggested that the Maldives were at one time the focal point of a busy maritime trade.

A basketful of cowrie shells from the 'Money Islands'. In ancient times a universal currency and the Maldives' most important export, they have been found as far north as Scandinavia.

race of seafarers. They appear to have been fair-skinned (though not necessarily European), red-bearded, and usually depicted with artificially extended ear lobes.

Not enough is known to gather all the myriad references to these people into a single anthropological theory, and Thor has never attempted it. Nevertheless he is prepared to conjecture on the possibility that these long-eared men and women with their amazing navigational skills might all have been kith and kin, even though they appear to have spread so widely across the ancient world – from the Indus valley to Mexico, to Peru, to Easter Island. And now he had unearthed evidence of a people with the same characteristics once again: on the Maldives archipelago, far out in the Indian Ocean.

25

BEFORE THE
BEGINNING

'There is only one ocean. We speak of seven, but they are all part of the same sea, and the continents are islands.'

Thor Heyerdahl is something of a scientific gambler; not, of course, with the facts, but with the prospect of success. Often with little more than his own instincts to guide him he will trace the slenderest of clues to its source, where more conventional archaeologists would certainly wait for some sort of corroboration. Three years after the Maldives expedition Thor was off again, and this time I was fortunate enough to go with him.

A stranger had sent him a tip that a prehistoric seafaring people called the Reidan had once ruled the entrance to the Red Sea in South Yemen. The fabulous riches of the biblical Queen of Sheba had been based on the caravan route through Yemen, and when the Reidan discovered the sea route to India they caused the collapse of this kingdom. Could the Reidan be the elusive Redin?

In Aden, capital of the People's Democratic Republic of Yemen, we found the symbol of the winged sun that Thor knew so well from the Maldives. But no one, not even the director of the Aden Museum, could tell us its significance. The name 'Reidan', however, did mean something to him: it was one of the six kingdoms of ancient Yemen. Since this region was now in a war zone he recommended instead a visit to Shibam, the former capital of Sheba – founded in about 1200 BC, but still flourishing. 'The old houses that form the town', wrote Thor, 'stood like sun-baked towers packed side by side along shaded streets, so narrow that we had to disturb

The former sultan's palace in South Yemen is now a museum. Here Thor was shown cowrie shells that he was certain had come from the Maldives in prehistoric times.

the goats from their slumbers to let us pass.' And here again there were many examples of the winged sun symbol.

An old man, considered the historian of Shibam, at last told us what this symbol meant. 'It is Sin,' he explained, adding that this was the South Yemeni word for God. But in the language of the highland region of the country it meant the sun-god. The concentric circles represented *shames*, the sun, and the three lines on either side *asha'a*, its rays.

In the nearby museum, formerly the sultan's palace, we found some objects recently excavated in the locality by Russian archaeologists. Among them was a little pile of cowrie shells – typical money cowries from the Maldives. There was no doubt in Thor's mind that these, like the ones discovered at the port of Lothal in the Indus valley, had been brought by prehistoric voyagers from the Maldives. But could the earliest waves of migration have been in the opposite direction? Could the Reidan, who reputedly found the sea route to India, have called in at the Maldives? If so these people, who carved the symbol of their sun-god on the oldest structures in the Maldive archipelago, must have been its first settlers.

There was an even greater discovery awaiting us in the National Museum. Here we saw a number of alabas-

RIGHT The alabaster statue of a king found at Mohenjo Daro in the Indus valley. The ring held by a narrow band on his forehead and upper arm was clearly a symbol of rank, if not of divinity.

FAR RIGHT In South Yemen's National Museum Thor was astonished to find a statue with precisely the same symbol on the upper arm. It represented further evidence of early cultural links across the Indian Ocean.

ter statues of kings with shell-inlaid eyes, strikingly reminiscent of Mesopotamian art; each had a distinctive thin moustache like those Thor had seen on stone heads in the Maldives. But one of them really excited him: dating from the fifth century BC, this king had a ring in a band carved round his arm. Thor had seen this same embellishment on a statue of a priest-king at Mohenjo Daro.

By now he was certain that there had been very early contact between the Indus valley, South Yemen and the Maldives, in fact all round the Indian Ocean, three thousand years before the Arabs had guided medieval Europeans into this part of the world. As we know from the Old Testament, foreign trade was the basis of the wealth of ancient Yemen, and although the hinterland was savage and inhospitable the region had a long coastline. According to Roman records, ships from the Indian

The city of Shibam in South Yemen, a medieval Manhattan made entirely of mud.

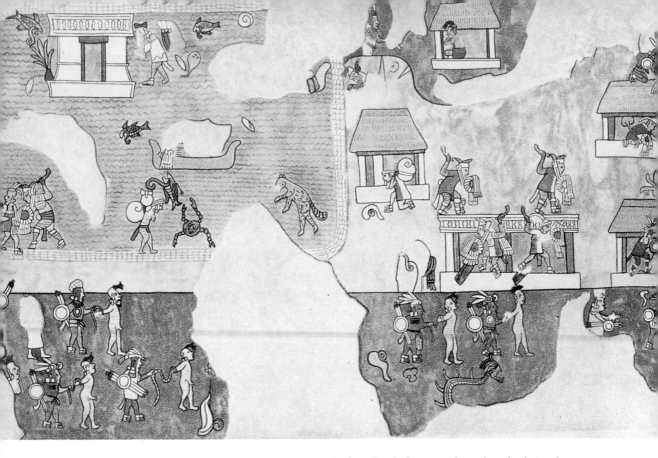

A mural from a temple wall in Yucatan, Mexico. In the lower half, naked, light-skinned people are shown being captured by a dark-skinned race who are clothed and heavily armed.

Ocean entered the Red Sea and unloaded in Lower Egypt; clearly this had once been a major gateway to the Indian Ocean. 'There is no barrier to seaworthy ships as long as the water of the ocean continues,' wrote Thor. 'There is only one ocean. We speak of seven, but they are all part of the same sea, and the continents are islands.'

When he set out to cross four thousand miles of Pacific Ocean on the *Kon-Tiki*, Thor Heyerdahl had no idea that one day he would embark on a crossing of the Atlantic. Similarly, at the time of the *Ra* voyages he had no idea that in the years to come he would sail *Tigris* across the Indian Ocean. Yet in retrospect, each voyage fits neatly into an expanding pattern which is now global in its proportions.

Nor did that young explorer who set out for Fatu Hiva in 1936 have any reason to think that islands would play such a crucial part in his life. If, from Easter Island, you drilled a hole down through the centre of the earth, you would come up on the opposite side of the planet at the Maldive Islands. It is a curious fact that these two geographical antipodes, each as far away as it is possible to get from any continent in their respective oceans, have

provided Thor Heyerdahl with evidence that unlocked the secrets of an entire region.

In one sense he has always been working backwards from his own personal winning post – a solution to the age-old mystery of Easter Island. The growing conviction that the earliest settlers could have come from America, bringing aspects of their culture with them, led him to consider those early American civilizations in much greater detail. From there it was the many parallels with the Old World that became impossible to ignore. So moving eastwards once more, intellectually as well as physically, and always backwards in time, he concentrated his attention on the Indian Ocean, and particularly on the three great civilizations that had sprung so miraculously into existence around 3000 BC.

A mosaic is made up from thousands of tiny coloured stones which have no apparent meaning until they take their place in the grand design. In one sense, all historical and archaeological research is like the piecing together of a mosaic. But in Thor Heyerdahl's work there is something too of the modern graphic artist who puts one transparent gel on top of another, each one adding a new meaning and dimension to those beneath.

A watercolour by Torriani, dated 1590. It shows a group of Guanches, the primordial inhabitants of the Canary Islands. European navigators were surprised to find that many of them had fair skins and blond hair and beards.

A typical fair-skinned Berber youth from the Kabyle area of the Atlas Mountains (ABOVE), and (OPPOSITE) a Berber family, their looks more Scandinavian than North African, in traditional dress. Before their conquest by the Arabs the Berbers controlled large tracts of North Africa, and could have been the first to navigate the Atlantic.

The process has now reached the point where the entire planet has become his theme.

The biggest change has been in his attitude to the sea. The little boy who was once scared of water has grown into the man who stripped away the prejudices contained in the concept that, for early man, the ocean was 'land's end', an impassable barrier which marked the end of the only world he knew. Thor is convinced now that long-distance navigation began five thousand years ago – perhaps in the Mediterranean, perhaps in the Indian Ocean. Aided by powerful currents, ships and men could have spread rapidly westwards across the Atlantic and the Pacific. But just who those intrepid early navigators were is a puzzle that preoccupies him still.

Since the unexpected discovery of the Indus valley civilization a few decades ago, it has usually been listed with those of Egypt and Mesopotamia as one of man's three independent sources of civilization. But why independent? Thor kept on asking himself. In a reed ship and with an unskilled crew he had sailed between all three places in a few months. And while all three of these civilizations started in full bloom, modern archaeologists have found traces of earlier maritime cultures on islands in the Mediterranean, in the Persian Gulf and on Britain's northern islands. 'We have been blindfolded too long by the European attitude that everything *began* with us,' he wrote. 'In reality, many great civilizations throughout the world *terminated* with our arrival.'

The Aztecs and Mayas based their sacred national history on the arrival of white and bearded culture bringers, who came from across the Atlantic long before the Spaniards. This history was properly recorded with their own kind of script on the pages of proper paper books; Europeans called them heathen savages and burned those books. But their inscriptions on pyramids and stone stele remain. And today we know that history meant more to them than to the conquistadores. The Mayas were astronomers and had a calendar system more exact than that of Europe. The beginning of time, according to this system, coincides to the very century with the zero date in the ancient Hindu calendar, and

The dry, rocky plateau at the top of the Tassili escarpment, six thousand feet above the Sahara Desert.

ABOVE *The magnificent cave paintings at Tassili show that thousands of years ago the region was green and fertile, abounding in game.*

OPPOSITE *One of the famous rock paintings of Tassili, showing what many consider to be the earliest-known depictions of reed boats.*

with the estimated date of 3100 BC for the founding of the first dynasties of Egypt and Mesopotamia.

Thor believes we should be more open-minded about the history of those who preceded Europeans in America. The aboriginal population of the Canary Islands – after whom the Canary Current, which flows into the Gulf of Mexico, was named – were white and bearded. These people, known as Guanches, were descendants of Berbers from Africa. After Phoenician, Roman and Arab invasions and population influxes the Berbers are now a minority in North Africa, but many of those who remain have light colouring. Thor found it hard to believe that the blue-eyed, blond-haired Director of Public Relations for OPEC to whom he was introduced in Sweden was no Scandinavian but a pure-blooded Berber from Algeria. His new friend, Abdel Kaher Benamara, invited him to come to the Atlas Mountains to see these people, the Kabyle Berbers, for himself.

After visiting Benamara's family they flew deep into the Sahara, to the Tassili Mountains – six thousand feet high and one of the driest places on earth. Thor wrote of it as resembling 'a space platform of concrete, sailing in the blue high above a moon-like desert'. And yet they had gone there to see the world's oldest-known paintings of boats – reed boats.

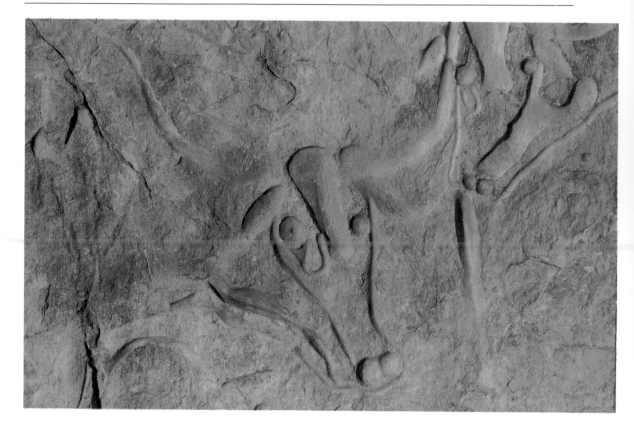

Not far from the oasis of Djanet stands a rock carved with the image of a weeping cow – a fitting symbol for the climatic catastrophe which befell the once green Sahara.

❛On smooth surfaces were prehistoric paintings of men and animals – cattle, water-buck, elephants, rhinoceroses, giraffes, lions, even hippopotami and fish. The only possessions that these early artists had depicted apart from their herds were reed boats. Some were sickle-shaped like the pre-pharaonic petroglyphs in the Red Sea canyons; others tusk-shaped, as in Chad and Ethiopia today.

The oldest of these rock paintings were dated to about 7000 BC, and represented 'negroid people' in procession or taking part in ceremonial dances. The reed boats, however, and the animal paintings, belonged to about 5000–4000 BC, when the 'white people' arrived with cattle. Presumably this is when the Berber cattle rangers arrived.

Then, about 3000 BC, the climate changed drastically. Former forests disappeared as rivers and lakes dried up and the landscape was turned into desert. From this period probably dates a relief of cattle heads bent down as if trying to drink out of a water-hole in the sand between the rocks. One cow was carved with its muzzle down in the dried-up hole, a large tear welling from its eye. I could not imagine a better and more gripping monument to the disastrous climate changes of this distant time.

When I looked at my fair-haired African friend as he bent down to gaze at the weeping cow, I saw in him the desperate Berber of antiquity who left this message for posterity before joining the mass migration of his reed boat-building people to the narrow stretch of green land along the seashore. It is understandable that fleeing Berbers, black and white, had ended up in the Canary Current and the Canary Islands. With North African Berbers afloat in the current that runs like a vast river to the Gulf of Mexico, the bearded men of Maya, Aztec and Inca traditions have a legitimate place in aboriginal American tales about the Atlantic – but more as fact than as fiction.

The Berbers were not Europeans, nor were they the only non-European people who were fair and bearded. There are many who believe that the seafaring Phoenicians were blond. Certainly the tomb paintings of the ancient Etruscans show many with blond and reddish hair, yet they came to Italy from some unidentified port in the Middle East before Roman history began. Frescoes of reed boat-builders in ancient Egypt show some with fair skin and red hair working side by side with others of darker skin and black hair.

How can we expect to identify the white and bearded Atlantic voyagers from Aztec and Mayan texts and illustrations until we know the origins of the Etruscans, the Berbers, the Phoenicians, the Guanches and all the other people who sailed on and around the Mediterranean in antiquity – not to mention the Redin and other early merchants on the other side of Africa? We shall lack many answers until we know why the climate in North Africa and the Middle East changed so drastically about three thousand years before Christ, and why so many civilizations around the Atlantic and Indian Oceans changed direction or started their zero year at the same time. **9**

26

THE VIEW FROM THE PYRAMIDS

'Somewhere along the way modern man has gone
wrong by failing to acknowledge the huge difference
between progress and civilization.'

At the time of writing, Thor Heyerdahl is in his seventy-fifth year; but only a very rash man would say that he is in the evening of his life. His mental and physical stamina are as legendary as ever. His attention to detail never falters, and his memory seems as accurate as a computer. Perhaps his only concession to advancing years is an afternoon siesta. But even then he usually grasps a pen or a spoon in his hand. When the object slips from his grasp, he knows that he has nodded off for long enough; it is time to be up and about.

And now all this energy and drive has found a new outlet, ironically in the very country from which the *Kon-Tiki* voyage began – Peru. The drab and dusty little town of Tucume lies on the edge of the desert, between the mountains and the sea four hundred miles north of Lima. In this unlikely spot Thor has built himself a traditional adobe-brick home which he has named 'Casa Kon-Tiki'. On one side of the house two superb doors open on to extensive grounds which include what must be the only prehistoric pyramid in the world in private hands. On each of the doors local carpenters have carved the symbol of a lion and the mask of the man-god Kon-Tiki, both emblems of a pre-Inca culture which may once have stretched for thousands of miles down the western coast of South America.

A windmill is under construction to drive the electricity generator. Very soon the property will be entirely self-sufficient in food. At half-past six every morning,

'Casa Kon-Tiki', the traditional adobe-brick house which Thor has designed and built for himself at Tucume in north-west Peru.

owls watch impassively as their landlord goes jogging round his estate. After breakfast he saddles his horse and rides out to supervise the work in progress.

Here, in his own words, written specially for this book, is the story of how Thor Heyerdahl decided to uproot himself from Europe and begin a new phase of his life in this remote corner of Peru.

❝ The Pacific – the 'Peaceful' Ocean; what a name to give the largest and most ferocious of all oceans! Yet in spite of my own memories of violent storms and towering seas, the name given to this ocean seemed fitting when I recently returned to Peru. I was sitting on the cliffs beside the endless beach of the Lambayeque valley, where the Spaniards had gone ashore in the sixteenth century when they marched inland under Pizarro and conquered the mighty Inca empire. Here they were given a pious but fatal welcome by the Incas, who thought they were descendants of the white and bearded men who long ago had come sailing down this same coast and brought civilization to their forefathers.

I had never been to the Lambayeque valley before, but in a sense I felt at home here. Down along this ocean current lay Tahiti and the Marquesas, where my interest in Pacific migration routes had been fired. Out there lay also the Tuamotu atolls, linked to this coast by the elements that had pulled and pushed the *Kon-Tiki* from

here to there. Much closer and a bit further north lay the Galapagos; it was there that we had first found pot-sherds proving numerous voyages by pre-Inca mariners from just this part of the coast. Much further out and yet only half the distance of the *Kon-Tiki* voyage lay Easter Island; for voyagers from this coast it was the nearest inhabitable land. And Easter Island happens to be the only oceanic island in the Pacific hemisphere with vestiges of prehistoric civilization: script, architecture, engineering, art, astronomy.

The Polynesians had not reached Easter Island that early – perhaps not many centuries before the Europeans arrived. But they insisted that another people, who erected stone statues and built masonry walls, were there to receive them when they came. Our excavations indicated that these earlier stone carvers had come from ancient Peru, with their masonry technique, their bird-man cult, their custom of ear extension and their ancient Peruvian root plants like the sweet potato, yucca and gourd.

But our excavations had also opened up a problem not apparent until archaeological digging began. There were traces of three different cultural periods on Easter Island. The Polynesians could only be associated with the Late Period of decadence and civil war. The Early Period showed striking affinities to the Tiahuanaco culture of southern Peru. The Middle Period was somewhat different but clearly related, as if a new wave of invaders had come from almost the same area, yet with different ancestors and not the slightest respect for the earlier temples and images which they destroyed. Could these Middle Period mariners with their bird-man cult and ear extension have come from the great maritime cultures that dominated the north coast of Peru before being devastated by the Inca invaders from the highlands?

The most consistent and deeply rooted claim of the Easter Islanders was that their ancestors had come from a large desert country to the east and discovered their island by steering towards the setting sun. The royal discoverer, King Hotu-Matua, had brought with him on board his large rafts people with artificially extended ear lobes. I had just come from Easter Island to visit the

OPPOSITE *Every day Thor rides out to supervise work on the estate and excavations. His horse Raya is a Peruvian pacer, trained never to go faster than a trot.*

desert coastline of Peru; but I had not escaped the traditions of the seafaring long-ears, for this coastline was full of stories about them. The Incas of the royal line claimed to have inherited the custom of ear extension from the founder of the pre-Inca kingdoms, Con-Tici Viracocha, before he departed with all his long-eared followers on his final voyage into the Pacific. All the pre-Inca art of the Lambayeque valley depicted men with large discs in their extended ear lobes, nearly always engaged in fishing or travelling on the upper deck of huge reed ships with a double stern, and with passengers and a huge number of water jars on the lower deck.

Many thoughts and visions occurred to me as I sat on the cliffs above the beach where such great reed ships had once been launched, capable of navigating anywhere up and down the South American coast and downwind to any other part of the Pacific. Yet I could not rid myself of the memory of an even more amazing sight I had recently experienced.

I had accepted an invitation from Walter Alva, director of the Brüning Museum, and Guillermo Ganoza, who wanted to show me something that might be of interest to my research. The tropical sun was already low in the sky when we arrived at the outskirts of a village where some children were playing football in a dusty field at the foot of a large hillock. There was nothing strange about this hillock except for the way it towered in majestic solitude above an immense plain. It was a ghostly grey, like the walls of the village houses and the sun-dried mud on the ground. But just behind, the luxuriant green flats of the irrigated river valley stretched to the horizon. An uninterrupted landscape of sugar cane, maize and all sorts of vegetables and tropical fruits waved like a windswept ocean right up to the desert beach at our feet.

Then Walter Alva pointed in the other direction. There our view was barred by a sparse forest of evergreen, ever-dry algarrobo trees with fringed, mimosa-like foliage and long, spiny branches. There was no road, but ample space to walk in between the trees. If our guide's story were true, we were about to face one of the wonders of the ancient world, but one not listed in any tourist guide.

'There are twenty-six pyramids here,' said Walter Alva. He added that some were over 120 feet high, and none had yet been dug by either archaeologists or grave robbers. The sun was now so low that its rays marked out dark ravines that ran in parallel lines down the slopes, as if a giant dragon had drawn its claws down every side of the mighty closed structures. This was man-made all right. In the eroded ravines we could see how everything was built up from hundreds of millions of sun-baked adobe blocks – like the village houses. But each of these gigantic structures was compact inside, with a base as large as a football field and the upper platform of the truncated pyramid towering as high as a ten- or twelve-storey building.

This incredible place is not marked on any map, not even archaeological ones. The nearby village is known as Tucume, and the local people refer to this prehistoric

Part of the huge pyramid complex at Tucume. It is Thor's hope that excavations here will provide answers to some of the mysteries which still surround the birth of civilization in South America.

315

The Tucume pyramids at sunset. Pizarro and his conquistadores came this way shortly after defeating the Incas, but since there was apparently no gold to be found they passed on.

metropolis as 'El Purgatorio' – Purgatory, a name inherited from the Spanish conquistadores who chose the locality for the execution of Indians who refused Christian baptism.

Such pyramids seemed to belong to the Arab world. Although abode pyramids were rare in Egypt, they were common in Mesopotamia. There the Sumerian, Babylonian and Assyrian sun-worshippers built their ziggurats just like this, astronomically oriented to the sun and in tall steps or terraces with a ramp leading to the upper platform. Even the construction technique was the same: a floor of poles or reeds was inserted at intervals of twelve to sixteen feet up through the compact pyramid to prevent sagging as a result of the immense pressure from on top. This system had also been used on the Sakara pyramid, the oldest one in Egypt, which was constructed in superimposed terraces unlike the tombs raised by later pharaohs.

We had a few more minutes before the sun went down. The rays had already painted the pyramid walls so they reflected a warm golden glow. We wondered what was hidden inside. Nothing, is what authorities would have insisted a few decades ago. But then, in 1947, the Palenque stone pyramid in Mexico was found to have a secret entrance with a stairway leading down to a splendidly decorated burial chamber.

Walter Alva could testify to the fact that Peruvian pyramids also held tombs – he had just stopped grave robbers at the pyramid in Sipan, only an hour's drive away. There the greatest gold treasure of the century was said to have been discovered by grave robbers only a few months earlier. The local people had sold an estimated four million dollars' worth of pure gold to unknown Americans before it was discovered. Walter had courageously interfered and notified the police. The village was surrounded and ransacked; one man was shot dead.

Tucume, Walter told us, had not yet been assaulted by robbers. In fact, the medicine men from the surrounding area gathered among these ruins once a week to drink and conduct their rituals. The site was apparently both respected and guarded by the people in the nearby village.

When I saw the amazing art treasures that Alva had

OPPOSITE *Thor with the late Guillermo Ganoza at the entrance to the burial chamber at Sipan. Inside, tomb robbers had discovered the greatest gold treasure of the century. Some of the gold masks and jewellery were recovered by the police and are now on display in a local museum.*

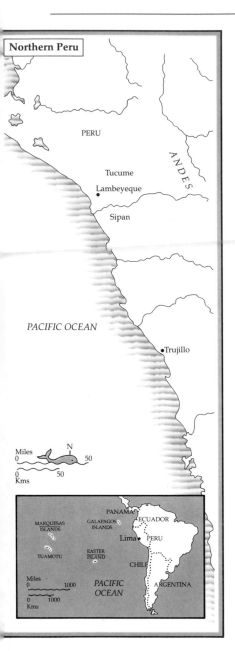

Northern Peru

just rescued from the pyramid in Sipan, I was over-whelmed by the skill and sophistication of these ancient artists. Nothing better had been produced for Egyptian pharaohs or Sumerian kings. Yet the raw materials used seemed to have more to tell. Gold was not available locally, though it could be found in the interior high-lands by experts who knew what to look for. But the gold masks had inlaid eyes of blue lapis lazuli, the nearest source of which was 1,250 miles away in Chile. Furthermore, the masks had teeth of pink spondilus shell, available only in Panama and Ecuador, in the opposite direction. Worked into the jewellery was an abundance of turquoise, which could only have come from Argentina or the southern United States. As for the colourful plumes of the splendid feather-cloaks buried with the kings and princes, these were taken from jun-gle birds from the opposite side of the Andes or from Ecuador.

Up to now the orthodox view of the many pre-Inca civilizations on the Pacific coast has been that they developed in isolation and independently. But already the evidence is pointing to some kind of complex inter-relationship. The peak of Peruvian civilization ante-dated the coming to power of the Incas. When the conquistadores landed in Peru in the sixteenth century they were blinded by all the gold and other wealth they found. They were amazed by the stupendous ruins they found everywhere from the coast to Tiahuanaco. Yet they considered it no more than fables when the Incas explained that these were vestiges from a still greater time when all the land was ruled by the founders of Peruvian civilization.

The conquistadores disembarked on the north coast and followed the old Inca road up into the highlands to the rich old mines and the Inca headquarters. This road passed the pyramids of Tucume, and had already served the pre-Inca rulers of the Lambayeque valley for access to the mines. Two of the early chroniclers actually referred to Tucume as the most impressive ruins they saw in the land. But as new roads were built, Tucume went into oblivion and slept for an additional four and a half centuries undisturbed.

In due course, at Walter Alva's instigation, the Peruvian authorities gave me permission to organize the first-ever archaeological project at Tucume, as a joint venture between the Kon-Tiki Museum in Oslo and the National Institute of Culture in Peru. Here was an exciting challenge, perhaps the greatest I had ever confronted. Where else could anyone today run into an unexplored pyramid valley, with colossal structures not yet known to the modern world and yet as impressive as anything discovered in America since the days of Columbus? We are living on a fairy-tale planet indeed. We think we know it, and we think we know its unwritten past because we have been to the well-trodden tourist paths in Egypt and Mexico, and have at least seen pictures of Machu Picchu in Peru. We send explorers to the moon in the hope of discovering something exciting; there we find only rocks and sand. But on this marvellous planet, where beasts and mankind have lived and left their traces for millions of years, it is still possible to locate unmapped temple cities and capitals of lost civilizations merely by island-hopping among the atolls of the Maldives or by taking a short walk away from the Panamerican Highway. **9**

Apart from heads of state, I doubt if there is another

Ceramic jars and other household objects intended for use after death were left behind by the Sipan tomb robbers, who were only interested in gold and precious stones.

321

Among art treasures seized from the grave robbers was this puma mask (RIGHT) covered in gold leaf, with teeth of spondilus shell from Panama. The puma was a symbol of royalty. Also recovered was another mask (BELOW) with eyes of lapis lazuli, which could only have come from Chile. An almost identical mask was rumoured to have been sold on the black market for US$60,000.

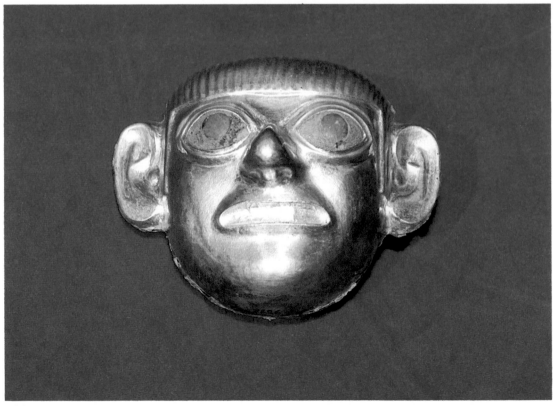

In the innermost burial chamber Walter Alva found an exquisite brooch (LEFT), one of the finest examples of pre-Columbian workmanship ever discovered. The central figure, perhaps the king himself, carries a ceremonial staff and wears a necklace of tiny owls' heads. At the same time Alva found a gold necklace (BELOW) with a moon-shaped emblem which might also represent a reed boat. Similar designs carved in wood have been found on Easter Island.

Fishermen on the beach at Lambayeque, where reed boats are still in daily use. Here a legendary king called Naymlap is supposed to have landed after sailing down from Mexico with a great fleet of rafts. According to local tradition, the pyramids at Tucume were built by Naymlap's descendants.

man on earth who would find it so easy, if he chose, to travel the world without a passport. It is not just that Thor Heyerdahl is known and admired almost everywhere, by schoolchildren and scientists alike; in some indefinable way he actually seems to have become a citizen of the world. He told me once that he never feels homesick because he wouldn't know where to feel homesick for. Home is where he happens to be at any given moment.

It is, of course, no accident that on so many of his voyages the flag of the United Nations has fluttered at the masthead. He passionately believes that the problems

besetting this planet are now so great that they cannot be solved by nation states from within their own borders. To give but one example, much of his work has been involved with migration. Massive changes in climate such as prolonged drought or flood have caused whole peoples to abandon their traditional homelands and move elsewhere. If such natural calamities were to occur again – and there is growing evidence that they will – then any large movement of populations will be effectively blocked by the artificial frontiers of the modern world. If the 'greenhouse effect' causes the level of the sea to rise so that half of Bangladesh is submerged,

One of the adobe pyramids at Tucume, with the ramp leading to the upper platform clearly visible. The excavation programme, jointly undertaken by the Peruvian government and the Kon-Tiki Museum in Oslo, is expected to last several years.

will the other nations of the world be ready to welcome their homeless and destitute neighbours, not by the thousands but by the millions?

These are enormous questions which preoccupy Thor Heyerdahl in a way that ordinary current affairs do not. At 'Casa Kon-Tiki' in Peru there is at present no radio, no television and no regular delivery of newspapers. If he has a political viewpoint – in the sense of being for or against capitalism, for instance – I have never heard him express it. World leaders of the left and of the right have been his friends. As he sees it, rivalry between man and man is not the greatest danger, unless it leads to a nuclear holocaust. A far greater threat to the survival of this planet is the war that man is constantly waging on his own environment.

Thor has been 'green' from a very early age. His first expedition to the island of Fatu Hiva was a deliberate attempt to find out if there was another way of living in the twentieth century which did not disturb the delicate balance of nature. Since then he has monitored the pollution of the oceans, and used his prestige on countless occasions to proclaim the creed of a balanced existence, which means living in some kind of harmony with every other form of life around us. In Thor's view, 'somewhere along the way modern man has gone wrong by failing to acknowledge the huge difference between progress and civilization'. If the message is not heeded, 'we will chop off the very branch we are all sitting on'.

If there is a link between Thor Heyerdahl, defender of the future, and Thor Heyerdahl, unraveller of the past, it is probably best understood within the context of natural evolution. To put it in his own words: 'If we try to suggest that man was primitive for millions of years, and became civilized almost overnight, then that runs counter to the normal process of evolution as we see it in the natural world. Personally I don't believe that civilization simply sprang into existence five thousand years ago.' What then, should the archaeologists of the future be looking for?

❛There were probably many beginnings. One day some of them will surely be found beneath the desert sand. And with the help of new technology, there is no reason at all why something of enormous importance may not be discovered on the ocean bed. We are too accustomed to think of Atlantis in the same science fiction terms as men from outer space. I don't believe anybody ever visited this planet from space. But I know that the ocean has not always had the same shape that it has today. Once there was land in many places where there is no land now. The myth of the 'Lost City of Atlantis' is not one that we should dismiss lightly. **9**

Thor Heyerdahl is a wandering spirit. The day when he exchanges a dusty ride across the desert for a comfortable fireside with a good book will probably never come. Others may consider that his most important work is behind him, but it is a view that he does not share. There will always be more mysteries to solve; more pieces of the great mosaic to fit into place. One has the feeling that before passing through the gates of Paradise, if that proves to be his reward, he will stop and examine them for any symbols or hieroglyphics that might throw some light on man's remote ancestry. Nor will it come as any surprise if the boat which carries him across the Styx is made of reeds.

With Thor are (left) Walter Alva, who is now working at Tucume, and (right) the late Guillermo Ganoza, who originally had the idea of inviting Thor to Peru.

Come, my friends . . .

'Tis not too late to seek a newer world.

Push off, and sitting well in order, smite

The sounding furrows; for my purpose holds

To sail beyond the sunset, and the baths

Of all the western stars, until I die.

Alfred, Lord Tennyson

INDEX

Italic page numbers refer to illustrations

BIBLIOGRAPHY

By Thor Heyerdahl:

The Kon-Tiki Expedition: By Raft Across the South Seas, 1950

American Indians in the Pacific: The Theory Behind the Kon-Tiki Expedition, 1952

Aku-Aku: The Secret of Easter Island, 1958

(joint ed. with Edwin H. Ferdon Jr) *The Archaeology of Easter Island: Reports of the Norwegian Archaeological Expedition to Easter Island and the East Pacific*, vol. I 1962, vol. II 1966

Sea Routes to Polynesia, 1968

The Ra Expeditions, 1971, revised edn 1972

Fatu Hiva: Back to Nature, 1974

The Art of Easter Island, 1975

Early Man and the Ocean: The Beginning of Navigation and Seaborne Civilizations, 1978

The Tigris Expedition: In Search of Our Beginnings, 1980

The Maldive Mystery, 1986

About Thor Heyerdahl:

Arnold Jacoby, *Señor Kon-Tiki*, 1968   Dates refer to first English-language edition

PICTURE CREDITS